Visual Planning and the Picturesque

VISUAL PLANNING AND THE PICTURESQUE

Nikolaus Pevsner

Edited by Mathew Aitchison

THE GETTY RESEARCH INSTITUTE
PUBLICATIONS PROGRAM
Thomas W. Gaehtgens, Director, Getty Research Institute
Gail Feigenbaum, Associate Director

Visual Planning and the Picturesque
Michele Ciaccio, Manuscript Editor

The excerpt from Nikolaus Pevsner, "Il Festival di Londra,"
Comunitá, 12 October 1951, 48–51, was translated by
Sabine Eiche.

Published by the Getty Research Institute, Los Angeles
GETTY PUBLICATIONS
Gregory M. Britton, Publisher
1200 Getty Center Drive, Suite 500
Los Angeles, California 90049-1682
www.getty.edu
Printed in China

14 13 12 11 10 5 4 3 2 1

Front Cover: Detail of the cover of *Architectural Review* 110
(1954). Architectural Press Archive/RIBA Library
Photographs Collection
Back Cover: Plan for the precinct of St. Paul's. See p. 191
Frontispiece: Fell Tower, 1949. See p. 55

Library of Congress Cataloging-in-Publication Data
Pevsner, Nikolaus, 1902–1983.
  Visual planning and the picturesque / Nikolaus Pevsner ;
edited by Mathew Aitchison.
     p. cm.
  Includes bibliographical references and index.
  ISBN 978-1-60606-001-8 (hardcover)
  1. City planning—Philosophy. 2. Picturesque, The,
in architecture. I. Aitchison, Mathew. II. Title.
  NA9031.P48 2010
  711'.4—dc22
                           2009039523

Contents

Acknowledgments

The text contained within this volume represents the belated publication of materials that may have laid dormant were it not for the generosity and assistance of several individuals and groups. First and most important is John Macarthur, supervisor of my doctoral research, who first pointed me toward Nikolaus Pevsner's work on the picturesque, its influence on mid-twentieth-century British architectural and urban design discourses, and, inasmuch, the greater Townscape movement. With this suggestion, Macarthur was partly recalling the advice of his onetime doctoral supervisor at the University of Cambridge, Joseph Rykwert, who had pointed out that it was Pevsner's ideas on the picturesque that lay behind Gordon Cullen's well-known illustrations of Townscape—a connection to which the present volume attests. I am deeply grateful to Macarthur not only for his direction but also for helping me to evaluate and situate the copious materials subsequently discovered and to secure the financial support essential for research.

As the transcription and editing of *Visual Planning and the Picturesque* were initially begun as part of my doctoral dissertation, much of the funding was concurrent with my PhD program. This consisted of a three-year full-time research scholarship from the University of Queensland and fellowships from both the Center of Metropolitan Studies Berlin and Syracuse University's School of Architecture. Queen's University Belfast also provided valuable research support. In October 2004, a generous University of Queensland Graduate School Traveling Scholarship allowed me to view the materials held within the Nikolaus Pevsner papers at the Getty Research Institute (GRI). A Getty Library Research Grant enabled me to return to Los Angeles in May 2006 to complete the transcription of the manuscript and carry out final corrections. At this time, *Visual Planning* was proposed as an independent volume to GRI Publications. This brought me in contact with Julia Bloomfield, then head of that department, who greeted the project with excitement. Since that time John and I have enjoyed Julia's untiring support and enthusiasm in bringing to light an unpublished manuscript by her former neighbor in London.

Without the support and foresight of Wim de Wit, it would have been impossible to transcribe and edit Pevsner's manuscript or to assemble its numerous illustrations. I must also thank the staff of special collections at the GRI, most notably Ted Walbye and the other librarians who tolerated my extended and erratic demands. Many thanks to Thomas Gaehtgens for his ongoing support of the project; the staff at the Getty Center for assisting with my stays in Los Angeles; Sabine Eiche for her translation of one of Pevsner's texts; Jobe Benjamin, who photographed the Pevsner papers with an expert eye; Amita Molloy, whose attention to the details of production is in evidence throughout this volume; Stuart Smith for an innovative design that recalls the *Architectural Reviews* of the period; and John Hicks, Alicia Houtrouw, Daniela Loewenthal, Rachelle Okawa, Laura Santiago, and Jannon Stein, who provided editorial support and diligently acquired rights to reproduce the images herewith. Michele Ciaccio deserves special thanks for her sensitive and immaculate copyediting and her frequent and always insightful suggestions.

The introduction to this volume has a longer history. It emerged from Macarthur's research into the picturesque (conducted under the auspices of a generous Australian Research Council Discovery grant), my own doctoral research begun in 2003, our joint research, and several papers published both jointly and separately from 2004 onward. We would like to thank the members of the ATCH (Architecture Theory Criticism History) research group at the University of Queensland and the Society of Architectural Historians,

Australia and New Zealand, who have been inquiring and supportive audiences for preliminary versions of the introduction. We owe a particular debt to Andrew Leach of ATCH, my associate supervisor, who has followed this project closely. In May 2008, we were able to travel to Los Angeles to finalize publication details and work on the introductory essay: Macarthur through the support of the School of Geography Planning and Architecture at the University of Queensland, and I through a research grant from Syracuse University. Apart from those groups within the GRI who have supported the research and publication, we would like to thank several individuals who have provided assistance and support essential to the realization of the project. Robert Elwall of RIBA Library's Photographic Collection supplied much useful background information regarding both Pevsner and the Architectural Press archives; Lynne Jackson, editorial coordinator of the *Architectural Review* (*AR*) provided archival materials concerning Pevsner's role at the *AR*; Jean-François Bédard assisted in sourcing eighteenth-century French engravings; and Ben Wilson helped shape the draft version of this book with funds from the ATCH research group.

Finally, I would like to thank those who have accompanied me in person and in spirit over the last few years—in particular, my family and my friends in Australia, Germany, Ireland, and the United States. Among these, many thanks to Fritz Neumeyer, Erik Ghenoiu, Jasper Cepl, Jana Schmidt, and Angela Hirst for their support. It would also be remiss of me not to acknowledge Pevsner himself, whom I began to study as a historical figure as part of my doctoral studies. I thank the family of Nikolaus Pevsner and his estate for their kind permission to publish the materials contained in this volume—which I anticipate will go some way toward correcting the estimation of his significance and impact on twentieth-century architecture and thus balancing aspects of his reception since his passing some twenty-five years ago.

—MATHEW AITCHISON, BERLIN, APRIL 2009

Pevsner's Townscape

JOHN MACARTHUR and MATHEW AITCHISON

THIS VOLUME PRESENTS a previously unpublished work by Sir Nikolaus Pevsner (1902–83), one of the most prolific and influential architectural historians of the twentieth century. Much of the book that follows was published as journal articles in the *Architectural Review* (*AR*) in the 1940s and 1950s during Pevsner's term as editor, but it is nevertheless surprising that he did not complete the book for publication under one cover and that the manuscript has remained largely unknown. Seen as it was first intended, *Visual Planning and the Picturesque* provides a good example of how Pevsner related his roles of historian and critic, and its publication now answers some of the criticism that stymied his reputation late in his career and since his death. Had *Visual Planning* been published at the time of its writing, it would have shown more clearly that Pevsner's interests often strayed from his core fields of art and architectural history to include a substantial body of work on town planning. Moreover, it would have seen him assume an influential position within the mid-twentieth-century British Townscape movement, with which he is rarely associated.

Visual Planning is a book not of history per se but of history put to use in a present-day argument about architecture and town planning, and it is intended to make the past available as precedent and inspiration for Pevsner's contemporaries. The book is something of an anomaly among Pevsner's vast oeuvre of history writing in its straightforwardly instrumental character. This is interesting with regard to his detractors' claims that Pevsner tended to surreptitiously mix his roles as historian and critic. Whatever distance there ought to be between these roles, they are clearly articulated in *Visual Planning*. Some readers will be surprised that the book's argument, and indeed its raison d'être, is what is now known as Townscape. Attentive readers of the *AR*, of which Pevsner was an editor and prolific contributor, would know that he was involved in the journal's campaign for a new concept of urban design. Throughout the 1940s, Pevsner wrote a number of historical essays on the picturesque and exegeses of theories that provided a pedigree for Townscape. *Visual Planning* shows that Pevsner was not merely involved but a central figure of the movement—albeit he was commissioned for the task by Hubert de Cronin Hastings (1902–86), the owner and editor of the *AR*. In the early years of World War II, Hastings ruminated on a body of opinion about modern architecture and urban design that had run through the journal in the 1930s, and he aimed to form this into an actual program relevant to postwar reconstruction. Hastings hired Pevsner to assist him in editing the journal in 1942, and it is likely that *Visual Planning* was commissioned as the core text of the new movement and was to be published as a book by the *AR*'s parent company, the Architectural Press. The book went unrealized for reasons on which we will speculate shortly.

After several name changes, including "Visual Planning," "Exterior Furnishing," "Sharawaggi," or even "Picturesque Planning," the movement was finally launched under the banner "Townscape" in 1949.[1] Parts of *Visual Planning* were published as articles before and after this time, while Pevsner continued into the 1950s to develop the manuscript for publication as a book. Although work on the manuscript appears to have ceased in the early 1950s, he alluded to the project in following years and was still thinking about it in the 1970s. He left a plan for the book, complete drafts of Parts I and II, illustrations, and notes for Part III. The book that follows has been transcribed and edited by Mathew Aitchison, and the incomplete Part III was created by excerpting Pevsner's published works.

Pevsner intended *Visual Planning* to address several issues: to reveal Britain's unacknowledged contribution to planning history, to prove the fundamental role of the picturesque in Britain's cultural production and artistic dispositions, and to show the commonalities of these fundamentals with the modernist architecture of his own day. These intentions were to be linked to provide the historical and theoretical premises for a new approach to urban design. Apart from the intrinsic value of such ideas, *Visual Planning* is also of interest for its historical value. In its mode of history writing and its place at the origins of Townscape, *Visual Planning* offers opportunities to revise our understanding of Pevsner and the role of history in midcentury modernism.

Pevsner

Sir Nikolaus Bernhard Leon Pevsner (fig. 1) was born in Leipzig in 1902 and educated there before going on to study at universities in Munich, Berlin, Frankfurt, and finally Leipzig, where he completed his doctoral thesis in 1924.[2] From 1929, Pevsner held the position of *Privatdozent* (privately funded lecturer) at the University of Göttingen. The election of the National Socialist party in Germany, and their subsequent race laws, saw Pevsner's removal from his lectureship in 1933. In the same year, he traveled alone to England in an attempt to find safety in a country (and language) with which he was relatively familiar, having carried out research in Britain in 1930 and lectured extensively on English subjects in the proceeding years at Göttingen.[3] With the help of Philip Sargant Florence of Birmingham University, he held a two-year research fellowship from 1933 to 1935 funded by the Academic Assistance Council, and his family joined him in 1935.

In 1940, Pevsner was briefly interned as an enemy alien, but his local contacts—including Frank Pick, Kenneth Clark, and J. M. Richards—had soon secured his release.[4] In his résumé, Pevsner claimed to have lectured at University College London and the Courtauld Institute of Art as early as 1933.[5] During the blitz on London of 1941, he worked as a rubble clearer and street sweeper by day and a fire watcher by night.[6] The master of Birkbeck College, University of London, where Pevsner spent his nights watching for fires, is reported to have remarked, "I hear we've got a rather bright chap on the roof; I think we might invite him down."[7] In the same year, Pevsner became the editor of the King Penguin series, having been introduced to Allen Lane, founder and proprietor of Penguin Books, by Richards in 1939.[8] In 1942, Pevsner was appointed part-time lecturer at Birkbeck College. Having contributed numerous articles to the *AR*, in 1942 he was appointed the acting editor of the *AR* for the duration of the war, succeeding Richards. From 1947, Pevsner held a position on the *AR*'s board of directing editors, retiring in 1971.

In 1945, he began broadcasting on BBC radio, an association that would last until 1977 and a position that provided him with greater exposure outside of academic circles.[9] He was naturalized in 1946 and returned in the same year to Birkbeck College, where he taught until 1959.[10] He was also appointed Slade Professor of Fine Art at Cambridge in 1949.[11] In the mid-1940s, Lane again approached Pevsner for suggestions regarding forthcoming series on art and architecture, and it was from this meeting that Pevsner's most monumental projects emerged: *The Buildings of England* and *The Pelican History of Art* series, the production and publication of which would span almost until the end of his professional life.[12] The 1950s and 1960s saw an enormous number of publications from Pevsner and a slew accolades and honorary titles awarded to him. Significant among these were being chosen as the BBC Reith Lecturer of 1955, receiving the Royal Gold Medal awarded by the Royal Institute of British Architects (RIBA) in 1967, and being knighted for services to art and architecture in 1969. Pevsner died on 18 August 1983 in London.

Fig. 1. Nikolaus Pevsner, 26 November 1954

Pevsner was one of the earliest and most influential historians to write about architectural modernism in English. His *Pioneers of the Modern Movement: From William Morris to Walter Gropius* (1936) was one of the first books to give modernism a historical lineage and influenced schools of architecture that had begun to integrate history courses into their newly modernist design studios.[13] Pevsner showed how the British Arts and Crafts movement had developed concepts of appropriate use of materials and the social implications of design and manufacture. Furthermore, he showed how these ideas had been taken up in Germany and, when stripped of handicraft and made industrial, had become the basis of European modernism. The book flattered Pevsner's new compatriots at one level and chastised them at another, as it and a later article argued that Britain had failed to develop architecturally after 1900.[14] Pevsner then released *An Enquiry into Industrial Arts in England* (1937).[15] In 1942, the year he most likely began research on *Visual Planning,* he published *An Outline of European Architecture,* the first major historical synopsis to include modern architecture.[16] *Visual Planning* is consistent with his other works in arguing the merit and historical inevitability of modernism.

Modern architecture had made an indelible impression on Pevsner as early as 1925, when he first met Walter Gropius and visited the *Exposition internationale des arts décoratifs et industriels modernes* (1925), where he encountered Le Corbusier's Pavilion de l'Esprit Nouveau.[17] In fact, Pevsner's *Pioneers* originally grew from a clue offered by Gropius himself, who told Pevsner that William Morris was a source of inspiration.[18] Perhaps more important than Pevsner's early commitment to modernism were his aims, scope, and method as a scholar. His education in Germany within the discipline of *Kunstwissenschaft* (the science of art) had brought Pevsner in contact with the seminal works in the field and their influential proponents. These included such well-known academics as Heinrich Wölfflin and August Schmarsow, along with Pevsner's own professor and role model, Wilhelm Pinder (1878–1947).[19] *Kunstwissenschaft*, as opposed to *Kunstgeschichte* (the history of art), was a scientific approach to art, which focused on the formal and chiefly visual aspects of artworks largely to the exclusion of the artist, whose biography and traits had been the basis of art history since Giorgio Vasari. *Kunstwissenschaft* drew on the thought of Georg Wilhelm Friedrich Hegel and his claims that historical change in art was not coincidental but a holistic development of culture and of "spirit." Thus, one could understand an artwork contributing to or hindering this development, and *Kunstwissenschaft* could even lead to predictions by identifying progressive art that was a symptom of an imminent shift in the Zeitgeist, or the spirit of the time. Wölfflin claimed that art since the Renaissance had an internal problematic that could be studied abstractly from the individual artists and their social and political circumstances and that explained the rise of abstraction and expressionism in his time.[20] Pevsner's use of historical knowledge as an action in the present that could identify advanced art is very similar to what his contemporary Sigfried Giedion, a student of Wölfflin, was doing with his first English-language book, *Space, Time and Architecture* (1941).[21]

Two other traits of Pevsner's work grew from his education. He followed the anthropomorphic and empathetic understanding of architecture that Wölfflin, Schmarsow, and Theodor Lipps had developed and which was also known in progressive British circles through the work of Vernon Lee and Geoffrey Scott.[22] Empathy supposes that the feelings that an artwork arouses occur at a bodily level anterior to ideation. What we feel about an old artwork has something in common with the feelings of its makers and audiences despite the different concepts they had of art, and indeed of affect. Present empathy with an artwork was then an objective knowledge on the basis of which historical change could be understood. When Pevsner writes of the "unconscious planning" that underlies urban ensembles like the Inns of Court in London and of the unconscious continuity of the picturesque into modern planning ideas, he means this presence of the past as felt, which can be brought from perception to cognition by historical understanding.

Wölfflin ended *Kunstgeschichtliche Grundbegriffe* (1915; *Principles of Art History*, 1932) by stating an issue beyond the scope of the book, namely, how to account for national and regional differences in artistic development. Wölfflin proposed that Western art had developed holistically and systematically since the Renaissance, but worried about how northern Europe often seemed to be behind Italy and the Mediterranean; he hoped that in his own time it had marched ahead. It seemed to Wölfflin that regional differences powered the dialectical development of art. Pevsner's teacher Pinder made it his major task to develop this idea into a *Kunstgeographie* (the geography of art), which Pevsner explained as "the history of art in its relationship with the Nation."[23] These ideas underlie *Visual Planning*. As the book's foreword suggests, English cities still seem medieval in their barely coordinated form and thus behind the French development of baroque urban planning based on axes and rond-points that dominated Europe from the seventeenth century. But Pevsner argues that the English have a kind of feeling for planning and a theory of it—the picturesque—and *Visual Planning* attempts to show that an understanding of the particularities of English planning can drive the historical dialectic toward a modernist concept of cities. For Wölfflin's problem, Pevsner's solution is categorical and perhaps overly simplistic but interesting nonetheless. In 1947, Pevsner published the article "Modern

Architecture and Tradition," which provides useful context for *Visual Planning*.[24] There he proposes that modern architecture is international and the kind of total form of a period that Wölfflin proposes but that regional differences exist in the more place-bound study of town planning. This division, and simplification, of the distinct roles of architect and planner subsequently underpinned much of the Townscape movement: the acceptance of modern architecture as the *only* valid idiom for new building, which was to be incorporated and "compromised" by traditional or circumstantial urban patterns.

What education Pevsner would have had in *Stadtbaukunst* (the art of city building) is also interesting. He certainly knew Camillo Sitte's famous *Der Städtebau nach seinen künstlerischen Grundsätzen* (1889; *The Art of Building Cities: City Building According to Its Artistic Fundamentals,* 1945), which held enormous currency in twentieth-century urban design.[25] Sitte's recommendations closely resemble those of *Visual Planning* and were clearly an important precedent for Pevsner and the greater Townscape movement. Pevsner was unequivocal in placing Sitte at the beginning of a lineage that extended from the late nineteenth century to the work of Raymond Unwin and other British town planners of the early twentieth century. This acknowledgement, however, was largely absent from Townscape's developmental period and appears to have been obscured by the perceived need to galvanize nationalist sentiment during and immediately after the war. This war-time chauvinism was then complicated and given an unlikely longer impact by Pevsner's assumptions about national character in art. That *Stadtbaukunst* was downplayed in the 1940s belied an important influence: Sitte's argument can be seen as a development of picturesque sensibilities, and *Visual Planning* witnesses the return of the picturesque to Britain through Pevsner.

Pevsner was extraordinarily productive in his long career, producing some sixty books, around forty contributions to books, and over 450 articles that we can only briefly characterize.[26] His interests were necessarily in the whole of visual culture, but they fall into the usual divisions of art, architecture, and design. *Visual Planning,* and the published articles associated with it and the Townscape movement, show that he had considerable investment in the history of town and city planning. Of his major works, *Visual Planning* is closest to *The Englishness of English Art,* which was first given as the Reith Lectures in 1955 and then published as a book in 1956.[27] The chapter "Picturesque England" is a compression of the argument of *Visual Planning*.[28] These works are the fullest development of Pevsner's *Kunstgeographie,* and they strongly link Englishness to the aesthetic and practice of the picturesque. The picturesque was a major research topic for Pevsner, a subject on which he gathered an enormous number of notes throughout the 1940s.[29] His idea was that the eighteenth-century picturesque brought together earlier tendencies in English art and crystallized these as principles that were yet to be fully realized but could be in the development of architectural and urban modernism.

It is not absolutely clear what the title of Pevsner's book should be—the manuscript has no title. The editor's choice of one of the titles by which Pevsner referred to the manuscript reflects on not only the content of the book but also Pevsner's reception in architectural culture. The politics of architectural discourse in Britain in the 1950s was largely divided between the neo-picturesqueness of the *AR* and a classicist/modernist tendency based on the work of Rudolf Wittkower and applied to contemporary architectural issues by Colin Rowe. Reflecting the effect of Pevsner's dominance of the debates of the time, Reyner Banham titled his review of the period "The Revenge of the Picturesque."[30]

Pevsner's reputation and that of his work went into steep decline in the few years before his death in 1983. *Kunstwissenschaft,* with its claims to understand history as a causal process and to predict the future, was debunked as a portentous ideology of modernism. Younger scholars such as Banham, Rowe, and Peter Collins reread the sources and found there was little conceptual or historical coherence to modernism that matched the grand programmatic accounts of Pevsner and Giedion. More directly, Pevsner, as one of the most prominent proponents of modernism in Britain, was attacked by antimodernists as public and academic confidence in the modernist movement cracked. In the controversial book *Morality and Architecture* (1977), Pevsner's onetime student David Watkin deftly pointed out some of the unlikely presuppositions of *Kunstwissenschaft* and connected these methodological failings to what he saw as the totalitarian nature of modernism and its dictatorial professors.[31]

Several publications have dealt with Pevsner's reception, particularly with regard to his foundations and reliance on *Kunstwissenschaft,*[32] but despite his leading role in twentieth-century art and architectural history, there is still no comprehensive biography that sets both Pevsner's life and work in their full context.[33] *Pevsner on Art and Architecture: The Radio Talks* (2002) carries an extended introduction by the volume's editor, Stephen Games, which, along with Timothy Mowl's comparison of John Betjeman and Pevsner, *Stylistic Cold Wars: Betjeman versus Pevsner* (2000), remains one the most detailed treatments of Pevsner's life and work.[34] The *Oxford Dictionary of National Biography*'s entry by Brian Harrison adds several useful insights.[35] An admirably thorough bibliography by John Barr, published in 1970, has unfortunately not been updated.[36]

Generally, the biographical accounts show Pevsner's personality in a similar, or at least comparable, light. They illustrate the life of a modest, somewhat humorless, dry, diligent, systematic, patient, scholarly, industrious, and, above all, professional historian of art, architecture, and design.[37] It should be no surprise that such qualities are also the standard British stereotypes for Germans, and most accounts are certain to note Pevsner's German heritage and that he retained his accent in both speech and writing. Betjeman—largely out of professional jealousy and national chauvinism—gave Pevsner the nickname of "Herr Doktor Professor."[38] In a private letter from the early 1950s, Betjeman labeled him "that dull pedant from Prussia."[39] Despite this stereotyping, Pevsner became a household name in Britain, mostly due to *The Buildings of England* series along with his numerous BBC radio talks, and the county guides have been renamed *The Pevsner Architectural Guides* in his honor. While Pevsner undoubtedly enjoyed the esteem accorded to him, he was aware of his limits and modest about the merit of his work. In the foreword to the bibliography of his works, which encompasses over one hundred pages of entries, Pevsner remarks, "although I know that I have nowhere propelled my subject […] I hope to have recognized some needs and provisionally fulfilled them."[40]

The Manuscript and Its Context

Today Pevsner's papers are kept at the Getty Research Institute (GRI) in Los Angeles, and his extensive personal library—a collection of over 4,600 volumes—is also held by the GRI's Research Library.[41] Pevsner's papers were acquired by the GRI in 1984 and consist of a combination of typewritten and handwritten notes, clippings, photographs, scrapbooks, correspondence, lecture notes, research materials, and manuscripts.[42] There are 143 boxes of material available to scholars, and his library is fully cataloged and available to researchers via the Internet. It remains a curiosity—one that we will attempt to illuminate in the course of this introduction—that this manuscript has remained unpublished and generally unrecognized for so long. By the early 1950s, when most work on the project was stopped, Pevsner had published two best sellers in architectural history (which remain in print today) and was poised to launch two series that continue to hold sway over art and architectural publishing to the present.[43] As one of the twentieth century's most renowned and prolific art and architectural historians, Pevsner was never short of publishing connections and became something of a patron himself in the 1950s.[44]

The manuscript is kept in box 25—already expressing the ambiguous nature of its contents—in a folder titled "Visual Planning and the City of London, 1945" and "Reassessment 4. Three Oxford Colleges, 1949?" This folder contains around seventy shabby-looking pages, mostly handwritten on ruled foolscap paper with a fountain pen (fig. 2).[45] In addition to the manuscript folder, several others contain Pevsner's notes and outlines for the various parts of the manuscript, along with the selection of photographs and placeholder illustrations he had intended for the publication.[46] The manuscript was begun in the mid-1940s, and the scraps of paper, receipts, and reused typing paper testify to wartime rationing. As if trying to further raise efficiency, Pevsner's minute handwriting (which he admitted was "appalling"[47]) was compressed, often rendering it illegible to the unaccustomed eye. A product of the age of the handwritten manuscript with foldout addenda, inserts, and cross-references, the pages often resemble a collage and were obviously assembled at different times.[48] Later we will describe in detail when Pevsner worked on the document; in brief, it was begun in the mid-1940s and altered and added to until the early 1950s, after which time *Visual Planning* appears to have remained dormant for another half century. The project was not forgotten; Pevsner went on to lecture on the subject numerous times thereafter, always using the same examples and the same order of exposition and argument.[49]

It was in a footnote of *The Englishness of English Art* that Pevsner first publicly announced he was working on *Visual Planning*; it is from this announcement that the title of the present volume has been drawn. With reference to his earlier articles on the picturesque, Pevsner wrote, "I am working on a book on Visual Planning and the Picturesque. Of the historical parts some material has been published in the *Architectural Review* [...]."[50] A close reading of his earlier and more minor articles and reviews reveals that Pevsner had come close to publishing his intentions on several occasions. In February 1944, using the pseudonym Peter F. R. Donner, Pevsner waged a vehement critique of Isabel Wakelin Urban Chase's *Horace Walpole, Gardenist*, writing, "The art of gardening is a visual art. To write of it an author's primary interest should be visual."[51] Beginning a pattern to be continued in following years, Pevsner used the occasion to outline what needed to be done in the field and gave several suggestions for such a book, which mirrored his own plans for *Visual Planning*. Of eighteenth-century landscape gardening he wrote, "No comprehensive book exists yet. [...] An intelligent summing-up of all this [...] material is needed and [...] it should be done as a strict history of the visual development, monographically and biographically—with a good number of illustrations."[52] In December 1946, in a review of the first English translation of Camillo Sitte's *Der Städtebau*, Pevsner suggested updating aspects of the book's visual presentation and in doing so again alluded to his own plans.[53] The next occasion came with a review of the second volume of Pierre Lavedan's *Histoire de l'urbanisme* (1941; History of urbanism) in September 1947. Criticizing Lavedan, Pevsner wrote, "The truth of the matter is that it is high time for a book on visual planning in England."[54] The last allusion to the manuscript in the 1940s comes with another review in September 1949 of *Amsterdams Bouwkunst en Stadsschoon, 1306–1942* (1948; The architecture and urban beauty of Amsterdam). Pevsner wrote a little bitterly, "It is a dazzling thought that a book of this kind might be produced on London. But which publishers would dare do it?"[55]

In 1974, after resigning himself to the book's incompleteness, Pevsner recalled the period of his appointment as editor of the *AR* in the mid-1940s and the circumstances surrounding the inception of *Visual Planning*:

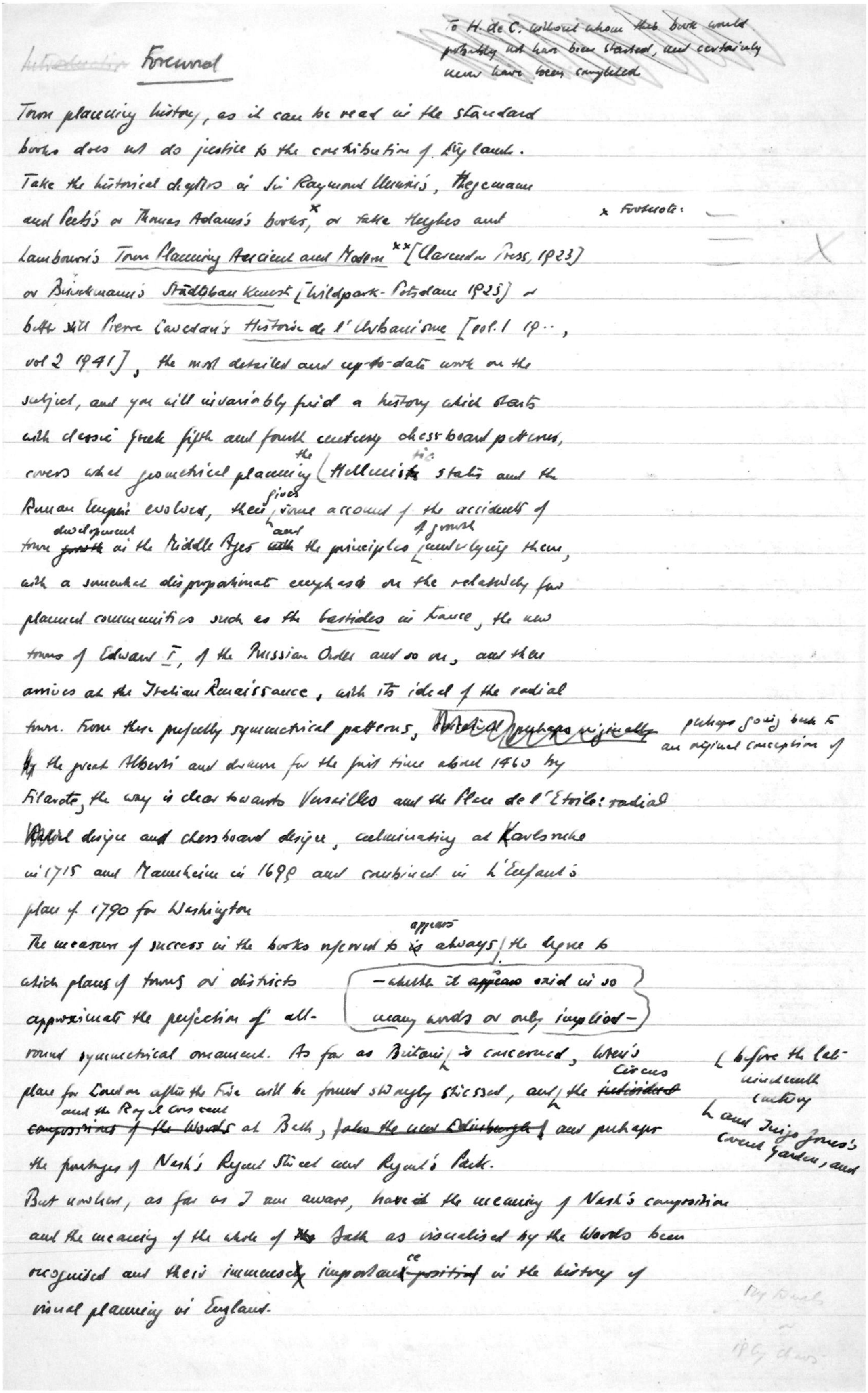

~~Introduction~~ <u>Foreword</u>

To H. de C. without whom this book would probably not have been started, and certainly never have been completed

Town planning history, as it can be read in the standard books does not do justice to the contribution of England. Take the historical chapters in Sir Raymond Unwin's, the German and Peets's or Thomas Adams's books,* or take Hughes and Lamborn's *Town Planning Ancient and Modern* **[Clarendon Press, 1923] or Brinckmann's *Städtebau Kunst* [Wildpark-Potsdam 1925] or better still Pierre Lavedan's *Histoire de l'Urbanisme* [vol. 1 19·· , vol 2 1941], the most detailed and up-to-date work on the subject, and you will invariably find a history which starts with classic Greek fifth and fourth century chessboard patterns, covers what geometrical planning (the Hellenistic states and the Roman Empire evolves, their some account of the accidents of town growth in the Middle Ages and the principles underlying them, with a somewhat disproportionate emphasis on the relatively few planned communities such as the bastides in France, the new towns of Edward I, of the Prussian Order and so on, and their arrives at the Italian Renaissance, with its ideal of the radial town. From these perfectly symmetrical patterns, perhaps going back to an original conception of by the great Alberti and drawn for the first time about 1460 by Filarete, the way is clear towards Versailles and the Place de l'Étoile: radial design and chessboard design, culminating at Karlsruhe in 1715 and Mannheim in 1699 and combined in L'Enfant's plan of 1790 for Washington.

* Footnote:

The measure of success in the books referred to is always the degree to which plans of towns or districts approximate the perfection of all-round symmetrical ornament. As far as Britain is concerned, Wren's plan for London after the Fire will be found strongly stressed, and the and the Royal Crescent compositions of the Woods at Bath, John Wood Edinburgh and perhaps the prestige of Nash's Regent Street and Regent's Park.

— whether it appears said in so many words or only implied —

(before the nineteenth century and Inigo Jones's Covent Garden, and the Circus)

But neither, as far as I am aware, have is the meaning of Nash's composition and the meaning of the whole of Bath as visualised by the Woods been recognised and their immensely important position in the history of visual planning in England.

Fig. 2. The first page of Nikolaus Pevsner's *Visual Planning* manuscript. Los Angeles, Getty Research Institute

Some time after the beginning of the Second World War the *Architectural Review* lost its principal editor J. M. Richards […]. He suggested me as his—temporary— successor and moved to Cairo. I did what I could, and this would have been entirely in matters of contemporary building, if it had not been for the co-owner of the *Review,* H. de Cronin Hastings. […] He had read Christopher Hussey's *The Picturesque,* the great classic of the movement. . . . I also had of course read the book—even several years before I settled down in England, but purely as a piece of English art history. It was de Cronin Hastings who dropped a remark in his stud- iedly casual way indicating that surely Hussey's *Picturesque* and our day-to-day work for the *Review* were really the one and same thing. This is what set me off. With de Cronin's blessing I started on a book whose subject was just this aside of the great pathfinder. In the end the book was never written, and instead only a few papers on the Georgian Picturesque came out, all but one in the *Review*.[56]

Clearly, *Visual Planning* was a commission from Hastings, the owner and chief editor of the *AR,* and Pevsner dedicated the book to him (or "HdeC," as he was known). As Hastings owned the Architectural Press, it seems almost certain that the book would have been published in-house. In an unpublished tribute to Hastings, Pevsner went further in describing the project and its commissioning, writing in 1974 that "My Picturesque was to be a book, half historical, half topical. [Hastings] gave me leave from the *Review* for that […] But in the end I never wrote the book."[57] In the 1970s, Pevsner, with the sup- port of Richards, initiated a study of the professional history of the *AR.* Pevsner's chosen researcher, Brian Hanson, recorded that in the year 1944, "[Pevsner] was engaged on a book called 'A History of Visual Planning' which he prepared but never finished. HdeC makes Pevsner's life easy so that he can finish it. The idea was to start with the Picturesque and end in Townscape."[58]

The cover page of the manuscript makes clear that the book was intended to have three parts with a brief foreword. All three parts were intended to each have a very dif- ferent style of presentation, which is reflected in this volume. Part I was to be "mostly presented in pictures," Part II "mostly presented in quotations," and Part III "occasion- ally submitting solutions."[59] The foreword and Part I appear to have been written at the same time, most likely from the beginning or middle of 1945.[60] It is unclear when work on this part stopped, but archival evidence suggests that it could have been sometime before August 1947.[61] As per Pevsner's instructions, Part I was to consist of photographs interspersed with passages of running text. Here Pevsner devised photonarrative tours of examples of English planning that he thought contained the essence of visual planning. These included Oxford, both the city and its colleges; Bath; and London, in particular Lincoln's Inn and Regent's Street and Park. The text in Part I gives instructions for the visual presentation of this part, and most illustrations for it are held in box 25 and cross- referenced accordingly.

Part II of the *Visual Planning* manuscript was more scholarly in nature and used Pevsner's favored method of exegesis: the florilegium (an anthology of the "flowers" of a literary field). Part II contains only four notes for illustrations, none of which Pevsner obtained, and consists mostly of lengthy quotations framed in a coherent narrative by running prose. The text of Part II is divided into seven sections and appears to be com- plete. Pevsner devised a cross-referencing system for this part to avoid writing quotations longhand.[62] It is largely by this system and the other cited publications that it is possible to apply a date of production to Part II. On the first page, Pevsner listed a series of relevant articles as "recent and detailed studies."[63] The most recent of these studies was that by Osvald Sirén in 1950.[64] As discussed above, research for the content of Part II was begun as early as 1942, but the production of the text appears to have only begun in 1950. In the period in between, Pevsner published several historical studies of the picturesque and its associated personalities.[65]

Part III was never completed and was the least clear in terms of its intended mode of presentation and content. Extrapolating from Pevsner's notes, articles, and descriptions for this part, we can assume that it was to be a mix of both visual and textual media, which aimed to explain the development of *Visual Planning* and its application and usefulness up to his own day. As the above description stated, "The idea was to start with the Picturesque and end in Townscape."[66] Pevsner's directive of "occasionally submitting solutions" also indicates that he intended to show the subject's topicality with recourse to examples. The numerous notes and quotations Pevsner prepared in which he partially set out the order, significant projects, places, and personalities, along with aspects of his argument, have been consulted in the preparation of the text for Part III. Although the synopses in Pevsner's notes are preliminary, their analysis and interpolation reveals three main lines of thought: they are chiefly historical, polemical, and exemplary in nature, and they allow for the most straightforward and coherent breakdown of the relevant works.

With regard to the historical content of Part III, it is clear that Pevsner intended to continue his portrayal of the development and history of visual planning from the beginning of the nineteenth century, where he had ended his presentations in Parts I and II. This historical account was concerned with three main areas. First was the introduction of the picturesque to the town and city via landscape and, in particular, parks and landscaped squares. Second was the development of picturesque architecture and building from the early nineteenth to the early twentieth century. Last, and most relevant to his thesis of visual planning, were the historical studies of the development of planning in the nineteenth and twentieth centuries leading on to its application to mid-twentieth-century problems.

It is to these problems that Pevsner's thought for Part III came to bear in his argument for the interpretation and uptake of picturesque principles and the continuity and relevance of the visual-planning tradition for modern concerns—as Pevsner phrased it in the foreword, "an account of how this theory and this tradition influenced the nineteenth century in England and might influence the twentieth." Pevsner's arguments here were wide ranging, including themes surrounding functionalism, suitability to the spirit of the time, attention to the genius loci and national character, and extended to include formal recommendations. Perhaps most important was Pevsner's stark advocacy of modernism and his plea for its adaptation along the lines of national character, along with his complete rejection of historicism and imitation in the architectural and planning problems of his own day.

Following these historical and polemical texts, Pevsner intended Part III to also be exemplary, "occasionally submitting solutions." It is this aspect of Part III that brings Pevsner in close contact with *AR*'s concurrent Townscape campaign. These examples draw on the many projects and designers listed in Pevsner's notes and publication, many of whom were also intimately associated with Townscape, such as Hugh Casson, Gordon Cullen, William Holford, Thomas Sharp, and Hastings.

The text in Part III takes the form of a florilegium, Pevsner's favored method for Part II and other articles on the picturesque and its important personalities.[67] In the absence of a complete draft, Part III of this volume can only ever be an interpretation, as it appears Pevsner was either unsure of its intended content or felt it to be rendered superfluous through the passage of time and other publications.

Apart from text and notes for Parts I to III, box 25 also contains the numerous illustrations Pevsner had selected for publication in *Visual Planning*. There are seventy-seven images in total, the majority of which have been included in the present volume; the

Photographs of Lincoln's Inn

Entering from the main Chancery Lane
entrance

1.(We have not discussed this) An exterior
view from Cursitor Street showing the
forbidding old front towards Chancery
Lane with the Gothic Entrance arch.

2. Inside this entrance arch and framed by
ht a view of the Old Hall with the narrow
passage on the left (through which we
are going to carry on in a moment) the
wider passage on the right and the left
end of the Chapel.

3. From inside the passage on the left of
the Old Hall take a view towards N.W.
On left the tall corner buttress of the
building opposite and on the right if
possible the bay window of the Old Hall.
The view should be upright and towards
the gardens.

4. View from about the door of Old Hall
towards W. N. W.   Take the whole range
of new halls and Library with the corner
of building No.8 as right hand frame.

5. From about N.W. corner of Old Hall
looking W.   Take the Gate towards

Fig. 3. Nikolaus Pevsner's instructions to the photographer of Lincoln's Inn, London. Los Angeles, Getty Research Institute

remaining illustrations were not decisively marked for inclusion or not suitable for publication.[68] The illustrations were mostly intended for Part I, but there are also several that were intended for Part III, such as those for Ladbroke Grove and London's squares.[69] Many of the illustrations appear to have been directly commissioned by Pevsner and followed a tour predetermined by him (fig. 3).[70] Pevsner used a range of photographers and also worked from stock images.[71] It is not clear exactly when these tours were commissioned or when the photographs were taken. Considering the Ladbroke Grove tour photographs intended for Part III were dated 28 June 1946 and were most likely the last of the tours to be completed, others may have been carried out before this date. The most likely date for these earlier photographs is the winter of 1944 to 1945. The text from Part I—which appears to have been begun in early 1945—was written to the images that were already at hand, and it was winter when the photographs were taken.[72]

There are several examples from the period that have assisted in recreating what Pevsner had in mind in terms of layout and visual presentation for *Visual Planning*. An example is found in Pevsner's tour of Oxford published in the *AR* in August 1949.[73] In the manuscript, Pevsner has crossed out sections of the original text and made a note to replace the text with the 1949 article.[74] This tour reveals a combination of large and small illustrations, showing specific detail and general shots for orientation, accompanied by running commentary with a brief introduction and conclusion. Pevsner's photographs are from similar viewpoints to those published by Raymond Unwin in his tour of Oxford in *Town Planning* (1909), which Pevsner clearly knew.[75] Pevsner's photographs are also used in Thomas Sharp's *Oxford Replanned* (1948), which uses a greater number of images from the same shoot and which has served as a guide for the layout of Part I of the present volume.

Apart from Pevsner's own recollections, few scholars have pointed to the existence of the *Visual Planning* project or the existence of the manuscript, and fewer still have attempted to analyze the work within Pevsner's oeuvre. Lionello De Luigi's essay "Townscape e tradizione pittoresca nella cultura urbanistica inglese" (1960; Townscape and picturesque tradition in English town planning culture) is the first publication to mention the project.[76] With reference to Pevsner's *The Englishness of English Art,* De Luigi wrote, "Nikolaus Pevsner moreover gave advanced notice of a book of his, *Visual Planning and the Picturesque,* but I have yet to see it published."[77] In Pevsner's obituary published in 1984, Robin Middleton appears to have known of the *Visual Planning* manuscript when he wrote, "he failed to complete that study of the Picturesque in English art for which he gathered notes over a number of years, considering it to be the key to all proper understanding of English architecture."[78]

More recently, scholarship surrounding the manuscript, Pevsner, and his role in the greater Townscape movement (as played out on the pages of the *AR*) has increased. Erdem Erten's doctoral dissertation, "Shaping 'The Second Half Century': *The Architectural Review,* 1947–1971" (2004), is the best work to date on the editorial policy of the *AR* in these years.[79] This work, along with Erten's earlier conference paper, "From Townscape to Civilia: The Evolution of a Collective Project" (2002), has provided many new insights and first introduced Pevsner's manuscript to scrutiny.[80] As we shall see, Pevsner published aspects of the argument and text from *Visual Planning* on several occasions; however, Erten's transcription of a passage from the manuscript's foreword represents the first verbatim publication.[81] The present authors became aware of the manuscript in 2003 and have examined different aspects of its significance in publications since that time.[82]

It is unclear why the manuscript remained unfinished and unpublished. Pevsner's first public announcement of the project in 1956 in *The Englishness of English Art* also appears to be the last in which it was cited as an ongoing work. It is possible that Pevsner was ambivalent about the project, and his interest was dependent on his relationship with the project's patron, Hastings. In his unpublished tribute to Hastings of 1974, Pevsner wrote,

> The Donner criticisms (by me) were [Hastings's] idea, though I fear I never fully understood what he wanted them to be. *Outrage* was his idea, splendid as Ian Nairn's realisation was. To a more limited degree he stood godfather to Jim Richards' Vernacular and my Picturesque. […] My Picturesque was to be a book, half historical, half topical. He gave me leave from the *Review* for that (and engaged Ian MacCallum at my suggestion). But in the end I never wrote the book. So in his later years instead of relying on others, he published direct (though as I. de Wolfe): *Man Plan* first, *Civilia* then, a thrill but also hell for his assistants.[83]

Pevsner seems to have used the pseudonym Peter F. R. Donner when he was more than usually following Hastings's instruction, which he did not always understand or have complete sympathy for. The statement that in the end Hastings had published the idea directly, and in books nothing like *Visual Planning,* suggests some differences between publisher and author. So despite referring to the manuscript as "my Picturesque," Pevsner may never have been entirely committed to it.

Other scholars who have cited the manuscript have offered theories. Remarking on Pevsner's talents and shortcomings, Middleton's obituary pointed out that "Pevsner's was not a philosophic approach."[84] Erten's hypothesis also points to a lack of aptitude, though of a different kind, in writing of the manuscript's incompleteness: "The third part, however, was left unwritten and, most probably due to lacking collaboration from a coauthor involved in planning, Pevsner did not speculate on the application of Picturesque theory into town planning. His articles that reflected on such an application were only written later, as criticism of the planning developments in Britain."[85] The notes for Part III do reveal a level of indecision and tentativeness completely absent from his notes for Parts I and II, but Erten's theory is questionable as Pevsner had published articles and lectures that concretely speculated on the application of the picturesque in urban planning, using the catchphrase "visual planning" as early as 1944.[86] Nevertheless, it is true that many of Pevsner's more mature and reflective articles on the application of visual planning to contemporary issues (from which Aitchison, as editor, has constructed Part III) did come about from the mid-1950s onwards, possibly after the book had been abandoned.

A combination of these circumstances probably explains the failure of the project when put in the context of Pevsner's workload, his other publishing projects, and the growing publications of other Townscape authors. In the early 1950s, Pevsner began the two series of publications, *The Pelican History of Art* and *The Buildings of England,* which were to dominate his productive output for many years. Additionally, he was not only the editor of the *AR* in these years but also a professor of art and architectural history. It could easily be imagined under this workload that *Visual Planning* slipped from high priority in the late 1940s to a lower one by the mid-1950s. Pevsner's only public reference to the book in 1956 in *The Englishness of English Art* is also interesting in this regard. As mentioned above, the last chapter of that book, "Picturesque England," ultimately does much that *Visual Planning* sets out to do.

By the end of the 1940s, Pevsner, by his own admission, had published in the *AR* and elsewhere most of the historical material intended for Part II of the manuscript;[87] and as the introduction to Part II equivocally suggested, "No attempt will be made to provide another history of the Picturesque after Mr. Hussey's fascinating and comprehensive book of 1927." Additionally, by the end of the 1940s, Pevsner had published interpretations of the practical traditions of English planning that he thought constituted *Visual Planning.*[88] By the end of the 1950s, it could be argued that the book's topicality had all but dissipated.

Sometime around 1960, Pevsner must have heard that Hastings's Architectural Press was to publish a book of Townscape by another member of the *AR* team, Gordon Cullen. *Townscape* (1961) made the same general arguments as *Visual Planning* and for the same audience, but it was not scholarly or historical in its presentation. Hastings had swapped horses, and whether this was because Pevsner had advised him that he could not complete *Visual Planning* in a timely way, or whether Hastings preferred Cullen's populist approach, we cannot know. Pevsner, however, does not refer to Cullen in his later reminiscence of Hastings's commission for the book.[89]

Townscape and Visual Planning

Townscape is closely identified with Cullen because of the enormous success of *The Concise Townscape* (1971), an abridgement of his *Townscape* (1961), which was, in turn, an elaboration of his "Townscape Casebook" (1949) and other projects undertaken as the *AR*'s art editor.[90] The context surrounding the publication of Cullen's book is interesting because it has rarely been acknowledged that it is actually a compendium of articles and studies carried out in the pages of the *AR* from the 1940s onward and not, as is customarily held, a stand-alone volume. In that way, these editions greatly resemble the development of *Visual Planning* as a publishing project.

Due to the manner of *Townscape*'s abridgement and the context in which it arrived, the 1971 book had a remarkably different meaning and uptake from Cullen's 1949 article. *The Concise Townscape* arrived among a number of books critiquing modern architecture in the name of community life and traditional forms, and at the beginnings of postmodernism in architecture. Today, a majority of architects would identify Townscape with Cullen and those values. Cullen's "Townscape Casebook," however, was intended as a visual essay to illustrate the article "Townscape" by Ivor de Wolfe—that is, Hastings—who was leaping over Pevsner to put their joint project into print.[91] For Hastings and Pevsner, and at that time Cullen, Townscape was explicitly modernist. This is plain in Cullen's 1961 *Townscape*, which contains scores of Cullen's illustrations from the *AR*'s imaginary Townscape schemes of the 1940s. These illustrations show buildings in a modern idiom, quite like those that Casson had developed for the Festival of Britain, inserted into historic city fabric. The modernist schemes were dropped from *The Concise Townscape*, leaving only Cullen's case studies of precedents in historic and vernacular urban forms. Although *Townscape* went through several printings, it is now quite rare, while *The Concise Townscape* is a cheap paperback that has never gone out of print. A large part of the significance of *Visual Planning* today is that it shows how modernist Townscape was intended to be in the 1940s, and indeed into the 1970s. In Pevsner's remarks quoted above, he states that the project was continued by Hastings (as Ivor de Wolfe) in later publications, including *Civilia* (1971).[92] This book, published in the same year as *The Concise Townscape*, is a design of a hypermodernist megastructure on picturesque principles and shows how much Cullen had diverged from the path that Hastings and Pevsner had stuck to.

These issues of publishing history and attribution are a part of a wider confusion regarding the reception of both Pevsner and Townscape and their interrelations. On the one hand, Pevsner has been criticized in recent decades for his views on architectural history, his promotion of modernism, and his "blinkered" approach to its application.[93] On the other, Townscape is generally held to be quite the opposite of modernism: conservative, reactionary, and nostalgic. Acknowledging and discussing Pevsner's involvement in the movement challenges some of these misconceptions; Pevsner's input shows neither him as a dogmatic modernist nor Townscape as an exercise in purely historicist urban design. It will be useful, then, to show the breadth, general character, and development of Townscape so as to clarify the role and significance of *Visual Planning*.

The term *townscape* denoted an approach to architecture and urban design that had its historical corollary in landscape gardening applied to the urban realm.[94] From Pevsner's recollection, it was Hastings's insight in seeing a direct connection between Hussey's description of eighteenth-century picturesque theory and the work of architects that the *AR* admired. An early and explicit statement of this argument came from Hastings in 1944, with the little-known and anonymous article "Exterior Furnishing or Sharawaggi: The Art of Making Urban Landscape."[95] The early date, whimsical title, and lack of a named author have kept this article obscure, but it is, nonetheless, the single most significant essay of the Townscape movement. Of the emerging campaign, Hastings wrote,

> the purpose of this article is [to point out] the fact, obvious to foreigners and historians, that a national picture-making aptitude exists among us, and has done for centuries. In *Picturesque Theory*, evolved on this island early in the eighteenth century and imitated all over Europe round about 1800, a quite unmistakable national point of view asserted itself. It was expressed at first exclusively in landscaping improvements of private grounds and country estates, and though in the nineteenth century certain of its conventions were applied to the town square, the

well-to-do-suburb, and the garden city, these were in forms so debased as to justify one in saying that true Picturesque theory has never been applied to the
urban scene.

What we really need to do now [...] is to resurrect the true theory of the
Picturesque and apply a point of view already existing to a field in which it has not
been consciously applied before: *the city*.[96]

The interdependence of Hastings's and Pevsner's arguments is implicit in Part III. Much
of the role of *Visual Planning* is to show how a modern picturesque is different from and
superior to the nineteenth-century scenographic architecture of G. G. Scott and G. E.
Street, and the Sitte-esque town planning of Unwin. But such niceties of historical memory
were put aside when de Wolfe published "Townscape" in December 1949, accompanying it with Cullen's picture essay "Townscape Casebook." Part of Cullen's initial fame
must rest with the impenetrability of de Wolfe's essay, which confuses the argument of
"Exterior Furnishing or Sharawaggi" by wrapping it in a portentous discussion of the theory
of liberalism. However, the full title "Townscape: A Plea for an English Visual Philosophy
Founded on the True Rock of Sir Uvedale Price" and some remarks about the Englishness
of the picturesque and the modernity of its principles suggest that Hastings was keenly
incorporating the research that Pevsner had done for *Visual Planning*. The strength of the
argument lies in two points that are not, in the first instance, picturesque.

First, Pevsner and Hastings take the picturesque to be a visual formalism in which
objects and their relations are subsumed into relations of pictorial composition from particular points of view.[97] With some qualifications, this is true of what Georgian gardeners
such as Humphry Repton were able to do in "unifying a scene" by removing discordant
elements and hiding property boundaries. De Wolfe, however, meant something slightly
different in that visual planning was meant to make a pictorial unity out of disparate elements, particularly modern, historic, and vernacular buildings that were in themselves
aesthetically disjunct and ideologically antagonistic.[98] The pictorial formalism proposed
here is one modeled on collage and not the unity of the subject that was at the basis of
eighteenth-century painting composition.[99]

Second, de Wolfe's "Townscape" argues in rather strong terms for the method of its
companion, Cullen's "Casebook." Picturesqueness was said to be English in the same
way as English law: that is, case law based on precedent and contrary in principle to the
codified law of post-Napoleonic Europe. Alluding to Cullen's "Casebook," the editorial
introduction to "Townscape" jested that "[de Wolfe's] method *or lack of it* is demonstrated
in miniature in the section which follows."[100] Pevsner's *Kunstgeographie* led him to believe
that a characteristic empirical frame of mind underlay law, politics, and gardening, and that
this had a natural affinity with modern architecture. In de Wolfe's text, this idea combines
rather too easily with the history of contrasting French and English gardening along the
lines of an inevitable tyranny of ideals and becomes quite chauvinistic. Nevertheless, if
we read de Wolfe's "Townscape" with *Visual Planning*, we can see Pevsner's larger point:
English empirical modernism would be on the functionalist side of the modern movement.
Pevsner's doctoral student Reyner Banham would later argue that modernism up to the
war had been largely a rationalist discourse, that is, based on rationalization of structure
and normative in its ideas and forms.[101] The much-spoken-of functionalism had yet to
be achieved and could not be normative. It is in this light that we should see the *AR*'s
later series "The Functional Tradition," which looked at nineteenth-century and vernacular
functional buildings and at Pevsner and Hastings's insistence on an architecture of case law
and precedent.[102] Such an approach also gives a strong voice to the historian.

Using *Visual Planning*, it is possible to strengthen the original Townscape article and recover some aspects that did not survive Cullen's popularization. This is even more the case if we take a wider view of Townscape. The word *Townscape* was first used in the *AR* in December 1948 as a rubric for critical articles and projects published in the magazine, although the term had already been used on several occasions previously.[103] In his *Oxford Replanned,* Thomas Sharp has a claim to having defined the term, stating rather convincingly,

> To-day we are attending the rebirth of an art which is of significance to the whole community. It has the virtue that it can be practised by anyone who has a weakness for architecture or a personal interest in a given town. By an analogy with an equivalent art practised by the eighteenth-century Improver of land (we, after all, are Improvers of cities) it might be christened TOWNSCAPE.[104]

Although published in 1948, *Oxford Replanned* was written earlier; its prefatory note is dated March 1947.[105] At this time, its manuscript probably passed under Hastings's nose. Alternatively, Sharp was familiar with the *AR* and its activities and might have at least deduced the concept from the *AR*'s various campaigns. Although lexically equivalent, Sharp's usage does not carry the load that Hastings puts on the term. Later, in his 1949 "Townscape," Hastings finishes the article with a jibe at Sharp, stating with reference to the "Casebook" by Cullen: "To bring the thing down to practical politics the section which follows tries to demonstrate in a purely token way the Case-Book idea applied to town planning as a visual art, termed by Thomas Sharp Civic Design and by the *Review,* I think, Townscape."[106]

Other than as a pique at Sharp, it is unclear why Hastings chose the title "Townscape" over "Visual Planning" in 1949. In any case, Hastings's article was preceded by numerous thematically linked editorial campaigns across issues of the *AR* throughout the 1940s, including "Exterior Furnishing," "Urban Landscaping," and "Sharawaggi." It was during this period that Pevsner first used the terms "picturesque planning" and "visual planning," and references to the "visual planner" became commonplace in the *AR*.[107] In the 1950s, this movement became known under several other rubrics: "The Functional Tradition," "Outrage," and "Counter-Attack." The 1960s and 1970s reveal related campaigns such as "The Italian Townscape," "Civilia," and "Sociable Housing." There is a strong case for seeing all of these campaigns and catchwords as part of a greater and indeed longer-lasting movement with its beginnings in the 1930s and which ultimately went through several transformations and revisions until the early 1980s. More remarkable than the shifting headline of the campaign is its scale. Aitchison has shown that from the 1930s to the early 1980s, the *AR* published 1,400 publications related to Townscape by about two hundred authors.[108] Regular and significant installments in these related campaigns include those not only of Hastings, Pevsner, and Richards but also of Lionel Brett, Kenneth Browne, Hugh Casson, Sylvia Crowe, Gordon Cullen, Eric de Maré, Frederick Gibberd, Osbert Lancaster, Ian Nairn, Paul Nash, John Piper, Thomas Sharp, Raymond Spurrier, and Christopher Tunnard, among others.[109] Analysis of this discourse shows remarkable consistency and a coherent, if not entirely systematic, development of the ideas of Townscape from its origins in the late 1930s into the mid-1970s.

Hastings, whose father owned the Architectural Press, became an editor at the *AR* in 1927 at the age of twenty-five. In 1935, he became executive editor and began to shape the journal with the prescient choice of Richards as his assistant editor, and then acting editor in 1937. Hastings had worked with Betjeman as an assistant editor at the *AR* in the early 1930s; the painter John Piper was a major contributor from 1936, when he and Richards began countryside tours together, and Betjeman commissioned Piper for books for the Shell Guides to the English counties.[110] Pevsner, another friend of Richards, also wrote his first articles from 1936, contributing about twenty before joining the editorial group in 1942 to replace Richards, who had joined the services. Richards, Betjeman, Piper, and also the artist Paul Nash initiated the *AR*'s strong interest in the preservation of historic buildings and the relation of this with modernism, which was one of the underlying issues that became Townscape. From 1942 until 1946, however, Hastings and Pevsner ran the journal alone, a collaborative setting from which Townscape's proto-manifesto, "Exterior Furnishing or Sharawaggi," emerged in 1944, along with a range of Pevsner's introductions to the picturesque. Pevsner returned to academia in 1946, and Hastings restructured the management into an advisory board of himself, Pevsner, Lancaster, and Richards, with Richards as full-time editor and Ian McCallum as assistant editor. With few changes, this pattern and Pevsner's involvement with the *AR* and its Townscape campaigns was to last for the next twenty-five years.

There is little doubt that Hastings was the mastermind behind most of the major campaigns pertinent to the greater Townscape movement.[111] In 1971, Pevsner stated that "The brilliant ideas creating what was called *Architectural Review* policy were mostly H. de C.'s."[112] Richards recalled that "the adaptation of the English Picturesque tradition to urban instead of garden landscapes [was] a principle the *Architectural Review* had been advocating since Hastings and Pevsner had campaigned about it during my war-time absence between 1942 and 1946."[113] Hastings's particular personality manifested itself in an enthusiasm for pseudonyms. In the 1920s, he published a series of articles in the *AR* under the pen name Hermann George Scheffauer and as The Editor before settling on Ivor de Wolfe for the 1949 "Townscape" article, a pseudonym that he would use (with the minor variation of Ivor de Wofle) for his ruminations on Townscape-related matters until 1973.[114] This preference for anonymity also extended to several important figures within the *AR*. Pevsner used the pseudonym Peter F. R. Donner in the *AR* throughout the 1940s, John Summerson used John Coolmore, and Richards used James MacQuedy.[115]

As mentioned above, the clearest statement of Townscape is not the eponymous article of 1949 but the 1944 article "Exterior Furnishing or Sharawaggi," signed by The Editor and written when Hastings and Pevsner were working closely together and when *Visual Planning*'s Part I was being researched and written. Comparing "Exterior Furnishing or Sharawaggi" with *Visual Planning* provides a sense of which aspects of Townscape Pevsner was not responsible for. The diagnoses of the situation differ, as The Editor writes directly of the contemporary unpopularity of modernism, a fact that does not trouble *Visual Planning*. The cure, however, is much the same. Modern architecture is let down by its planning consequences in an excessive and exclusive idealism that provides no way for modern and historic buildings to live together. What is required is a new picture in which, despite their ideological and technical incompatibility, modern, historic, and vernacular buildings can be visually composed together. Both the resources and the authority for this lie in the picturesque and its national character. There are clear differences between Hastings's polemic tone and Pevsner's scholarly one, but the most significant is the high value Hastings puts on the incongruity of the elements to be subsumed into the new picturesque.

> The fear of one's modern cupboard clashing with the Victorian atmosphere of a room, or one's Victorian chandelier looking out of place in an Aalto environment is wholly unjustified. Even more undesirable is the fear that any object, in itself not up to a discriminating contemporary aesthetic standard, would be a blot on a whole interior. The aesthetic qualities of the individual items are quite irrelevant. Let them be ugly, let them be incongruous. What matters alone is the unity and congruity of the pattern. A frankly vulgar little bronze poodle on an Italian marble

pedestal might even hold a place of honour on the mantel-shelf, either because of
its value as an accent in a picturesque whole, or [. . .] because of some equally
legitimate sentimental value.[116]

It is doubtful whether it would have occurred to Pevsner that the picturesque could master vulgar poodles in this way, but the *AR* circle knew that the picturesque was in part a
discourse against beauty, and Hastings (mis)quotes Uvedale Price on the aesthetics of
ugliness in Rembrandt van Rijn's painting *The Carcase of an Ox* (late 1630s; Glasgow,
Glasgow Art Gallery), claiming enthusiastically that "the eighteenth-century intelligentsia
cut right across the centuries linking Salvator Rosa with Salvador Dalí."[117] Most likely this
interest in incongruity began around 1936, when Richards involved the painters Nash
and Piper, key players in a debate that moved from abstraction to surrealism to neo-
romanticism in the last years of the 1930s.[118] In 1936, the year of the London International
Surrealist Exhibition in which he was prominent, Nash contributed the article "Swanage
or Seaside Surrealism."[119] Piper, who had designed the modernist journal *Axis* for his wife
Myfanwy Evans, was partly responsible for the typography of the *AR* from 1936, and he
and Betjeman made the *AR* famous for its adoption of florid Victorian typefaces within
a modern page design and the occasional inclusion of bad Victorian architecture, preferably popular uneducated appropriations of historical styles. Kenneth Clark's *The Gothic
Revival* (1928) had begun the reappraisal of the Victorian period and this had, for some,
joined with the impact of European surrealism in a second front against ideas of "good
form" and was echoed by the *AR*'s editors' case for flouting "good taste" in their statement
of editorial policy in 1947.[120]

This surrealist-tinged attitude to disquieting affects of the past has a strong lineage in
British thought on historic preservation, as Piper explained in his article "Pleasing Decay"
(1947).[121] The ethic of evidencing the full life of a building and not judging that history with
current aesthetic prejudices is itself an aesthetic of age, decay, and incongruity confluent
with the picturesque and with surrealism. Pevsner was well aware of this discourse and
claims in an article excerpted in Part III that the English have an aesthetic preference to see
the varied and incongruous stages of building, as opposed to the European preference for
formal completion.[122] Pevsner's account, however, does not have the color with which writers like Herbert Read and painters like Nash and Piper were attempting to naturalize surrealism. For Pevsner, the English interest in landscape is an affirmative aesthetic of pleasure,
but the *AR*'s first interest in genius loci came from Nash, by which he meant uncanniness
of a landscape as an active force that could affect the deep unconscious.[123] His painting
Monster Field (1939; Durban, Durban Art Gallery) of a fallen tree as a malevolent creature
was first published in the *AR* as a photograph and essay.[124]

It is these loosely surrealist traits that in the postwar period came to be classed as neo-
romantic following Piper's title for his book of 1942, *British Romantic Artists*.[125] Whimsy,
psychological introspection, and a mythic concept of place are aspects of Townscape that
we do not find in *Visual Planning*. Perhaps Pevsner would have found them uninteresting
or distasteful, but he was also making a historical judgment. Pevsner's insistence that the
picturesque was an empirical aesthetic is correct. The eighteenth-century picturesque
was concerned with visual effects rather than affecting a subject—it was pre-romantic is
this regard, and Pevsner wanted it to stay that way. The picturesqueness that interested
Pevsner had a defined place in the history of eighteenth-century ideas, but his British
colleagues were acculturated in a nineteenth-century romantic picturesque flavored by
William Blake and Samuel Palmer, Lewis Carroll and Edward Lear. The series of articles
on the picturesque that Pevsner published through the 1940s, which make up a good deal
of Part II, should be seen in this context. Making Price, Repton, Joshua Reynolds, William

Temple, and other figures available in their historical specificity was intended to put a solid base under the sensibilities that Pevsner found among his colleagues.

The development of *Visual Planning* and Townscape largely played out against the backdrop of World War II with the damage caused to British cities and debates about reconstruction. Richards and Summerson published in the *AR* regular reports on war damage, which were a startlingly aesthetic account of the strange beauty of destruction.[126] In 1944, the circle around the *AR* made a case for bombed churches to be preserved in ruin as war memorials.[127] Later, Pevsner gave a radio talk on the subject on the BBC,[128] and around the same time, Casson would turn up the pitch on this curious mixture of war, art, and architecture with his "Art by Accident: The Aesthetics of Camouflage" (1944).[129] The *AR* saw reconstruction as the time when modern architecture would achieve its historic role. But they were equally concerned that doctrinaire modernists would take the occasion of extensive bomb damage to make a true tabula rasa of British cities, stating in the foreword to their first extensive plan for the city of London, "How can this aged structure be rebuilt? A timid preservationist attitude aiming at mere street improvement falls as short of what is required as the fantasies of the brave-new-worlders. Constructive compromise is what the *genius loci* calls for, not *tabula rasa*."[130] Of the utmost importance here was the insistence by the *AR*'s contributors on a nonrevivalist idiom of architecture, along with an empirical appreciation of the diversity and heterogeneity of the urban scene. Townscape's early discourses criticized the deleterious effects of modernization in both town and country while championing the proliferation of modern architecture.

The *AR*'s search for a reformed modernism found precedent in Scandinavian modernism, which the *AR* had labeled the "new empiricism" in the late 1940s because of its less dogmatic adherence to the international style and its incorporation of local motifs, materials, and traditions.[131] As early as 1941, Pevsner—as his alter ego, Peter F. R. Donner—could say the following in the editorial introduction to his "Criticism" series:

> These monthly articles are frankly about aesthetic aspects of architectural design. They are written in the belief that we can now take the practical basis of modern architecture for granted. They claim […] that we have got beyond the stage when we were so thankful for the sheer reasonableness and efficiency[,] that these were sufficient recommendation in themselves, and that there is room now, in criticism as in actual design, for study of the graces that all good architecture displays, whether in the precedents set by the past or the growing maturity of the present.[132]

This reform was developed parallel—but in stark contrast—to the new monumentalism in the United States of America, which proposed a return to the grand and formal aspirations in architecture and planning that the more modest formulation of modernism as utilitarian had undermined.[133] The development of Townscape resulted in the precarious balance of striking visual qualities of modern architecture and its placement within a more traditionalist mode of urban planning. These ideas tended to result in projects that were developed with more consideration of their visual qualities and in consultation with their sites and the genius loci—an idea that went on to be known as contextualism. They also displayed a striking mixture of new and old and sought to invoke the moving spectator rather than the static viewer. More generally, these ideas resulted in designs that were informal, irregular, and ungainly, and involved contrasting compositions of mass, materials, and texture. The architect was expected to innovate and invent, the planner to incorporate and moderate. Hastings referred to this as the "cultivation of significant differences" from which the "radical planner has to produce his practical surrealist picture."[134] This implied an approach to architecture and planning that was no longer ideal, rational, or pure, but synthetic, mixed, and compromised: qualities gleaned, not incidentally, from the interpretation of the picturesque. In this campaign, Pevsner's argument about irregularity is a crucial one and perhaps his major contribution. Although de Wolfe was largely concerned with the Englishness of the picturesque and its anti-idealism, it is Pevsner who links functionalism and nonsymmetrical plan forms with the eighteenth-century visual value of "irregularity," an issue to which we will shortly return.

This brief review of Townscape reveals a movement with an eclectic and somewhat eccentric range of sources and an almost irreconcilably wide range of interests. These interests also implied a new scope for designers and a new scale of operations. Rather than focusing on architecture and planning alone, Townscape proposed to examine all aspects of what is today termed the built environment. Townscape, it was felt, should attend to all the visible artifacts within the urban scene, from which the visual planner could create "a humane kind of urban scenery, a humanized townscape."[135] Many positions taken up by Townscape in the 1940s—those concurrent with *Visual Planning*—are perhaps more familiar to postmodernism in architecture and urbanism from the 1960s onwards. Today, this feature supplies Townscape with not only a historical but a topical interest as well.

The Principal Ideas of *Visual Planning and the Picturesque*

Pevsner's text is intended to recommend visual planning as a method of urban design and, at that level, it is a simple idea. Planning should serve the views it creates, and planners and architects should think in terms of human engagement in sequences of views rather than with orthographic plans that represent abstractions. The second part of the title, "and the Picturesque," complicates the idea because it announces that Pevsner intends to argue with the authority of history over and above whatever efficacy he can claim for visual planning. What the difference is between visual planning and the picturesque, and what potential lies in an historical understanding of their similarity, is the tension that drives the book.

Before looking at how Pevsner's ideas and argument intersect, it would be useful to summarize what visual planning is. We could begin with what it is not: what is not planned visually is much of what one would expect of town planners; that is, there is no discussion of demographics and density, land use, water supply and sewage, or traffic and transport. Pevsner's approach is consistent with de Wolfe's idea that all practicalities of planning cannot be considered until there is a "picture of the kind of world the physical planner will make."[136] Pevsner qualified this view in stating that the usual planning concerns of "housing, slum clearance, traffic regulation, etc. [...] are indispensable, but visual planning is also indispensable, and if the whole of a town is in the end not visually pleasing, the town is not worth having."[137]

Pevsner's planning can be scenographic because it excludes the structures and quantities that can only be made visible in orthographic plans. Visual planning is then purely formal, but in the sense of a primary relation of space and the subject rather than the spatial properties of objects. Pevsner emphasizes the sequential views of a peripatetic viewer, whose sense of spatial form occurs in duration. To read Pevsner's descriptions of Oxford in Part I is to momentarily think that the city is a device that choreographs the movement of a subject. While Pevsner is proposing to take landscape design techniques, such as those of Repton, into urban design, one could equally say that his approach was cinematographic. Pevsner describes the admixture of textures, forms, historic styles, and everyday life (and, we must assume, all the practical matters of town planning) as being composed by the sequential attention of the moving spectator. A radical corollary of Pevsner's approach is that planning does not necessarily involve a plan or planner. Rather, the visual qualities of a place can develop through a mutual awareness of values and opportunities by generations of builders. Visual planning is thus additive, and tactical, based on an empirical observation of opportunities to strengthen existing qualities rather than on preformulated ideals. This idea is a clear development over Raymond Unwin, Barry Parker, and Camillo Sitte, for whom the forms of old cities were themselves a kind of ideal. For Pevsner, with his radical split between architecture and planning, the ideals and formal language of different periods of architecture are the better for that difference: their belonging together is purely visual, and to understand the contingency of viewpoint which seems to form a city is to more truly grasp its historicity.

Given the emphasis of the book on the picturesque and landscape design, it is notable that the examples of visual planning are largely enclosed open spaces, collegiate courts, and Georgian squares, not a landscape-like connection of objects in a field—*Visual Planning* might also have been called precinctual planning. The book assumes a degree of knowledge of the examples, and thus it clearly addresses a British readership. This nationalism is not, however, exclusive; it has its meaning in contrast to geometrical planning, and it plays a part in Western art and architecture as a whole.

The structure of the book is clear. In Part I, Pevsner describes places with the terms of pictorial composition and in a mode learned directly from eighteenth-century sources, particularly William Gilpin and Repton. Part II gives a history of the picturesque as a mentality and practice that developed in England from the late seventeenth century. This concrete history is important to Pevsner, but more important is his idea that the principles of the picturesque are abstract and ahistorical. Part III shows how a correct understanding of picturesque principles could allow the development of an urban-design theory appropriate to modern architecture.

Part I is an introduction, but a substantial and inventive one where Pevsner gives the reader an experiential account of the kind of urban form that the book proposes. The book thus relies on the reader's initial complicity in agreeing to share the pleasure that Pevsner describes in wandering the streets of Oxford and the Inns of Court in London. In Part III, he proposes a twentieth-century picturesque that should not be confused with images of rustic landscape. It is thus quite important that in Part I the reader sees directly the visual qualities of Oxford in the photographs and in Pevsner's prose without the identifications of rural landscape that the word *picturesque* carries or the conceptual terms and the understanding of the historical development that Pevsner will later introduce. Oxford and the Inns of Court are not picturesque in the historical sense, as Part II will tell us—this began in the late seventeenth century. While Part I risks several confusions, Pevsner is laying the ground for two important aspects of his argument: first, that urban form can be understood purely visually, in an open sequence, and from everyday terrestrial viewpoints; second, that this visual experience of towns is picturesque, when most readers in his time and since would understand this term to apply to rustic subjects.

Had *Visual Planning* been published in Britain in the late 1940s, its sequential views would have drawn comparisons to Unwin's representation of nine views of the town of Buttstedt in his well-known *Town Planning in Practice*[138] or even closer ones to Sharp's *Oxford Replanned*.[139] There are less obvious precedents in August Choisy and Repton; however, Pevsner's emphasis on sequence is a crucial development. Sharp, Unwin, and Sitte before him, and Gibberd a little later, all used multiple views keyed to plans, but the views are not necessarily in sequence.[140] Rather, urban experience is described as significant views from a variety of viewpoints that one can then correlate with the plan. In this sense, the plan is necessary for using the views, and we could imagine more viewpoints being added, or some elided. It is the plan that provides a conspectus of the urban experience, and the views illustrate this—the plan is the gestalt within which the percepts find their place. Pevsner's walk through Oxford, by comparison, has its structure in the walk, and the views are related in their succession. We might wonder as to his choice of the beginning and end of the walk, but each view is related to the next, and the urban form is described by this sequence. Pevsner began work on *The Buildings of England* guidebooks in 1945, the first three volumes appeared in 1951, and the itinerary in *Visual Planning* undoubtedly resembled the tourist's itinerary.[141] The manuscript materials for *Visual Planning* did not include finished plans for Pevsner's tours, and in many ways the book would stand without plans in the same way that plans in guidebooks are unnecessary once one has located one's self. But the greater point is that town planning can be done without plans. In a city of baroque axes and rond-points, visual experience is a kind of filling out of an already known gestalt, and terrestrial views are subjugated to an abstract viewpoint overhead. In Pevsner's picturesque urbanism, all one's experience would be immediate and replete, perception and cognition undivided, and the "plan" would merely be the outcome of planning for vision.

Part II gives a history of the picturesque, and this is the part of the book that is most familiar, as versions of it were published as articles in the *AR* as the book was being written and in support of the Townscape campaign for a modern picturesque. How Pevsner presents this history, and more so its geography, is crucial to his argument and not entirely apparent in the text.

The picturesque is an aesthetic concept but one embedded in a range of cultural practices and famously elusive of definition. It began in Britain in the late seventeenth century and took its current form when, in the mid-eighteenth century, Gilpin drew on French debates about painting for descriptions of gardens and the countryside.[142] Aesthetically, the picturesque is used to approve of scenes neither beautiful nor sublime, and these tend to be things ordinary or undesirable, which can be the subject for admirable paintings or photographs because of their purely visual qualities. Pevsner's *Visual Planning* is, overall, a serviceable introduction to the idea, and Part II is very useful as Pevsner edits and assembles a chronological selection of the major theoretical sources.[143] With recourse to Pevsner's notes, it is possible to track his attempts to locate the origins and outcomes of picturesque "principles," as he referred to them, principles including intricacy, surprise, impropriety, variety, contrast, piquancy, incongruity, roughness, sudden variation, and irregularity. A recent book by John Macarthur attempts to lay out the picturesque with a fuller treatment of its conceptual complexity, but this is not incompatible with Pevsner's useful account.[144] The classic treatment of the topic is Hussey's *The Picturesque: Studies in a Point of View* (1927), which was Pevsner's first source.[145] As we mentioned above, Pevsner recounts the commission of *Visual Planning* as a remark by Hastings as to their mutual admiration for Hussey's book and its relevance to the work of the *AR* in the 1940s. Although Hussey's is the better conspectus of the idea, *Visual Planning* has two aims that take it beyond Hussey.

Hussey's is a sympathetic and subtle exposition of what he saw as an underappreciated continuity in English taste and cultural production. The book begins with Hussey's awakening to the designed qualities of his grandfather's house, Scotney Castle in Kent. For Hussey, the works of late-eighteenth-century thinkers such as Price bear quite directly on the present—in every sense, Hussey's book is an autochthon's account. By contrast, Pevsner comes to the picturesque as an outsider, but this is not as self-evident as one might think. If we treat the picturesque as an aesthetic concept, then its history and its nationality are not of pressing interest—it ought to be relevant (or not) to a person's sensory apprehension of the art of ancient Greece or modern Java. The concept of the picturesque had been completely naturalized in Germany and many other places by Pevsner's time. If we think of the picturesque as a cultural and artistic activity in which the aesthetic concept is at play, which is to say as the art historian that Pevsner was, then both the time and the place of the picturesque are quite crucial. This conceptual instability is reflected in the word's etymology. While the root words *pittoresco* and *pittoresque* refer to painters, in English the word *picturesque* was assimilated to pictures, leaving the confusion that it means both what is suitable to be pictured and the qualities of pictures. This equivocation between picturesqueness as an aesthetic differentiation applicable at any time and the picturesque as an artistic culture with a definite history runs through and, to a degree, confuses *Visual Planning*. Thus, while the idea of the picturesque that emerges in *Visual Planning* is quite compatible with Hussey's, in Pevsner's hands the mild contradictions of the terms are strained. They develop into a historical argument about Englishness and a theory about the necessity of irregular spatial forms in modern architecture: two strands of argument Pevsner wanted the picturesque to be strong enough to link.

Pevsner's insistence on the Englishness of the picturesque was a matter completely assumed by Hussey. Consequent on this Englishness was Pevsner's search for the first occurrence of ideas that he and Hussey both knew largely from publications of the 1790s. Finding the genesis of the picturesque in the late seventeenth and early eighteenth centuries, and in arcane joke words such as *sharawaggi*, established precedence and stitched the picturesque into a more fundamental account of English cultural history. In this, Pevsner was following his teacher Pinder's concept of *Kunstgeographie*, of understanding art through its distinctive development in geographical regions and racial and national character. In 1934, only a year after his emigration, Pevsner published "Das Englische in der englischen Kunst," and *The Englishness of English Art* became the title of his Reith Lecture on the BBC and the subsequent book of 1956.[146] The chapter "Picturesque England" contains many of the arguments and some of the prose of *Visual Planning* and, as posited above, may be the reason the book was not published by Pevsner. Whether or not this is the case, it is clear in both works that Pevsner does not take the Englishness of the picturesque for granted. His arguments have a degree of simplistic naturalism (that the damp fertility of the British Isles, or the English love of sports and gardening was a cause), but he also addresses more serious aspects of intellectual history. He tried to show that the picturesque is intimate with the empiricism of British philosophy and science and with the pragmatic liberalism of its political institutions. Pevsner saw in Reynolds the beginnings of a "heritage of compromise" at the core of English art.[147] Hastings most likely took this (among other thoughts of Pevsner's) when The Editor wrote that "exterior furnishing" "lends itself to compromise, which is the English form of synthesis."[148]

Pevsner also held an abstract conceptual account of the picturesque as an aspect of art forms, on the basis of which he thought that modernism was picturesque, just as he had shown Oxford and the Inns of Court to be in Part I. Modernism was asymmetrical because it was, in the first place, functional. Pevsner intended to show that the picturesque was the aesthetic of functionalism, combining *locus* and *usus* as he put it.[149] Modernism was at odds with the taste of the British public and commissioning classes who, if they thought at all of a "modern" picturesque, would have followed Hussey's admiration for Edwin Lutyens. But Pevsner, drawing on the picturesque aesthetic concept of irregularity, believed that the asymmetrical forms of modernist architecture, because they could not be easily grasped as simple symmetrical figures, were easier to appropriate in a purely visual manner and hence picturesque. Now this is a picturesque principle, but not necessarily an English one.

Pevsner and the other originators of Townscape were greatly influenced by Sitte, whose book is studded with observations of *malerische* urban structures, which was translated quite straightforwardly as "picturesque" by Raymond Unwin. The picturesque idea had been greatly generalized and acculturalized in German aesthetic discourse on what we would now call the spatial affects of seventeenth-century Roman architecture, first discussed in these terms by Jacob Burckhardt.[150] Pevsner would have known the role *das Malerische* played in the most famous text on the method of art history: Heinrich Wölfflin's *Principles of Art History* (1915).[151] Wölfflin, together with Alois Riegl and Pinder's teacher August Schmarsow, were competing around the beginning of the twentieth century to explain the relation of building form and appearance. Thus, a version of picturesqueness lies at the origin of the idea that spatial form can be distinguished from object form. Pevsner's contemporary Sigfried Giedion, a student of Wölfflin's, used these ideas to put space at the heart of the modernist project, and, as discussed above, *Visual Planning* shares many of the ambitions of Giedion's *Space, Time and Architecture*.[152] Throughout the book Pevsner distinguishes picturesque objects from the principles of the picturesque, but it is the relation of these two that is at stake. Pevsner aims to show that the widely recognized picturesqueness of landscape parks, asymmetric accented nineteenth-century buildings, and twee garden suburbs is historically related to earlier, quite different forms and has the potential to be realized in a modern idiom. Under this historical trajectory of the picturesque are common and unchanging principles.

Beyond historical awareness, there are two practical lessons Pevsner wanted his readers to take from *Visual Planning*. First, that the picturesque can show us the aesthetic potential of functional building planning. Second, that the loosely geometric, contingently connected urban pattern of squares that characterizes Oxbridge and parts of London is a planning idea distinct from the baroque axial planning and symmetrical squares of Europe, and that this planning idea can, despite some chronological problems, also be described as picturesque.

While modernists believed that form followed function, Pevsner thought that this had been proved avant la lettre by eighteenth-century English writers observing the pleasing irregularity of buildings that had grown through use and circumstance. In general, this is a sound historical argument, but Pevsner overreaches in tying his two strands of argument together. Passages of *Visual Planning* can give the impression that the qualities of buildings that arise from determinations of site and function are not simply that but the historically determined obligatory forms of the twentieth century, and that, having began in England, modernism in architecture will reach its fulfillment there.[153]

Part II begins with quotations from Henry Wotton and Francis Bacon and writing about irregularity, announcing an agenda that runs through the entire book. The principle of the picturesque is a visual empiricism like the scientific empiricism with which Bacon critiqued scholasticism and began modern epistemology. Pevsner's point throughout is that symmetry has a cultural authority but is fundamentally irrational. On the one hand, if we designed buildings without preconceptions and by observation of the relation of building forms and uses, building forms would follow their functions. On the other hand, if we "[i]mpose symmetry, impose axiality and grids, impose rules even where the artist is feeling his way, . . . you reduce usefulness."[154] Pevsner wrote that picturesque landscape and the buildings of Le Corbusier and Frank Lloyd Wright could be considered in the same way as a "free exercise of the imagination stimulated by the disciplines of function and technique."[155] He follows remarks on the "irregularity" of forms with evidence in the eighteenth century that the picturesque was not merely a visually intriguing formal variation but rather an attention to site and viewpoint. By the end of Part II, however, he expressed disappointment:

> This search for evidence in eighteenth-century literature of an appreciation of
> picturesque architecture has brought us but a meagre harvest. Even more disap-
> pointing is a search for any appreciation of visual planning in towns. What can

here be quoted does not exceed some four or five passages, and not one of them is Knight's or Price's.[156]

In fact, there is good evidence in the works of Uvedale Price and Richard Payne Knight that Pevsner overlooked when writing *Visual Planning* (and which he later acknowledged). Like Pevsner, Knight thought that symmetry, while having a basis in human and animal form, was largely customary in art, where it is "the result of arbitrary convention."[157] "The system of regularity, of which the moderns have been so tenacious in the plans of their country houses, was taken from the sacred, and not the domestic architecture of the ancients,"[158] he wrote. "[T]he villas or country houses of the Romans were quite irregular—adapted to the situations on which they were placed and spread out in every direction."[159]

Knight's observations are referenced to his understanding of Hadrian's villa at Tivoli, and this seems to have inspired his own irregular house, Downton Castle (see p. 143, fig. 17). Although Pevsner claims that Knight nowhere recommends that his readers follow his example, Knight refers to Downton explicitly and points out that it has "at once, the advantage of a picturesque object, and of an elegant and convenient dwelling[....] It has [...] the advantage of being able of receiving alterations and additions in almost any direction without injury to its genuine character."[160] That this is a recommendation rather than a mere reflection is clear when Knight writes, "The best style of architecture for irregular and picturesque houses, which can now be adopted, is that mixed style, which characterises the buildings of Claude and the Poussins."[161] It is odd that in *Visual Planning* Pevsner ignores these passages, which continue from the quotation he does take of Knight approving symmetry in animal forms. Susan Lang, Pevsner's student and collaborator, later made a fuller account of Knight's architectural significance, which Pevsner acknowledged.[162]

Of the numerous passages by Price explaining the principles of irregularity that Pevsner passes over, this is perhaps the clearest:

> Now if the owner of such a spot, instead of making a regular front and sides, were to insist upon having many of the windows turned towards those points where the objects were most happily arranged, the architect would be forced into the invention of a number picturesque forms and combinations, which otherwise might never have occurred to him.[163]

These remarks were well known to architects of the time and quickly became the license for pattern books such as James Malton's *Essay on British Cottage Architecture* (1798). Indeed, in the hundred or so pattern books for cottage, villa, and rural architecture published from 1780 to 1840, irregularity becomes a standard topic in which claims as to its scenic and functional benefits are debated. Pevsner must have known of this genre of architectural works because he refers to them in his article of 1943 on a late example, that of Richard Brown.[164]

It is also remarkable that Pevsner did not find Price's descriptions of improving villages of interest.

> [should the improver] choose to preserve the look of a farm or hamlet [...] any building of good form, rising higher than the rest amidst them, would probably answer to that purpose, and serve at once to vary and unite the whole group— [....] There may be cases also where an improver, with great property all round, may have only a small piece of ground in such a hamlet, and be unable to purchase any more: a building of the character I mentioned, might do all that a lover of painting would wish for, and give him a sort of property in the whole; and I know that manner of appropriating objects to be the source of much pleasure.[165]

Understanding and acquiring prominent sites in order to form a visual unity is the very basis of visual planning. The concept of appropriation that Price mentions was greatly elaborated by Repton as a technique of forming visual unities and imaginary property by controlling viewpoints.[166]

It is not clear what to make of these apparent oversights by Pevsner. The scholarship of *Visual Planning* is not perfect, and Aitchison has corrected the text at several points, as doubtless Pevsner would have done before he sent it to press. It is possible that research assistants who were insufficiently briefed prepared Pevsner's research notes. It is also possible that, consciously or unconsciously, he did not want to see the extent to which modern planning techniques were already conceptualized around 1800. To an extent, it suits his argument for the full potential of irregularity to remain imminent in the picturesque, so that it can escape the contagion of nineteenth-century style and have its apotheosis in modernism. In this, he echoes a sentiment similar to that of The Editor, who ends the seminal "Exterior Furnishing or Sharawaggi" with the lines "Any time he so desires the modern town-planner is free to pick up Picturesque theory at the point before its corruption by the Gothic Revival; pick up the theory, rediscover the prophets, and apply the principles."[167]

In Part III, Aitchison includes Pevsner's description of the development of nineteenth-century picturesque architecture that takes a line through Charles Barry the Elder, G. G. Scott, Aston Webb, and Norman Shaw to arrive at Charles Francis Annesley Voysey and the Arts and Crafts movement. Pevsner deals with these without prejudice. Picturesque architecture as it is represented in Part II, however, is presented more in the spirit of "Ivor de Wolfe" (Hastings, but probably aided by Pevsner), who wrote in 1949 that

> the full implications of the modern movement with all its baffling ambiguities *can only be brought out by reference to the eighteenth century,* in which, and not the nineteenth, were set up those basic contradictions which were to form the stuff of the modern dilemma.[168]

In any case, the quotations above are offered in support of Pevsner's overall argument that the organizational capacities of planning were discovered in the project of picturesque scenography.

Irregularity and landscape are important for the bigger claim of *Visual Planning*. Modern architecture did not, in Pevsner's mind, require the history of the picturesque to justify it, but modern planning was another matter. While the *AR* team approved of modern building, they saw modernist urbanism, epitomized by Le Corbusier's Ville Radieuse, as excessively geometric and idealized. For Pevsner, geometrical city planning is at odds with the organic irregularity of functionally designed buildings. But, beyond this formal issue, Pevsner and his colleagues were skeptical of the high level of rationalization that geometric planning promised.[169] Not only did this suppose implausible levels of political power and economic costs, but they opposed the ethos of a single vision, which connoted the absolutism of the ancien régime and contemporary dictatorships. This was the same complaint made of French gardening by English eighteenth-century writers such as Horace Walpole and William Mason, and it complements Pevsner's Englishness thesis, but this is more than symbolic politics.[170] Pevsner is opposing theoretical and empirical methods in planning. His claim is that planning by contingency, opportunity, and compromise on a site-by-site basis is ultimately more practical and rational than ideal patterns applied to particular circumstances. His regular refrain of the irrationality of symmetry in building planning is equally true of city design. We can see the impracticality of grand designs in the failure to implement Christopher Wren's baroque plan of London after the Great Fire. But Pevsner is not proposing that cities can be designed functionally and irregularly like buildings, as Camillo Sitte, Raymond Unwin, or Patrick Geddes might have. His point is, rather, that cities cannot be designed, in the sense of constructed to a figure, at all.

Pevsner's prime example, which he knew from the research of Summerson, is John Nash's rapid retreat from an axial layout for Regent Street to a picturesque route.[171] Nash designed some passages so that the street would be pleasingly picturesque, but the design was in fact determined by finding preexisting elements that could be stitched together with economical land purchases. This resulted in a different relation of architecture and planning to the typical European or colonial city. The architect cannot take charge of the urban territory in the manner supposed by Charles Garnier or Le Corbusier. Each architect and builder makes the urban environment directly in the coordination that they seek or ignore in their relation to neighboring sites. Thus, the tasks of city-making and building-making have quite different levels of agency, where every building design is already an urban design. When Pevsner draws our attention to the attractiveness of English towns in Part I, his point is that while there is no plan that has been implemented, over a long period the iterative and tactical design decisions of individual builders become appreciable. In this, Pevsner is remarkably close the contextualist urbanism of the 1960s and 1970s.

The visual attractiveness of picturesque townscape not only opens the important distinction between urban and architectural agency; for Pevsner and his colleagues, there are two other related aspects. The AR's opposition to modernist planning is also a critique of the modernists' tabula rasa approach to existing cities, and thus there is a good deal of preservationist discourse within the Townscape movement. When Pevsner presented his idea of a picturesque revival to the RIBA, Hussey gave his conditional support on the grounds that historic buildings would be preserved.[172] In the architectural politics of the time, the AR opted for a compromise between avant-garde modernists associated with the Modern Architectural Research Group (MARS Group) and the public and institutional clients who preferred historicist public buildings and Arts and Crafts–tinged interpretations of vernacular dwellings. The AR pushed the line that if architects and planners took up the planning principles that Townscape and Visual Planning described, then the modern buildings would be rightly popular because the unpopularity of modern building was largely explained by its association with the destruction of places of public sentiment.

In the excerpted texts that Aitchison has chosen to represent the uncompleted Part III, we have a further sense of the complex interaction of Pevsner's argument and historical narrative. Pevsner's main contribution to urban theory is the idea of precinctual planning. Again Pevsner draws a historical argument starting with Oxbridge collegiate planning, praising Georgian Bath and Edinburgh, and heading toward the work of Casson, Gibberd, Holford, and Leslie Martin. The genesis of the picturesque in the eighteenth century does not fit at all well into this chronology, nor does the fact that Price hated Bath, thinking its elegance very unpicturesque. There are two things of interest here: first, what Pevsner's idea of precinctual planning was, and second, how this interacts with his historical positioning of the picturesque.

Visual Planning advocates a broken or incomplete geometric building layout, the epitome of which is Holford's plan for Saint Paul's, with its syncopated courts and contrived views to significant elements of Wren's cathedral (see p. 191, fig. 32). The formal values here are similar to those of Sitte and his admiration for piazzas of Italian towns where basic simple forms are accented by irregular connections and asymmetric building placement. Pevsner also admires, indeed enthuses over, Casson's Cambridge Arts Faculty, which is orthogonal and only slightly accented but which fits loosely into its precinct, the irregular Sedgwick site (see p. 192, fig. 33; p. 194, fig. 34). This is like the Inns of Court and Oxford examples in Part I, but it is also very like the ideas of a later detractor of Townscape: Colin Rowe.[173] Rowe's more sophisticated explanation has it that good cities are irregular in the sense that Pevsner and Sitte describe, but this is not because of the scenic sensibility and visual planning that Pevsner details. Rather, this is caused by the overlay of incomplete figures, in a collage of urban fragments that gives Rowe the title for his famous book *Collage City* (1978). We will return to this connection. Here it is sufficient to point out that Pevsner's picturesque urbanism was figural and favored the loose nonaxial squares of medieval collegiate buildings, or the complete but topographically placed and irregularly connected arcs and polygons of Georgian Bath or Edinburgh. As he summarized,

> What is most English in English town-planning, and in fact amounts in my opinion to England's essential contribution to town-planning development [...] is not the Circus or the Crescent as such, but the picturesque way in which such set pieces are placed as accents in an informal composition.[174]

What makes this precinctual planning English is that, first, the squares are lawned and planted with trees and, second, although less explicit, they dispose space around them with irregular facades, unlike the squares of European cities, which have the sense of being spaces carved out of building. Pevsner is claiming that these are picturesque in the expanded aesthetic sense, but it is more difficult to put them in his history as the formal square clearly predates the picturesque landscape.

Pevsner's historical and conceptual intertwining of the picturesque and the urban square follows this sequence. The eighteenth-century fashion for picturesque forms in the country led to the Georgian city squares being gardened in a rural, irregular manner. Then the Garden City movement took the principles of scenographic planning to make cities that had no urban character at all.[175] It is significant, then, that the model of loosely figural courts, contingently connected, pre- and postdates the picturesque in the Tudor Oxford and Casson's modern Cambridge. As Pevsner puts it,

> There is a possibility of applying this informal planning to city problems, but if we want to derive maximum benefit from Price's principles we must apply them as principles, and not take over such actual objects as the picturesque cottage or the landscape square, or at least not excessively.[176]

This relation of picturesque principles to picturesque objects is the lesson that runs through the whole of *Visual Planning* and explains its title—visual planning is the principle of the picturesque.

The Significance of *Visual Planning*

There is not much in *Visual Planning* to surprise a modern reader; what will interest scholars is the conjunction and arrangement of material and its attribution to Pevsner. The simple fact that Pevsner and Townscape are connected so closely corrects two widely held misconceptions. First, that Townscape was historicist, antimodernist, and thus related to the beginnings of postmodernism. *Visual Planning*, along with a wider survey of the published material by Aitchison, shows that the original Townscape was partisanly modernist and remained so for Hastings and Pevsner into the 1970s. Townscape was in favor of historic building conservation and the aesthetic shock of the old and new rubbed together, but staunchly antitraditionalist in building form. Second, *Visual Planning* confronts the idea that Pevsner was an archmodernist whose interest in history was pedantry put to work to support his opinions on contemporary architectural culture. The book shows that Pevsner was critical of the town-planning outcomes of modernism and sought a new urbanism that would allow modernist building to coexist with historical fabric. He argues that modernism in architecture was incomplete without a picturesque critique of the remnant baroque aspects of modernist planning.

There is no doubt that some resources for postmodernism lie in Townscape. This is particularly the case with the would-be popularism of the movement. Townscape celebrated popular and mundane parts of the built environment such as signage, street furniture, and naive uses of architectural style. These aspects are missing from *Visual Planning* and distinguish it and Pevsner from Hastings and the wider movement. Nevertheless, to the extent that the historical high architecture that Pevsner does discuss was also popular and the context remained the unpopularity of modernism, the arguments are complementary. For Pevsner and the *AR*, the unpopularity of modernism was a mistake on both sides. The conceptual and technical differences between modern and historic building that architects exaggerated and which shocked the public did not mean that they were aesthetically incompatible, that they could not be unified visually on a case-by-case basis. By the 1970s, however, this faith in visual unity had worn thin for many architects who became persuaded that modernism was fundamentally incompatible with the social and cultural life of cities.

By foresight or fortune, Cullen, with his *The Concise Townscape* of 1971, had picked the tipping point in architectural discourse. For the next decades, it was impossible not to see the popularity of premodern urban fabric as a call for historicism in building design. For authors such as Aldo Rossi, Leon and Rob Krier, Robert Venturi, and Colin Rowe, the inability of modern architects to make urban space was a symptom of the failure of the modernist project altogether.[177] A raft of new theoretical concepts supported this contention, but they can be loosely grouped as the linguistic turn that also drove developments in anthropology, literary, and cinema studies.[178] The older concepts of building type and city morphology came to be seen to intersect like lexicon and grammar and to explain why, to be urban, building design needed to be based not simply on a present problem but on a historically developed typology.

Visual Planning observes much the same deficiencies in modernist city planning, but for Pevsner the irregularity and contingencies of historically developed cities were interesting not for what they meant to the populace but as models of the development of principles of functionalism and site specificity into urban design. Where Pevsner thinks of the built environment in terms of meaning, his is a softer version of Hastings's surrealist-tinged interest in incongruity—in the way that buildings of popular sentiment, mute engineering structures, and high architecture can have all their various significance sublated into a picture. Certainly, Pevsner did not attempt to think outside of the putative historical necessity of modernism and redirected his observation of its faults into an agenda for future developments. This is not merely ideology; it follows on an understanding of architecture as primarily visual and aesthetic. "Visual," "planning," and the "picturesque" all declined in importance from the late 1960s as the values of meaning and communication supplanted aesthetic pleasure, and structure and constraint replaced form and composition.[179] Postmodernists and other critics of modernism can be understood to have been recovering the rhetorical basis of the discipline as it existed from ancient times, and in this same light we could see *Visual Planning* at the end of the long period of the visual understanding of architecture that began with the rise of aesthetics and its applicability in the picturesque. The fact that "visuality" has returned with a vengeance at the beginning of the new millennium increases the relevance of *Visual Planning*, Townscape, and the critics of both.

The *AR*'s Townscape campaign lingered into the 1970s, when the newer urbanisms began to differentiate themselves against it. Townscape's reputation suffered not only from Cullen's abridgment but also from its caricature in Rowe's *Collage City*. When first published as special issue of the *AR* in 1975, it appeared to be yet another avatar of the Townscape idea.[180] But, by the time *Collage City* was published in book form in 1978, Rowe was strongly distinguishing his idea from a Townscape portrayed as nostalgic, placatory, and manipulative in its top-down popularism: "an open gaol conducted on compassionate principles."[181] Although there is still bite in Rowe's description, the polemical tone and the charge of nostalgia disguise the considerable continuities between Townscape and the contextualism of *Collage City*. Pevsner may not use the word, but it is the collage-like overlay of distinct planning ideas, his "set pieces" adjusted to their sites and to existing features, that he praises in *Visual Planning*. Rowe insists on the poverty of modernist object buildings that displace space around them when compared to the "concave" nature of traditional urban squares, but this is hardly different from Pevsner's ideas of the benefits of precinctual planning, except that, in Rowe, this is shorn of the Englishness argument.[182] Rowe's touchstone for the right relation of buildings is Hadrian's villa at Tivoli, where a series of courts, each with their own concept and form, are arranged contingently with regard to each other and the topography. This is similar to the descriptions of Oxford and the Inns of Court in *Visual Planning* and would have been more so had Pevsner noticed that Knight did make an explicit discussion of irregular building planning and claimed Hadrian's villa as a precedent. At the time of the publication of "Collage City" as a special issue of the *AR*, Banham quipped that its true author was Ivor de Wolfe.[183] Banham, Pevsner's former student, most likely knew of the joint authorship of Townscape and the *Visual Planning* manuscript.

In the 1970s, the issues of urbanism were strongly tied to a newly critical historiography of modernism and the return of the question of architectural meaning. Had *Visual Planning* been in print at the time, Pevsner's teleological understanding of modernism's progress from its origins in the eighteenth century and his visual formalism would have appeared quite dated and unsophisticated, as was the fate of many of his other works. Its publication now, however, tells a different story. In retrospect, it is possible to see how much the contextualists of the late twentieth century owed to Townscape and to the thought of Pevsner. The idea that urban design required partly enclosed exterior spaces has its strongest statement in Sitte, who was the frequently unacknowledged source for urbanists across the twentieth century. This ancient urbanism of piazzas was at odds with the modern infrastructure-driven urbanism of fields and networks. Casson, Martin, Gibberd, Holford, and others were working out possible compromises, and Pevsner in *Visual Planning* provides historical resources and terms to underpin this way of designing with mixed urban systems. Pevsner's terms and historical props for explaining this way of designing were obsolete by the 1970s, but they provided a space for thinking about and developing increasingly sophisticated methods of urban design that continue through the twentieth century, even as the terms and horizon for architectural thought changed, a change epitomized by *collage* replacing *picturesque*.

Today, the contextualism of the 1970s, with its hopes for a renewal of the language of traditional urbanism of Europe, seems naive and nostalgic—much in the same way Rowe had portrayed Townscape in the 1970s. This is particularly so when faced not only with massive urbanization in Asia (an issue that Pevsner would not have thought on) but also with the remaking of Europe on a scale not seen since the postwar rebuilding that was the context of *Visual Planning*. The linguistic moment is well and truly over in architecture, as is "theory" in the particular mode of evinced antiessentialism and critical historiography. The fashion in urban design is again antihistoricist and scenographic, and if the term *context* is used at all, it is likely to describe identity branding or major transport infrastructure rather than the building lots and street sections in which urbanism was sought in the 1970s. Some contemporary architects even use the word *picturesque,* perhaps to identify themselves against the contextualists of the late twentieth century, and with a further moment of historical symmetry, they introduce neologisms such as *SCAPE©* and *Drosscape,* which tend to prioritize the visual apperception of architecture or cities.[184] In this light, Pevsner's promotion of modernism might be read with less attention to his historicism and more to his "projective" impulse, his willingness to engage historical thinking in an imagined future.

The second major significance of *Visual Planning* is what it tells us of the work of Pevsner, particularly the charge that his use of history in the promotion of modernism was methodologically shoddy or actually immoral. In 1968, Pevsner was the target of two quite different younger historians. In *Teorie e storia dell'archittettura* (1968; *Theories and History of Architecture,* 1980), Manfredo Tafuri put Pevsner with Giedion and Bruno Zevi in a class of "operative critics." "Operative criticism is, then, an ideological criticism (we always use the term ideological in its Marxian sense): it substitutes ready-made judgments of value [...] for analytic rigour."[185] Tafuri claimed that modernism, an objective historical tendency, was being systematically distorted into an ideology by those promoting it. Pevsner and the other first-generation historians of modernism, by praising current developments that were ideologically consistent with what had already been written about pre–World War II modernism, were thus ill-prepared to deal with the rise of historicism in the late 1960s and 1970s.

David Watkin also began his critique of Pevsner, his former teacher, in 1968, in a lecture that developed into the controversial book *Morality and Architecture.*[186] Watkin, a proponent of classical architecture, represented exactly the critique of modernism that Tafuri feared it was unprepared for. Watkin pointed out in stark terms the hubris of historical determinist arguments, which supposed that actions in the present could be determined right or wrong on the basis of whether they accorded with a historical process. Watkin was thus attacking the belief in overarching historical processes that would explain the relation of individual lives in terms of the development of societies, economies, and mentalities.[187]

With Pevsner as his principal example, Watkin showed how judgments about current architecture have frequently been supported by historical argument in such a way as to appear inevitable. Pevsner is absolutely clear that the aim of the historian is to reveal to architects the historical circumstances in which they worked, but in Watkin's view such historicism erodes individual choice and responsibility in design.[188] Pevsner had an a priori belief in the logical and moral necessity of modernist architecture and then sought evidence in the past for a development toward this telos. But here Watkin's critique joins that of Tafuri in the claim that Pevsner distorts the past to serve the interests of his present argument, and this is the crux of the matter.

Tafuri's book was translated in 1980, and his position became integral to the American journal *Oppositions* and the critical (or at least self-conscious) revival of modernism under a neo-avant-garde position. Watkin's book was a great support for the British new classicists gathered around Prince Charles's promotion of a classical revival. Even the *AR,* Pevsner's former stronghold, joined in the critique, in terms that have since become familiar in works surrounding Pevsner's legacy. The *AR*'s feature article referred to Watkin's book as a "time bomb" and "a Nuremburg trial of academics."[189] Later Pevsner was blamed for the problems of modernist planning and taken to be a proponent of the Ville Radieuse by Timothy Mowl. Watkin's opposition to modernism was so jaundiced that he made it a more monolithic doctrine than any member of CIAM could have hoped for, and he wrote as if modernists were necessarily committed to tabula rasa redevelopment of urban sites and opposed to the conservation of historic buildings. Mowl, taking his authority from Watkin, sees Pevsner as a proponent of the point-block towers against which Betjeman was defending English particularism, which is a great misunderstanding.[190] Betjeman's antagonism toward Pevsner arose from their personalities and their rival guidebook series, but Hastings had put them both to work in the *AR*'s Townscape campaign against the Ville Radieuse. In Part III of *Visual Planning*, it is clear that a considerable body of Pevsner's writing denies this interpretation. Thus, in the 1980s, it seemed that left and right had combined to demolish Pevsner's authority, and he died with his reputation much diminished in 1983.

Visual Planning will not persuade any critic of Pevsner that subtlety and nuance underlie his historical method, but it does give us evidence of his fundamental honesty and of a much more complex relationship with modernism than one would understand from Watkin or Tafuri. It is precisely the point of *Visual Planning* to show architects what history would have them do and to give a historical frame to the contemporary architects that Pevsner preferred. But there is no sleight of hand here. Part I is a lesson in appreciation, Part II is a lesson in history, and Part III is a critical and evaluative study. The manuscript makes clear that Pevsner intended to put his various personas as guide, historian, and critic articulated under one cover, with the argument open to inspection. The criticisms of Tafuri and Watkin assume a degree of duplicity on Pevsner's part; as Stephen Games puts it, Pevsner "sometimes wrote as if the two activities were interchangeable. His historical works were also attempts at persuasion; his critical works were also attempts to secure a particular version of history."[191] This is not true of *Visual Planning*, which lays out the relation clearly.

Beneath his elaborate critique of "operative criticism," Tafuri does allow that there might be an honest form of history written with the aim of being "instrumental" in present architectural debates: "We do not think that the presence of a strongly distorted or instrumentalised critical and historiographical production is necessarily harmful or incorrect. If it were possible to use this kind of literature in assisting the comprehension of the methods and poetics in evolution, [...] we could accept its accentuated tendentiousness."[192] Although these terms might be odd ones with which to defend Pevsner, we can say nevertheless that *Visual Planning* offers the articulation Tafuri describes of an honestly instrumental history.

There is renewed interest in the history of architectural history and the role that historians played as actors in the development of modern architecture, particularly after World War II. Recent works by Nigel Whiteley and Anthony Vidler deal objectively with Pevsner, but largely in the context of the early career of his other famous pupil, Banham.[193] The present volume aims to contribute to that revision. But along with a more balanced view of what historians and polemicists such as Giedion, Pevsner, and Zevi were doing must follow a reopening of the question of the utility of history. The now-common suspicion and relativism concerning the authority of historians tells us little about how ideas and examples from the past can be made available to architects, an issue that Pevsner approaches in a refreshingly straightforward manner in *Visual Planning*.

Visual Planning also gives an opportunity to correct the impression that Pevsner was doctrinaire in his modernism. It is true that he thought it impossible to conceive of architecture outside of modernism, but this did not mean that he thought it a complete and stable concept or movement. *Visual Planning* makes clear that modernism has a stage further to go in its development from building planning into urban planning. This development was incomplete and open for Pevsner and his readers to explore and to experiment with the tools of historical precedent, just as the architects Pevsner praised were doing with designs.

Many think of Townscape as a resource for showing the inhumanity of modernism when compared to traditional urban forms. *Visual Planning* shows that this is not true of the earlier life of Townscape and its origins in Hastings's commission to Pevsner. For those who think Pevsner is a blinkered proponent of the modernism of Gropius's generation and an enemy of tradition, *Visual Planning* shows the need for a more nuanced account. Pevsner was a historicist who believed that buildings became obsolescent as the present was continuously realized, but he also believed that the past was a present and available resource—and, moreover, that past and present could be experienced together through visual planning.

NOTES

1. Ivor de Wolfe [Hubert de Cronin Hastings], "Townscape: A Plea for an English Visual Philosophy Founded on the True Rock of Sir Uvedale Price," *AR* 106 (1949): 354–62.

2. The following biography draws on *Pevsner on Art and Architecture: The Radio Talks*, ed. Stephen Games (London: Methuen, 2002), xiiv–xl; and Brian Harrison, "Pevsner, Sir Nikolaus Bernhard Leon (1902–1983)," in *Oxford Dictionary of National Biography* (Oxford: Oxford Univ. Press, 2004), 43:969–74. Where other sources have been used, they are referenced accordingly.

3. See Pevsner's résumé, which can be found in box 14b, folder "Notes," in the Nikolaus Pevsner papers, 1919–79, acc. no. 840209, Research Library, Getty Research Institute, Los Angeles; hereafter Nikolaus Pevsner papers.

4. *Pevsner on Art and Architecture* (note 2), xxxi.

5. See Nikolaus Pevsner papers, box 14b, folder "Notes."

6. Harrison, "Pevsner" (note 2), 43:969–74; and Peter F. R. Donner [Nikolaus Pevsner], "The Royal Gold Medal: Nikolaus Pevsner," *RIBA Journal* 74 (1967): 10. The Getty Research Institute holds Pevsner's private scrapbooks containing the clippings of his early articles, including those written under his pseudonym Ramaduri and those published in the German-language wartime newspaper *Die Zeitung* (on such topics as "rubble removalists" and "rubble removalist psychology"). See Nikolaus Pevsner papers, box 137.

7. *Pevsner on Art and Architecture* (note 2), xxxi.

8. J. M. Richards, *Memoirs of an Unjust Fella* (London: Weidenfeld & Nicolson, 1980), 133.

9. See a full list of Pevsner's broadcasts in *Pevsner on Art and Architecture* (note 2), 343–46.

10. Richards, *Memoirs* (note 8), 187.

11. *Pevsner on Art and Architecture* (note 2), xli.

12. See Seymour Slive, "Nikolaus Pevsner's Contribution as Editor of *The Pelican History of Art* Series," in Peter Draper, ed., *Reassessing Nikolaus Pevsner* (Aldershot: Ashgate, 2004), 73–74. See also Nikolaus Pevsner, "Foreword," in John Barr, ed., *Sir Nikolaus Pevsner: A Bibliography* (Charlottesville: University of Virginia Press for the American Association of Architectural Bibliographers, 1970), vii–xi.

13. Nikolaus Pevsner, *Pioneers of the Modern Movement: From William Morris to Walter Gropius* (London: Faber & Faber, 1936).

14. Nikolaus Pevsner, "Nine Swallows—No Summer," *AR* 91 (1942): 109–12.

15. Nikolaus Pevsner, *An Enquiry into Industrial Arts in England* (Cambridge: Cambridge Univ. Press, 1937).

16. Nikolaus Pevsner, *An Outline of European Architecture* (Harmondsworth: Penguin, 1942).

17. *Pevsner on Art and Architecture* (note 2), xx.

18. Pevsner pointed to this insight in a radio talk from 1949 titled "From William Morris to Walter Gropius," where, in regard to William Morris, he recalled that Gropius had said, "I owe him so very much." *Pevsner on Art and Architecture* (note 2), 36.

19. Pevsner was unequivocal in acknowledging his chief influences; see Pevsner, "Foreword" (note 12), vii–xi. For a discussion of Pevsner's *Kunstwissenschaft*, see Ute Engel, "The Formation of Pevsner's Art History: Nikolaus Pevsner in Germany, 1902–1935," in Peter Draper, ed., *Reassessing Nikolaus Pevsner* (Aldershot: Ashgate, 2004), 29–55.

20. Heinrich Wölfflin, *Kunstgeschichtliche Grundbegriffe: Das Problem der Stilentwicklung in der neueren Kunst* (Munich: F. Bruckmann, 1915); Heinrich Wölfflin, *Principles of Art History: The Problem of the Development of Style in Later Art,* trans. Marie Donald Mackie Hottinger (New York: Dover, 1950); and Martin Warnke, "On Heinrich Wölfflin," *Representations,* no. 27 (1989): 172–87.

21. Sigfried Giedion, *Space, Time and Architecture: The Growth of a New Tradition* (Cambridge: Harvard Univ. Press, 1941).

22. Harry Francis Mallgrave and Eleftherios Ikonomou, eds. and trans., *Empathy, Form, and Space: Problems in German Aesthetics, 1873–1893* (Santa Monica: Getty Center for the History of Art & Humanities, 1994); Vernon Lee, *Beauty and Ugliness and Other Studies in Psychological Aesthetics* (London: John Lane, 1912); and Geoffrey Scott, *The Architecture of Humanism: A Study in the History of Taste* (London: Constable, 1924).

23. Nikolaus Pevsner, "Das Englische in der englischen Kunst: Die retrospektive Austellung britischer Kunst in der Londoner Akademie," *Die Deutsche Zukunft: Wochenzeitung für Politik, Wirtschaft und Kultur,* 4 February 1934, 15.

24. Nikolaus Pevsner, "Modern Architecture and Tradition," *Highway,* August 1947, 228–32.

25. Camillo Sitte, *Die Städtebau nach seinen künstlerischen Grundsätzen: Ein Beitrag zur Lösung modernster Fragen der Architektur und monumentalen Plastik unter besonderer Beziehung auf Wien* (Vienna: Graeser, 1889). Pevsner owned the third edition of Sitte's book (1901); Pevsner's copy is now held in the Research Library at the Getty Research Institute. His earliest acknowledgement of his knowledge of Sitte can be found in Pevsner, *Pioneers* (note 13), 168. He also provided a précis of Sitte's argument and compared it with his own views on visual planning in his review of the first English-language publication of the book; see Nikolaus Pevsner, "A Pioneer of Town-Planning," review of *The Art of Building Cities,* by Camillo Sitte, *AR* 100 (1946): 186. Both of these texts are excerpted in Part III.

26. For the most comprehensive bibliography of Pevsner's oeuvre, see John R. Barr, ed., *Sir Nikolaus Pevsner: A Bibliography* (Charlottesville: University Press of Virginia for the American Association of Architectural Bibliographers, 1970).

27. Nikolaus Pevsner, *The Englishness of English Art: An Expanded and Annotated Version of the Reith Lectures Broadcast in October and November 1955* (London: Architectural, 1956).

28. This chapter is a reworked version of a BBC radio talk from 27 November 1955, originally titled "The Genius of the Place." See *Pevsner on Art and Architecture* (note 2), 230–40. Excerpts of this chapter are presented in Part III.

29. These notes—approximately five hundred pages of them—are now held in the Nikolaus Pevsner papers, boxes 25 and 26.

30. Reyner Banham, "Revenge of the Picturesque: English Architectural Polemics, 1945–1965," in John Summerson, ed., *Concerning Architecture: Essays on Architectural Writers and Writing Presented to Nikolaus Pevsner* (London: Allen Lane, 1968), 265–73.

31. David Watkin, *Morality and Architecture: The Development of a Theme in Architectural History and Theory from the Gothic Revival to the Modern Movement* (Oxford: Clarendon, 1977).

32. See the publications resulting from two conferences held in honor of Pevsner: most recently, Peter Draper, ed., *Reassessing Nikolaus Pevsner* (Aldershot: Ashgate, 2004); and Fulvio Irace, ed., *Nikolaus Pevsner: La trama della storia* (Milan: Guerini, 1992).

33. Stephen Games claims to have worked for several years on Pevsner's biography and has intimated that it is still forthcoming. See *Pevsner on Art and Architecture* (note 2), xi–xii. Internet searches show a book titled *Pevsner* by Susie and Meirion Harries was to be published by Sinclair-Stevenson in 2002. As far as we can see, this is yet to be published.

34. See *Pevsner on Art and Architecture* (note 2); and Timothy Mowl, *Stylistic Cold Wars: Betjeman versus Pevsner* (London: John Murray, 2000).

35. Harrison, "Pevsner" (note 2), 43:969–74. Additionally, numerous tributes and obituaries have been published. These include "Nikolaus Pevsner: 1902–83: A Symposium of Tributes," tributes by

J. M. Richards, Alec Clifton-Taylor, Philip Johnson, Hugh Casson, Jane Fawcett, *AR* 174, no. 1040 (1983): 4–5; and Robin Middleton, "Sir Nikolaus Pevsner, 1902–1983," *Burlington Magazine* 126 (1984): 234, 237.

36. Barr, *Sir Nikolaus Pevsner* (note 26).

37. In retrospect, it reads almost like an indictment of Pevsner's achievements that the most flattering term John Summerson could think of in his tribute to Pevsner upon his award of the Royal Gold Medal of 1967 was that of being a true "professional." See John Summerson, "Royal Gold Medal Award: Sir John Summerson's Tribute to Nikolaus Pevsner," *Architects' Journal* 145 (1967): 1523–24.

38. Mowl, *Stylistic Cold Wars* (note 34), 126–27.

39. Mowl, *Stylistic Cold Wars* (note 34), 149–50.

40. Pevsner, "Foreword" (note 12), xi.

41. His library contained 4,618 volumes.

42. Pevsner's library was acquired at the same time. Thanks to Wim de Wit for this information.

43. The editions still in print are Pevsner, *Pioneers* (note 13); and Pevsner, *An Outline* (note 16).

44. With *The Buildings of England* and *The Pelican History of Art* series, Pevsner divided up areas of research and directly commissioned several scholars to carry out these works.

45. The manuscript would have been much longer if Pevsner had included quotations. Instead, he cross-referenced to articles he had already published and to his store of typewritten notes kept in folders; see Nikolaus Pevsner papers, box 26, folders "The Picturesque in Architecture 1947 (notes)," "Price on Picturesque, 1949 (notes)," and "Richard Payne Knight, 1949 (notes, proof)."

46. See Nikolaus Pevsner papers, box 26, folders "Neue Baukunst and Bautraditon (1947)," "Visual Planning…(Illustrations)," "Visual Planning…(Illustrations: Bath)," "Visual Planning…(Illustrations: Lincoln's Inn)," "Visual Planning (Illustrations: Oxford)," "Visual Planning…(Illustrations: Ladbroke Grove)," "Visual Planning (Notes: General Points)," "Visual Planning (Notes: Part I–II)," and "Visual Planning (Notes: Part III)."

47. Using the moniker P. F. R. D (Peter F. R. Donner), Pevsner wrote of himself, "his filing [is] sometimes fallible and his handwriting is appalling." Donner [Pevsner], "The Royal Gold Medal" (note 6), 10.

48. This is most obvious in the variation in media: fountain pen, ballpoint pen, pencil, and the occasional typewritten insertion, along with the different stocks of paper that have been used.

49. See the lecture notes found in the following boxes in the Nikolaus Pevsner papers: box 52, folder "BBC Talk on Holford's Plan for the precinct of St. Pauls, 1956 (correspondence, notes, material)"; and box 54, folder "Birkbeck College (lecture notes: French)." Three series of lecture notes for "Visual Planning," from the late 1960s and mid-1970s, have also been located in box 74.

50. Pevsner, *The Englishness of English Art* (note 27), 199 n. 4.

51. Peter F. R. Donner [Nikolaus Pevsner], "Cincinnati Looks at Strawberry Hill," review of *Horace Walpole, Gardenist: An Edition of Walpole's "The History of the Modern Taste in Gardening" with an "Estimate of Walpole's Contribution to Landscape Architecture,"* by Isabel Wakelin Urban Chase, *AR* 95 (1944): 56.

52. Donner [Pevsner], "Cincinnati" (note 51), 56.

53. Pevsner wrote of Sitte's method, "the only deeply regrettable thing is that he evidently never had an opportunity to travel to England. What splendid examples he would have found in Oxford and Cambridge or at Bath." He continued his criticism, "If Sitte's sketch plans of squares were accompanied by photographs showing the visual effects of the planning devices which he so eloquently describes, what an invaluable contribution to town-planning history and town-planning today this belated English publication might have been!" Pevsner, "A Pioneer" (note 25), 186.

54. After initially praising the book, Pevsner went on to write:

> What he [the reader] will not see—and that seems to me the one major criticism of the
> book—is wherein precisely Britain's contribution lies. He will find some twenty pages

on London…and a few competent paragraphs on Bath and Edinburgh. But he will not get an idea of the English principle of informality and the free grouping of isolated units which is the clue to Oxford and Cambridge, and also to London and Bath. It is the principle which the *Architectural Review* some years ago decided to call Exterior Furnishing. But then what English book would expound that principle either? The truth of the matter is that it is high time for a book on visual planning in England.

Nikolaus Pevsner, "Lavedan Continued," review of *Histoire de l'urbanisme*, vol. 2, *Renaissance et temps modernes,* by Pierre Lavedan, *AR* 102 (1947): 103.

In mentioning "Exterior Furnishing," Pevsner refers to the influential article published by "The Editor"; see [Hubert de Cronin Hastings], "Exterior Furnishing or Sharawaggi: The Art of Making Urban Landscape," *AR* 95 (1944): 3–8. Pevsner notes, "Professor Lavedan has incidentally found for himself the same word—'le décor urbain meublé'—but without putting it to the best use." Pevsner, "Lavedan Continued" (this note), 103.

55. Nikolaus Pevsner, review of *Amsterdams Bouwkunst en Stadsschoon,* by J. G. Wattjes and F. A. Warners, *AR* 106 (1949): 196.

56. Nikolaus Pevsner, ed., *The Picturesque Garden and Its Influence outside the British Isles* (Washington, D.C.: Dumbarton Oaks, Trustees for Harvard University, 1974), 119.

57. Nikolaus Pevsner to Sherban Cantacuzino, 18 July 1974, Nikolaus Pevsner papers, box 6, folder "Correspondence: *The Architectural Review* [1974]."

58. See "*AR* Papers," cards 124, 125. These papers are now held by the *AR*'s current owners, East Midland Allied Press (EMAP). Thanks to Lynne Jackson for providing us with a copy.

59. See the first page of the *Visual Planning* manuscript, Nikolaus Pevsner papers, box 25, folder "Visual Planning and the City of London, 1945."

60. This has been deduced from the similarity of the paper and writing style in which these parts of the manuscript are written. An indication of the date for the writing of these parts also comes from the foreword, where Pevsner wrote, "As far as I am concerned, this importance [of visual planning] gradually presented itself to me while, over the last twelve or fifteen years, I went on travelling in Britain and watching towns and buildings as an outsider." As discussed above, Pevsner first traveled to Britain in 1930 and moved there permanently in 1933. Additionally, the argument and passages of the text are very similar to other publications and lectures by Pevsner from 1945, which are excerpted at greater length in Part III.

61. This chronology is supported by a letter from A. E. Brinckmann, dated 21 August 1947, that records Brinckmann's "thanks" to Pevsner for the "pages" of his study of "town planning" that Pevsner had previously sent. Brinckmann goes on to talk about his own study of Bath, presumably referring to Pevsner's study; see Nikolaus Pevsner papers, box 14a, folder "Correspondence 1940–1949." Unfortunately, Pevsner's letter and "papers" no longer exist in Brinckmann's archives at Cologne University.

62. The references—usually letters of the alphabet, roman numerals, or the first and last words of a blocked quotation—were kept in other folders (mostly box 26) or had been published previously.

63. These authors and their publications are dealt with comprehensively in the notes to Part II; see this volume, p. 146, n. 3.

64. Osvald Sirén, *China and Gardens of Europe of the Eighteenth Century* (New York: Ronald, 1950).

65. These are Nikolaus Pevsner, "Heritage of Compromise: A Note on Sir Joshua Reynolds Who Died One Hundred and Fifty Years Ago," *AR* 91 (1942): 37–38; Nikolaus Pevsner, "The Genesis of the Picturesque," *AR* 96 (1944): 139–46; [Nikolaus Pevsner,] "Price on Picturesque Planning," *AR* 95 (1944): 47–50; Nikolaus Pevsner, "The Other Chambers," *AR* 101 (1947): 195–98; Nikolaus Pevsner, "Humphry Repton: A Florilegium," *AR* 103 (1948): 53–59; Nikolaus Pevsner, "Richard Payne

Knight," *Art Bulletin* 31 (1949): 293–320; and Susan Lang and Nikolaus Pevsner, "Sir William Temple and Sharawaggi," *AR* 106 (1949): 391–93. A full bibliography of Pevsner's work concerned with the picturesque, visual planning, and Townscape is found in the selected bibliography to this edition.

66. "*AR* Papers" (note 58), cards 124, 125.

67. Pevsner published numerous florilegia (his first was written under the pseudonym Peter F. R. Donner), about which he wrote, "Florilegium: Thus medieval authors called a tome, chiefly composed of quotations; an anthology, a *catena*, a garner, a *thesaurus*. The term seems appropriate to indicate the intention of the following article and of similar articles to be published every now and then. Such Florilegia should prove equally illuminating whether dealing with individual books, or with problems of topical significance as treated by different writers or different generations." Peter F. R. Donner [Nikolaus Pevsner], "A Harris Florilegium," *AR* 93 (1943): 51.

68. The names of these folders in the Nikolaus Pevsner papers (box 25) and the number of images they contain are as follows: "Visual Planning (Illustrations: Ladbroke Grove)," 22 photographs and 1 plan; "Visual Planning (Lincoln's Inn)," 12 photographs; "Visual Planning (Illustrations: Oxford)," 23 photographs and 4 prints; "Visual Planning (Illustrations: Bath)," 4 photographs and 1 plan; and "Visual Planning (Illustrations)," 8 photographs and 2 prints.

69. See Nikolaus Pevsner papers, box 25, folder "Visual Planning (Illustrations: Ladbroke Grove"). These illustrations were listed for inclusion in Part III, see Nikolaus Pevsner papers, box 25, folder "Visual Planning (Notes: Part III)."

70. The photographs that still have the instructions to the photographer can be found in Nikolaus Pevsner papers, box 25, folders "Visual Planning (Illustrations: Lincoln's Inn)" and "Visual Planning (Illustrations: Ladbroke Grove)."

71. The photographers for the various tours were as follows: Ladbroke Grove, copyright Architectural Press, photographer Erich Auerbach; Lincoln's Inn, photographer Staniland Pugh; Oxford, combination of photographers Helmut Gernsheim (20 photographs) and Dell and Wainwright (3 photographs); Bath, Aerofilms Ltd.; and the reproductions held in the miscellaneous illustrations folder were mostly made by Spectrocolour Ltd.

72. There is a possibility that some, or all, of these photographs were taken later, perhaps the winter of 1945; however, this would also suggest the text was written an entire year later, which seems less defensible than the earlier date.

73. Nikolaus Pevsner, "Reassessment 4: Three Oxford Colleges," *AR* 106 (1949): 120–24.

74. Three pages are missing from the manuscript here (pages 5–7 of Part I). They were presumably taken from the *Visual Planning* manuscript for publication in this article in *AR*. It is also assumed that the illustrations for this part were either taken completely from the manuscript collection or partially augmented with new images.

75. See Raymond Unwin, *Town Planning in Practice: An Introduction to the Art of Designing Cities and Suburbs* (London: T. F. Unwin, 1909), 267–75. Compare this to Thomas Sharp, *Oxford Replanned* (London: Architectural, 1948), 21–26. Later, Pevsner points to this similarity and, tacitly, to his presumed reliance on it in Nikolaus Pevsner, "History: Unwin Centenary," *AR* 134 (1963): 207–8.

76. Lionello De Luigi, "Townscape e tradizione pittoresca nella cultura urbanistica inglese," *Urbanistica*, no. 32 (1960): 1–2, 9–12.

77. De Luigi, "Townscape" (note 76), 12. Kindly translated from the Italian by Andrew Leach.

78. Middleton, "Sir Nikolaus Pevsner" (note 35), 237.

79. Erdem Erten, "Shaping 'The Second Half Century': *The Architectural Review*, 1947–1971" (PhD dissertation, Massachusetts Institute of Technology, 2004).

80. Erdem Erten, "From Townscape to Civilia: The Evolution of a Collective Project" (paper presented at the "Cities of Tomorrow: 10th International Planning History Conference," University of Westminster and Letchworth Garden City, England, 10–13 July 2002).

81. Erten introduces the manuscript and its location; see Erten, "Shaping 'The Second Half

Century'" (note 79), 31–32. On pages 34 and 35, Erten provides excerpts and a synopsis of the tripartite structure of the book.

82. Aitchison's doctorate on the early phase of Townscape was completed under the supervision of Macarthur from 2003 to 2008. In 2003, they became aware of the *Visual Planning* manuscript from Pevsner's reference to it, and Aitchison located and transcribed the manuscript in 2004. For papers that discuss *Visual Planning*, see John Macarthur and Mathew Aitchison, "Ivor de Wolfe's Picturesque, or, Who and What Was Townscape?" in Harriet Edquist and Hélène Frichot, eds., *Limits: Proceedings from the 21st Annual Conference of the Society of Architectural Historians, Australia and New Zealand: Melbourne, 2004* (Melbourne: Society of Architectural Historians, Australia & New Zealand, 2004); Mathew Aitchison, "Visual Planning and the Picturesque: Sir Nikolaus Pevsner and Townscape Revisited" (paper presented at "Celebration: 22nd Annual Conference of the Society of Architectural Historians, Australia and New Zealand," Napier, New Zealand, 2005); John Macarthur, *The Picturesque: Architecture, Disgust, and Other Irregularities* (London: Routledge, 2007); John Macarthur, "Townscape, Anti-Scrape, and Surrealism: Paul Nash and John Piper in *The Architectural Review,*" *Journal of Architecture* 14, no. 2 (2009): 387–405; and Mathew Aitchison, "Visual Planning and Exterior Furnishing: A Critical History of the Early Townscape Movement—1930 to 1949" (PhD diss., University of Queensland, 2009).

83. Nikolaus Pevsner to Sherban Cantacuzino, 18 July 1974, Nikolaus Pevsner papers, box 6, folder "Correspondence: *The Architectural Review* [1974]."

84. Middleton, "Sir Nikolaus Pevsner" (note 35), 237.

85. Erten, "Shaping 'The Second Half Century'" (note 79), 35.

86. [Pevsner,] "Price on Picturesque Planning" (note 65), 47–50.

87. See Pevsner, *The Englishness of Art* (note 27), 199 n. 4.

88. See most notably [Nikolaus Pevsner,] "Frenchay Common or Workaday Sharawaggi," *AR* 98 (1945): 26–27; and Pevsner, "Reassessment 4" (note 73).

89. Perhaps reflecting this shift, Pevsner first tried to resign from the *AR* in 1961, writing, "as I am getting older, I find myself more and more out of sympathy with what is going on in architecture and what we, as a 'modern' paper, have to put in." Nikolaus Pevsner to Hubert de Cronin Hastings, 19 December 1961; Nikolaus Pevsner papers, box 6, folder "Correspondence: *The Architectural Review* (1961)."

90. See Gordon Cullen, "Townscape Casebook," *AR* 106 (1949): 363–74; Gordon Cullen, *Townscape* (London: Architectural, 1961); and Gordon Cullen, *The Concise Townscape* (London: Architectural, 1971).

91. De Wolfe, "Townscape" (note 1).

92. Ivor de Wofle [Hubert de Cronin Hastings], ed., *Civilia: The End of Sub Urban Man: A Challenge to Semidetsia* (London: Architectural, 1971). The change in name from "de Wolfe" to "de Wofle" resulted from a printing error that Hastings let stand. See D. A. C. A. Boyne, "Hastings, Hubert de Cronin (1902–1986)," *Oxford Dictionary of National Biography* (Oxford: Oxford Univ. Press, 2004). Like many of the Architectural Press editions relating to Townscape, *Civilia* was first published as a special issue of the *AR*. See Ivor de Wolfe, ed., "Civilia: The End of Sub Urban Man," *AR* 149 (1971): 326–408.

93. Of Pevsner, Timothy Mowl wrote, "Pevsner in one mood was a tolerant scholar of wide experience; in another a blinkered fanatic for a largely unproven Modernism." Mowl, *Stylistic Cold Wars* (note 34), 159–60.

94. Two articles exemplify this approach; see Gordon Cullen, "Hazards, or the Art of Introducing Obstacles into the Urban Landscape without Inhibiting the Eye," *AR* 103 (1948): 99–105; and Gordon Cullen, "Legs and Wheels," Townscape, *AR* 104 (1948): 77–80.

95. The Editor [Hastings], "Exterior Furnishing" (note 54). Erdem Erten has revealed that the author of this article was in fact Hastings; see Erten, "Shaping 'The Second Half Century'" (note 79), 35.

96. The Editor [Hastings], "Exterior Furnishing" (note 54), 3.

97. It is doubtful that the eighteenth-century aesthetes thought quite like this, as they were more concerned with concordance with genre than a strong idea of composition of the pictorial surface, but it was the basis of Wölfflin's idea that in the picturesque "appearance separates from the thing, the picture-form [(*Bild-form*)] becomes different to the object-form." Wölfflin, *Principles* (note 20), 25.

98. One such instance, written in Hastings's inimitable style, is the following: "one public-house gasolier, one bus stop, two public lavatories, one Underground station entrance, one manhole cover, one bend in the road to port, three brass balls, one Bass triangle, two bollards, six plane trees, Teas with Hovis, the neon sign of the flower shop, and a hundred and fifty horizontal windows in New Pelman Court. . . . From such assortments the radical planner has to produce his practical surrealist picture." De Wolfe, "Townscape" (note 1), 361. This argument, like many found in "Townscape," was offered earlier in "Exterior Furnishing": "We think most town-planners are themselves puzzled and embarrassed by their lack of realistic vision, their inability to *reconcile visually* in the mind's eye what appear to be irreconcilable elements in any town plan: quaint bits, new bits, monuments, traffic, tall buildings, short buildings, flat blocks, individual cottages, etc., etc." The Editor [Hastings], "Exterior Furnishing" (note 54), 3.

99. See Macarthur, *The Picturesque* (note 82), 19–56.

100. De Wolfe, "Townscape" (note 1), 355 (emphasis added).

101. Reyner Banham, *Theory and Design in the First Machine Age* (London: Architectural, 1960).

102. See the *AR*'s special issue, "The Functional Tradition," *AR* 107 (1950): 2–67. This term was in use in the *AR* in the late-1940s and throughout the 1950s.

103. The first article to appear under the rubric "Townscape," was Cullen, "Legs and Wheels" (note 94). For a comprehensive discussion of the development of *townscape* as a term and a concept, see the introduction to Aitchison, "Visual Planning" (note 82).

104. Sharp, *Oxford Replanned* (note 75), 36.

105. Interestingly, Cullen illustrated the book's dust jacket, and it was published by the Architectural Press. Several of the book's similarities to *Visual Planning* have already been noted above.

106. De Wolfe, "Townscape" (note 1), 362.

107. See note 86 above. It should be pointed out that while Pevsner appears to have invented the term *visual planning*, this was only a small step from Hastings's position: "There is an urgent need for a commonly accepted visual standard, *a visual policy for urban landscape*. Without a visual policy a physical planning policy is a kind of monstrosity." The Editor [Hastings], "Exterior Furnishing" (note 54), 8.

108. Aitchison, "Visual Planning" (note 82).

109. A comprehensive list of these authors and their various contributions is published in Aitchison, "Visual Planning" (note 82), appendix 1.

110. David Fraser Jenkins and Frances Spalding, *John Piper in the 1930s: Abstraction on the Beach,* exh. cat. (London: Merrell, 2003).

111. Erten's study shares this conclusion. Erten, "Shaping 'The Second Half Century'" (note 79), 36.

112. Nikolaus Pevsner, "Elusive JMR," *RIBA Journal* 78 (1971): 181. After Hastings's retirement in 1973, John Betjeman described him as "the most influential man I have ever met." John Betjeman, "Marginalia: H De C: Betjeman Recalls," *AR* 155 (1974): 120.

113. Richards, *Memoirs* (note 8), 241.

114. For a detailed discussion of Hastings's life and work, see his entry in Aitchison, "Visual Planning" (note 82), appendix 1.

115. See Aitchison, "Visual Planning" (note 82), appendix 1.

116. The Editor [Hastings], "Exterior Furnishing" (note 54), 6.

117. The Editor [Hastings], "Exterior Furnishing" (note 54), 5; see this volume, p. 157 n. 251, for

this quote. Hastings attributes this example to Richard Payne Knight, but it is in fact from Uvedale Price, *Essays on the Picturesque, As Compared with the Sublime and the Beautiful: And, on the Use of Studying Pictures, for the Purpose of Improving Real Landscape*, 3 vols. (London: printed for J. Mawman, 1810), 3:315–16. In the eighteenth century, feelings of disgust had a positive value as self-knowledge of aesthetic preference and orientation. Disgust plays a much larger role in the eighteenth-century picturesque and its reception then has generally been recognized. See Macarthur, *The Picturesque* (note 82), 57–109.

118. Macarthur, "Townscape" (note 82).

119. Paul Nash, "Swanage or Seaside Surrealism," *AR* 79 (1936): 150–54.

120. J. M. Richards et al., "The Second Half Century," *AR* 101 (1947): 21–26.

121. John Piper, "Pleasing Decay," *AR* 102 (1947): 85–94. On the aesthetic aspects in the early history of conservation, see Brian Ladd, "Urban Aesthetics and the Discovery of Urban Fabric in Turn-of-the-Century Germany," *Planning Perspectives* 2 (1987): 270–86.

122. Nikolaus Pevsner, "Why Not Harmonize the Old and the New?" *The Times*, 3 July 1961, xxii. See also Nikolaus Pevsner, "Scrape and Anti-Scrape," in Jane Fawcett, ed., *The Future of the Past: Attitudes to Conservation, 1174–1974* (London: Thames & Hudson, 1976), 34–53.

123. See Pevsner's invocation of Nash's revival of the concept in Part III, this volume, p. 208 n. 64 and p. 209 n. 65.

124. See Paul Nash, "Monster Field," *AR* 88 (1940): 120–22.

125. John Piper, *British Romantic Artists* (London: William Collins, 1942). Paul Nash was included, but he rejected the title.

126. Collected as J. M. Richards and John Summerson, *The Bombed Buildings of Britain: A Record of Architectural Casualties: 1940–41* (Cheam, England: Architectural, 1942).

127. "Save Us Our Ruins," *AR* 95 (1944): 13–14. Later republished as an independent volume: *Bombed Churches as War Memorials* (London: Architectural, 1945).

128. Delivered on 3 May 1946, the title of Pevsner's talk was "Reflections on Ruins"; see *Pevsner on Art and Architecture* (note 2), 343.

129. Hugh Casson, "Art by Accident: The Aesthetics of Camouflage," *AR* 96 (1944): 63–68.

130. "A Programme for the City of London: Introduction," *AR* 97 (1945): 159.

131. The first outing of "new empiricism" came in the unsigned article "The New Empiricism: Sweden's Latest Style," *AR* 101 (1947): 199–200. This was followed by Eric de Maré, "The New Empiricism: The Antecedents and Origins of Sweden's Latest Style," *AR* 103 (1948): 9–10.

132. Peter F. R. Donner [Nikolaus Pevsner], "Criticism," *AR* 90 (1941): 91.

133. See the article "In Search of a New Monumentality: A Symposium by Gregor Paulsson, Henry-Russell Hitchcock, William Holford, Sigfried Giedion, Walter Gropius, Lucio Costa, and Alfred Roth," *AR* 104 (1948): 117–28.

134. De Wolfe, "Townscape" (note 1), 361.

135. Cullen, "Hazards" (note 94), 99.

136. The Editor [Hastings], "Exterior Furnishing" (note 54), 3.

137. Nikolaus Pevsner, "Townscape," address at the Annual Meeting of the Council for Visual Education, *Journal of the Institute of Registered Architects* 10 (1955): 41.

138. Unwin was republishing images from Sitte's journal *Der Städtebau*. See Unwin, *Town Planning* (note 75), 215–20. Pevsner chose these images to republish in his article on Unwin, which are in turn published in Part III. See Pevsner, "History: Unwin Centenary" (note 75), 207.

139. See note 75 above on the similarities of the tours by Unwin, Sharp, and Pevsner of Oxford's High Street.

140. Frederick Gibberd, *Town Design* (London: Architectural, 1953).

141. These "perambulations," as Pevsner would later refer to his tours, would become an integral part of his *Buildings of England* guidebooks. See this volume, pp. 102–3 n. 7.

142. See Macarthur, *The Picturesque* (note 82), 19–56.

143. A comprehensive selection of period texts is available in Malcolm Andrews, *The Picturesque: Literary Sources and Documents* (Robertsbridge, England: Helm Information, 1994).

144. Macarthur, *The Picturesque* (note 82).

145. Christopher Hussey, *The Picturesque: Studies in a Point of View* (London: Frank Cass, 1927).

146. Pevsner, "Das Englische" (note 23), 15.

147. Nikolaus Pevsner, "Heritage of Compromise: A Note on Sir Joshua Reynolds Who Died One Hundred and Fifty Years Ago," *AR* 91 (1942): 37–38.

148. The Editor [Hastings], "Exterior Furnishing" (note 54), 7.

149. Nikolaus Pevsner, "C20 Picturesque: An Answer to Basil Taylor's Broadcast," *AR* 115 (1954): 227–29.

150. For a longer treatment of the picturesque in German language art, architecture, and planning, see Aitchison, "Visual Planning" (note 82), 73–111.

151. Wölfflin, *Principles* (note 20).

152. Giedion, *Space, Time and Architecture* (note 21).

153. See, for example, Pevsner's discussion of genius loci, excerpted in Part III, this volume, pp. 183–84.

154. Pevsner, "C20 Picturesque" (note 149), 229.

155. Pevsner, "C20 Picturesque" (note 149), 229.

156. See this volume, p. 145.

157. Richard Payne Knight, *An Analytical Inquiry into the Principles of Taste,* 4th ed. (London: T. Payne, 1808), 172.

158. Knight, *Principles of Taste* (note 157), 167.

159. Knight, *Principles of Taste* (note 157), 164.

160. Knight, *Principles of Taste* (note 157), 223.

161. Knight, *Principles of Taste* (note 157), 225.

162. Nikolaus Pevsner, *Studies in Art, Architecture, and Design,* vol. 1, *From Mannerism to Romanticism* (London: Thames & Hudson, 1968), 241 n. 82. The article referred to is Susan Lang, "Richard Payne Knight and the Idea of Modernity," in John Summerson, ed., *Concerning Architecture: Essays on Architectural Writers and Writing Presented to Nikolaus Pevsner* (London: Allen Lane, 1968), 85–97. For a fuller account of Knight's significance, see Andrew Ballantyne, *Architecture, Landscape, and Liberty: Richard Payne Knight and the Picturesque* (Cambridge: Cambridge Univ. Press, 1997). On the issue of irregularity, see Macarthur, *The Picturesque* (note 82), 110–75.

163. Price, *Essays on the Picturesque* (note 117), 2:268–69.

164. Peter F. R. Donner [Nikolaus Pevsner], "The End of the Pattern-Books," *AR* 93 (1943): 75–79.

165. Price, *Essays on the Picturesque* (note 117), 2:312.

166. Macarthur, *The Picturesque* (note 82), 176–232.

167. The Editor [Hastings], "Exterior Furnishing" (note 54), 8.

168. De Wolfe, "Townscape" (note 1), 360.

169. One of the earliest and most coherent articles to take up this argument within the *AR* was Lionel Brett, "The New Haussmann," *AR* 93 (1943): 23–26.

170. George Mason, *An Essay on Design in Gardening: First Published in MDCCLXVIII, Now Greatly Augmented; Also a Revisal of Several Later Publications on the Same Subject* (London: printed by C. Roworth for Benjamin & John White, 1795).

171. John Summerson, *John Nash: Architect to King George IV,* 2nd ed. (London: G. Allen & Unwin, 1949).

172. Nikolaus Pevsner, "The Picturesque in Architecture," *RIBA Journal* 55 (1947): 55–61.

173. Colin Rowe and Fred Koetter, *Collage City* (Cambridge: MIT Press, 1978).

174. Pevsner, "Reassessment 4" (note 73), 120.

175. This volume, see p. 166.

176. This volume, see p. 166.

177. Leon Krier et al., *Rational Architecture: The Reconstruction of the European City = Architecture rationnelle: La reconstruction de la ville Européenne* (Brussels: Éditions de Archives d'Architecture Moderne, 1978); Rob Krier, *Urban Space = Stadtraum,* trans. Christine Czechowski and George Black (London: Academy, 1979); Aldo Rossi, *The Architecture of the City,* trans. Diane Ghirardo and Joan Ockman (Cambridge: MIT Press, 1982).

178. Françoise Choay, *The Modern City: Planning in the Nineteenth Century,* trans. Marguerite Hugo and George P. Collins (London: Studio Vista, 1969); Françoise Choay, "Urbanism and Semiology," in Charles Jencks and George Baird, eds., *Meaning in Architecture* (London: Barrie & Jenkins, 1969), 26–37; and Roland Barthes, "Sémiologie et urbanisme," *L'architecture d'aujord'hui* 153 (1970–71): 11–13.

179. Perhaps the major exception to this schema is Kevin Lynch's *The Image of the City* (Cambridge: MIT Press, 1960). Despite obvious methodological differences, this book is an interesting counterpart to *Visual Planning* and arrives at similar arguments: "[Urban design] should be guided what might be called a 'visual plan' for the city or metropolitan region: a set of recommendations and controls which would be concerned with visual form on the urban scale" (p. 116).

180. Colin Rowe and Fred Koetter, "Collage City," *AR* 158 (1975): 66–91.

181. Rowe and Koetter, *Collage City* (note 173), 179.

182. In a letter of 1956, Rowe wrote of Townscape and "Englishness":

> After the insufferable tedium of Townscape, the dreary accumulation of public house *chi chi,* and the insipid neo-Regency aesthetic with which we have been blanketed since the war, it is the most extreme relief to be allowed to recognise that English architecture is not necessarily degraded nor essentially corrupt. The Connell, Ward and Lucas houses are so authentic and so English, and yet rise so far above that provincial quality of "Englishness" lately so much valued, that they have still, after all these years, the invigorating qualities of a manifesto.

Colin Rowe, "Connell, Ward, and Lucas," letter to the editor, *Architectural Association Journal* 72 (1957): 163 (emphasis added). The "Englishness" that Rowe refers to was none other than Pevsner's *The Englishness of English Art* (1956).

183. Banham wrote:

> Now that the authorship of "Collage City" is apparently up for grabs, may I press the strong claim of that genuinely mythical figure "Ivor de Wolfe"...the standpoint adopted by "de Wolfe" in his celebrated article "Townscape...a visual philosophy founded on the true rock of Sir Uvedale Price," equally suspicious of universal utopias and equally delighted by the juxtaposition of fragmentary designs. *And that was in the AR for December* 1949. Professor Rowe's attitude to these ideas at that time was consistently hostile—many a midnight hour he burned the ears of those of us who were prepared to listen with diatribes on the vast superiority of Le Corbusier's Utopian vision over English ad-hoc solutions and the Picturesque tradition....Unless this leopard has genuinely reversible spots, Rowe's claims to authorship, like those of Charles Jencks, are far less convincing than those of "Ivor de Wolfe."

Reyner Banham, "De Wolfe the Author?" letter to the editor, *AR* 158 (1975): 322.

184. *SCAPE©* is defined as "neither city nor landscape"; see Chuihua Judy Chung et al., eds., *Great Leap Forward* (Cambridge: Harvard Design School, 2001), 393. *Drosscape* is a term invented for the problem of "waste landscapes"; see Alan Berger, *Drosscape: Wasting Land in Urban America* (New York: Princeton Architectural, 2006).

185. Manfredo Tafuri, *Theories and History of Architecture,* trans. Giorgio Verrecchia (London: Granada, 1980), 153.

186. See David Watkin, *Morality and Architecture Revisited*, rev. ed. (Chicago: Univ. of Chicago Press, 2001), xvi.

187. In this, Watkin followed Karl Popper's attack on the historicism of Hegel and Herbert Butterfield's critique of British liberalism; see Karl Popper, *The Open Society and Its Enemies*, 2 vols. (London: G. Routledge & Sons, 1945); Karl Popper, *The Poverty of Historicism*, 2nd ed. (London: Routledge & Kegan Paul, 1960); and Herbert Butterfield, *The Whig Interpretation of History* (London: G. Bell & Sons, 1931).

188. See also David Watkin, "Sir Nikolaus Pevsner: A Study in 'Historicism'" *Apollo*, n.s., 136, no. 367 (1992): 169–72.

189. "Symposium: The Edifice Crumbles…" *AR* 163 (1978): 64.

190. Seemingly unaware of Pevsner's involvement in Townscape, Mowl attacks him, spuriously introducing two other early Townscape protagonists, Betjeman and Piper, to reinforce the charges against him:

> If an English poet and an English artist had the sensibility and the wit to envisage the horrific consequences of a cheap International Modernism back in 1939, then Pevsner, the expert from abroad, should have been able to stand back from the theory and cry for caution in 1950 when those consequences were actually unfolding. But should a man with no English social background have been encouraged so quickly to a position where he could exert an unwise and, in a very real sense, an "alien" influence?

Mowl, *Stylistic Cold Wars* (note 34), 115.

191. *Pevsner on Art and Architecture* (note 2), xv.

192. Tafuri, *Theories and History of Architecture* (note 185), 155.

193. Nigel Whiteley, *Reyner Banham: Historian of the Immediate Future* (Cambridge: MIT Press, 2002); and Anthony Vidler, *Histories of the Immediate Present: Inventing Architectural Modernism* (Cambridge: MIT Press, 2008).

VISUAL PLANNING AND THE PICTURESQUE

Nikolaus Pevsner

NOTE TO THE READER

Numbers in square brackets within the text, e.g., [13], refer to original page numbers of the manuscript. These numbers are only indicative of the page's location within the original text.

Square brackets, [ ], indicate an editorial intervention

Braces, { }, indicate Pevsner's own editorial interventions, comments, and text intended for notes.

Arrow brackets, < >, indicate Pevsner's marginal notes.

2 em dashes, ——, indicate missing or illegible words.

Notes with an asterisk, e.g., [43]*, contain Pevsner's instruction for a note, or content that he intended for a note. Within the endnotes, Pevsner's instructions and notes (in braces or in arrow brackets) appear in bold type, whereas editorial content appears in plain type.

Pevsner drew the bulk of the text for Part II from rare eighteenth-century volumes; this has made it difficult to verify the accuracy of his citations and transcriptions. Where possible, the original edition cited has been consulted, and the text corrected. Where it was not possible to consult Pevsner's preferred source, in some cases, the earliest or most authoritative edition has been consulted; in other cases, pagination has been adopted from the manuscript or from articles published by Pevsner in which the quotation also appeared.

TO H de C
without whose spiritual and material support
this book would not have been conceived
nor written.

MOTTO
It is not by copying particulars, but by attending
to principles, that lessons become instructive.
Sir Uvedale Price, *Essays on the Picturesque,* Vol. II.
1798; ed. of 1810, p. 115.

PART I,
mostly presented in pictures

PART II,
mostly presented in quotations

PART III,
occasionally submitting solutions

[1] Foreword[1*]

Town-planning history, as it can be read in the standard books[,] does not do justice to the contribution of England. Take the historical chapters in Sir Raymond Unwin's, Hegemann and Peets's or Thomas Adams's books,[2*] or take Hughes and Lamborn's *Town Planning Ancient and Modern*[3*] or Brinckmann's *Städtebaukunst*[4*] or, better still, Pierre Lavedan's *Histoire de l'urbanisme,*[5*] the most detailed and up-to-date work on the subject, and you will invariably find a history which starts with classic Greek fifth- and fourth-century chessboard patterns, covers what geometrical planning the Hellenistic states and the Roman Empire evolved, then gives some account of the accidents of town development in the Middle Ages and the principles of growth underlying them, with a somewhat disproportionate emphasis on the relatively few planned communities such as the bastides of France, the New Towns of Edward I, of the Prussian Order and so on, and then arrives at the Italian Renaissance, with its ideal of the radial town. From these perfectly symmetrical patterns, perhaps going back to an original conception of the great Alberti and drawn for the first time about 1460 by Filarete, the way is clear towards Versailles and the Place de l'Etoile: radial design and chessboard design, culminating at Karlsruhe in 1715 and Mannheim in 1699 and combined in l'Enfant's plan of 1790 for Washington.

The measure of success in the books referred to appears always—whether it is said in so many words or only implied—the degree to which plans of towns or districts approximate the perfection of all-round symmetrical ornament. As far as Britain before the late nineteenth century is concerned, Wren's plan for London after the Fire could be found strongly stressed, and Inigo Jones's Covent Garden, and the Circus and the Royal Crescent at Bath, and perhaps the frontages of Nash's Regent Street and Regent's Park.

But nowhere, as far as I am aware, have the meaning of Nash's composition and the meaning of the whole of Bath as visualised by the Woods been recognised and their immense importance in the history of visual planning in England.

[2] As far as I am concerned, this importance gradually presented itself to me while, over the last twelve or fifteen years, I went on traveling in Britain and watching towns and buildings as an outsider brought up on the orthodox tenets of town-planning and its most spectacular French examples. Looked at from the Parisian point of view, Bath is a scattering of individually laudable efforts, Regent Street a deplorable compromise, and Piccadilly Circus a pitiful failure. With Gabriel's École Militaire in one's mind, the colleges of Oxford and Cambridge are curious at best.

Yet to the unbiased traveller, Oxford and Cambridge and Bath are amongst the most impressive urban configurations to be seen anywhere in Europe. If the accepted criteria of town-planning history cannot explain the power of their effect, the fault must be with the criteria. Once this has been realised, the need is obvious for a revision of the categories under which town plans are treated. New categories have to be evolved, not from French and German but from English examples, their validity established and their applicability to topical problems tested.

This is the task which the present book sets itself. It consists of three parts. The first is an analysis, chiefly pictorial, of English town-planning tradition up to

1800, the second a florilegium of English planning theory—that is, the theory of the Picturesque—and the third an account of how this theory and this tradition influenced the nineteenth century in England and might influence the twentieth.

NOTES

1*. Pevsner crossed out an earlier dedication that read **<To H. de C. without whom this book could probably not have been started, and certainly never have been completed.>**

2*. **<footnote.>** Although Pevsner did not state exactly which titles he was referring to, the volumes under discussion are presumably Raymond Unwin, *Town Planning in Practice: An Introduction to the Art of Designing Cities and Suburbs* (London: Adelphi, 1909); Werner Hegemann and Elbert Peets, *The American Vitruvius: An Architects' Handbook of Civic Art* (New York: Architectural Book, 1922); Thomas Adams, *Recent Advances in Town Planning* (London: J. & A. Churchill, 1932); and Thomas Adams, *Outline of Town and City Planning: A Review of Past Efforts and Modern Aims* (London: J. & A. Churchill, 1935).

3*. **{Clarendon Press, 1923.}** Thomas Harold Hughes and Edmund Arnold Greening Lamborn, *Towns and Town-Planning, Ancient and Modern* (Oxford: Clarendon, 1923).

4*. **{Wildpark-Potsdam 1925.}** Albert Erich Brinckmann, *Stadtbaukunst: Vom Mittelalter bis zur Neuzeit* (Wildpark-Potsdam: Akademische Verlagsgesellschaft Athenaion, 1925).

5*. **{vol. 1, 19..., vol. 2, 1941.}** Pierre Lavedan, *Histoire de l'urbanisme*, vol. 1, *Antiquité–moyen âge* (Paris: Henri Laurens, 1926); and *Histoire de l'urbanisme*, vol. 2, *Renaissance et temps modernes* (Paris: Laurens, 1941).

PART I,
mostly presented in pictures

Fig. 1. Place de la Concorde, Paris. View toward the north

If any foreign traveller were asked what he considers the most beautiful towns of England, his answer would without doubt be Oxford and Cambridge. The truth of the answer will not be denied. Whether the appearance of Oxford and Cambridge is due more to accident or to planning can for the moment remain open. In any case, the two towns, in deference to their outstanding visual merits, deserve to be examined first. But how can a book and its illustrations do justice to the visual merits of Oxford [3] and Cambridge, which are not merely merits of individual buildings (often, indeed, these are negligible) but merits of sequences of buildings—interior and exterior spaces which can reveal their aesthetic qualities only to the roving eye? The immoveable eye of the camera cannot catch them. A formal composition, it is true, with one point fixed from which the whole, as it expands identically to the left and the right, can be taken in by the camera. Once the picture has been seen from that particular point, its job is done. Change of position does not help it; it only distorts. This is true of, say, the Place de la **Fig. 1** Concorde. Gabriel's two companion buildings on the north side must be seen with the Madeleine between, exactly in the central axis. Diagonal views are senseless. Turn round and look across the bridge to the Palais Bourbon. Again, a strictly axial viewpoint is essential. Or take the Hôtel des Invalides, the Champs Élysées with the Triumphal Arch in the distance, take the Louvre, take the Palais Chaillot: everywhere, a fixed point, or at least a straight line, is provided from which alone the composition can be appreciated. Place a camera into the right spot and you can be sure of a satisfactory reproduction of the architect's aesthetic intentions.

At Oxford or Cambridge you can do nothing of the sort. You have to walk through the quads and passages of college after college, looking forward and backward, left and right, up and down as you progress, in order to perceive what must be perceived to gain the impressions which matter. Replacing the continuous walk [with] a small selection of photographic shots is an inadequate substitute, but in conjunction with diagrammatic plans and some running commentary it may be possible to convey their spatial significance.

I have chosen Oxford rather than Cambridge examples because the pattern at Oxford is more compact. At the same time, Oxford has probably little to offer that, from the point of view of English planning, could compete with the view of King's from the river.

The following tour shall lead us through three colleges: Christ Church, Corpus Christi, and Magdalen, for a moment into a fourth: St. Edmund Hall, and then along the High Street from east to west and up one cross lane from the High to the Broad.[2]*

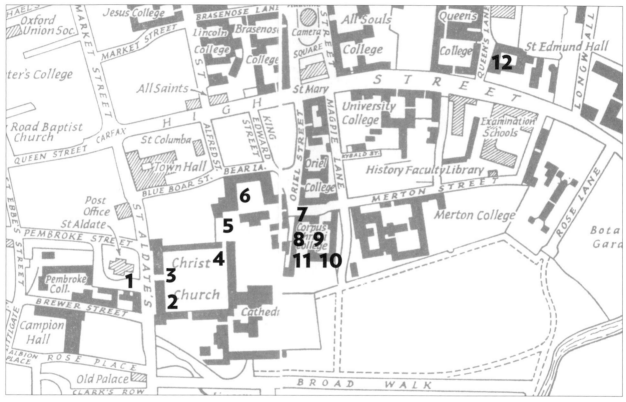

Oxford's Colleges. Key to 1–12

1. The tower of Christ Church starts in the Tudor Grand Manner, with a gatehouse as the middle accent of the long St. Aldate's front. It was meant by Wolsey[3] to have a tall centre, but not as tall as it is now, and two turrets left and right, reaching somewhat higher than the centre — that is the motif which also dominates the fronts at Hampton Court, at Trinity College, Cambridge, and many Tudor Mansions. Wren paid tribute to the *genius loci* by finishing the tower in the Gothick manner, though with a reversal of accents. The engraving below shows the gateway before Wren finished the tower. The old lime tree by St. Aldate's Church and the dark, rough wall of Pembroke against the much more polished wall surfaces of Christ Church are a setting after our picturesque tastes, but were no doubt not seeable or appreciable in Wolsey's time.

2. The monumental gate leads dead into the centre of the most monumental of Oxford quads—260 by 260 feet. The fact that the chapel is not placed in any relation to the gatehouse may be taken to have been, from Wolsey's point of view, an unavoidable snag, considering that he had to use the existing church of St. Frideswide: but the raised hall on the right—in no axially stressed place—is a deliberate breach of etiquette, the same which appears at Hampton Court. The nineteenth century could appreciate its planning value, and Thomas Garner's tower over Hall Staircase (of about 1880), which appears between cathedral and hall, is a bold and wholly successful addition. The gully separating it from the raised hall adds intricacy where one would least expect it but cannot help welcoming it. [Figure] 2a [below] shows this corner of the quad before Garner's tower was built.

3. Fell Tower, in the other corner, is an equally asymmetrical, if less prominent, [accent]. Garner might have repeated its height and turreted pattern on his side, but he did not. Through Fell Tower is the only way out of Tom Quad. You have entered the vast square by a grand gateway. You leave it by a narrow vaulted passage. Sunny breadth and smooth lawn are exchanged for a moment [for] a cool and confined space.

4. And then, again only for a moment, we seem in a wholly different scene. Rough walls on the left and right, trees rising behind them, and the trailing-down wild *Vitis Coignetiae* [Crimson Glory Vine] as a link to emphasize and get over the seeming incongruity between the rustic walls and the smooth, trim Palladian wing of Peckwater, appearing in front of us to prepare us for the sober dignity to come.

5. But there is yet another surprise in store before we reach Peckwater. Directly we pass the wild wall-creeper[,] we leave the zone of vegetation and return to pure stone-scape. And there, while we expect the gentility of Palladianism, there towers on our right the dramatic mass of the Library, twice as moving with its flaking stonework than it would be were it smoothed as the rest of Peckwater. No more poignant contrast than this in the whole of Oxford. It is heightened in its effect by the more deliberate contrast of giant orders with and without a ground-floor pedestal to stand on. English Baroque and Burlingtonian (pre-Burlingtonian) classicism side by side. Through the cleft, and we enter Peckwater.

6. A quad considerably smaller than Tom, but raised to equal dignity by its even classical facades: "Atrii Peckwateriensis quod spectas latus extruxit Antonius Radcliffe S. T. P.," says the main north facade. Smooth columns, fine masonry, large main pediments, and evenly alternating small pediments for the windows of the piano nobile, but, to our right as we now stand, still the glowering front of the Library—even here an unsolved antagonism. And the tour of Christ Church is not completed yet. In the gap between smooth and rough and moderate and immoderate appears a further building, Wyatt's[4] delicate gateway of Canterbury Quad. The quad is a classical backwater of only two stories, humble compared with the cliff of the library.

7. Through Wyatt's arch and a few steps down Merton Street and we are at the entrance to Corpus Christi College. The front quad, completed in 1520, is comfortably smallish and business-like. It is entered not in the centre of the north side, but the Pelican set up in 1581 restores symmetry. Only let nobody expect that that axiality would be carried on into a major formal composition. To reach the second quad, we have to slink out at the left corner, and then the tour begins to be exciting.

8. A narrow corridor ends under the arcades at the narrow end of a cloister, if [a] cloister it can be called. At first it seems only a rather meanly-sized courtyard in front of Fellows' Building, but a variety of striking effects are compressed into the narrow space. Founders' Building is a formal composition with two symmetrical, slightly projecting wings, but its symmetry can from nowhere be seen effectively. Also, the narrow sides of the quad do not continue the symmetry: on one side, the cloister in which we stand; on the other, a break in height which is not concealed in any way.

9. And the arcades of the long side of the cloister opposite the formality of Founders' Building are turned into a picturesque delight by dangling Virginia Creeper and Gothic wall and window above. Again, leafage intervenes between two characteristically opposed textures: peeling ashlar and coarse rubble. No Piranesi could have introduced impropriety with more zest than the designer of this cloister. As we look at this north wall of the courtyard, we stand in a long corridor of no more than five and a half feet width — the most incongruous centre feature of so representational a composition as Founders' Building.

10. Turn round and enjoy the surprise of one of the lushest of Oxford gardens at the end of the dark passage—an excellent piece of unpretentious landscaping with fine, sensitively chosen trees. The tulip tree in front stands out against the background of Christ Church Meadow.

11. Then walk along towards the President's nicely proportioned lodgings — neo-Stuart of 1905 — turn round and receive the parting shot: two-storied embattled rubble wall and three-storied balustraded classical wall; cosy Tudor windows and forbidding blank classical niches; and a foreground of lawn and a low wall hidden by flowering bushes. The tour has taken us from the comfortable square size of the front quad by way of the exceedingly compressed and intricate second quad to this scene of landscaped architectural variety.

12. Is it necessary to continue? It should not be. The same experience can be had in most of the other colleges, unless they are as exceptionally unlucky as Balliol. But remember standing on the spacious lawn in King's at Cambridge; between Henry VIII Chapel, Gibbs's[5] Fellows' Building, and Wilkins's Screen and Hall; or in the narrow, intimate, domestic quad of St. Edmund Hall at Oxford: the epitome of collegiate picturesqueness. The dominant feature here is a tall, broad acacia tree placed out of all axes and growing at an angle of sixty degrees. Buildings are of two, three, and four stories with cornices at ever-varying heights, the somewhat more formal building of 1680 tucked into one corner. Its warmer cream colour is in contrast to the greyer rubble on the left, and the branches and umbellate blooms of wistaria stand delicately against the rubble behind.[6]

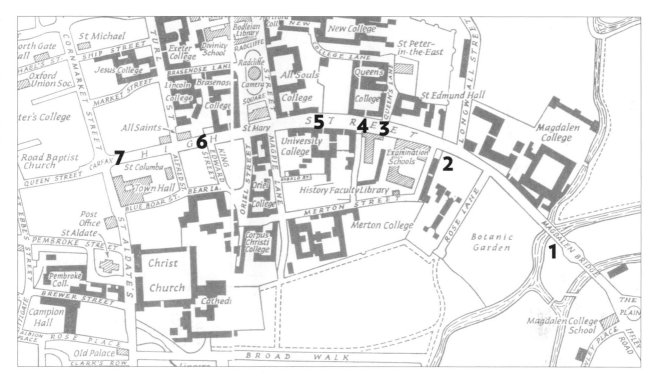

High Street, Oxford. Key to 1–7

1. Entering Oxford, as one should, from Magdalen Bridge, and through the tradesman's entrance from the station, the first picture of the city is significant of all that is to follow. Its visual values are so different from those, say, of the paragon city entrance, that of Rome by means of the Porta del Popolo. Instead of two churches of identical gravely porticoed facades separating three long, straight, fanning-out streets, you have here[,] across the bridge[,] a kind of green of uncertain shape. What you first see is not a street yet; it is still half-country, half-town. There is only one strong accent: Magdalen Tower, fixing what will be the line of one frontage of the High. But between it and the bridge there are lower outbuildings, their bell turrets and pinnacles at different heights half-hidden by trees, and opposite, on the left of the bridge, are the gateway and adminis-tration of the Botanic Gardens appearing behind a spectacular ——[8] tree and a lawn. Gateway and ad- [9] ministration again are of widely divergent character. Nicholas Stone in 1632 uses rustica-striping right across his columns, as Serlio had first recommended it, and crowns his composition with three pediments lustily trying to push each other out of position, the architect of the genteel tripartite administration building makes only one weak attempt at rusticity: in his weird panels of vermiculated rustication. Only behind the lawn in front of the Botanic Gardens appears on the left the corner house proper of the High. But when that point is reached, the Magdalen side juts back again. St. Swithun's Building and Magdalen School Hall, i.e., Garner[9] and Blomfield,[10] lie behind a screen of trees. The school hall is visible from the bridge already, as it stresses the bend of the High. For the High, with all its monumental buildings and the representational character which it might so easily have assumed, was never straightened.

2. On the left are the first proper street houses, stone-fronted, dignified, of moderate size and very different heights, and then smaller [properties], plain and plastered or bay-windowed. The other side makes an effort at period-commercial with Masonic Buildings. But one's eyes run quickly along these broken facades towards the grander point-de-vue in the distance, moving round slowly as the bend of the street develops: Queen's with its two identical wings and its curiously low cupola in between, and the dome of the Radcliffe Camera behind.

3. With the facade of Queen's, Oxford appears at its grandest. The motif of the far projecting wings, the screen between, and the lantern over the entrance is very formal and therefore, of course, once more of French origin — see, for instance, the Luxembourg in Paris. But the execution is baroque, in the oddly squat cupola especially.

4. Queen's is a monument in the French sense, but the High is not a [10] monumental street in the French sense.[11] For its buildings are not axially connected. They appear and disappear individually, each of its own peculiar character, and thus each a surprise. The one principle that seems to have guided [the] architecture is variety. On the left, this principle appears now for the first time in a more self-conscious way. Sir Thomas G. Jackson's Examinations Schools, with their carefully designed and mixed jollity of Tudor and Stuart, belong to an age [in] which picturesqueness in architecture had become a tenet.

   Meanwhile, the High goes on bending slightly. The rotund form of the Radcliffe disappears, and the broad, spiky steeple of St. Mary's appears instead—an irritatingly sharp contrast to Queen's and what lies between, that is, unpretentious warm domestic frontages, gabled or flat; one magnificent maple tree introducing nature where Paris would not tolerate her; a more ambitious Georgian stone facade of six bays; and the long, low south range of All Souls from the Warden's Lodge to the corner of St. Catherine Street. The contrast between this pleasantly haphazard picturesqueness and the more regulated picturesqueness of Barry[12] at University College should be noted in passing.

5. And then, while the south side of the High keeps a quiet accompaniment to the north—with the Greek Doric shop front of Halliday's antique shop as its prettiest feature—the flank of St. Mary's appears, screened at first behind a few trees and then coming out with its pinnacles at three different heights and with the barley-sugar columns of its porch. When will architects of the twentieth century have the self-confidence in their own style to place it so frankly next to one of contrary character? Meanwhile, All Saints has appeared behind Brasenose. The two spires are as consciously opposed to each other as porch and wall of St. Mary's. Aldrich's[13] spire is elegant, St. Mary's sturdy; Aldrich's smooth, St. Mary's bristling.

6. The west end of the High belongs chiefly to the nineteenth century. Standing by St. Mary's you have Champneys's[14] pompous Oriel front [11] on one side and Jackson's[15] more conventional Brasenose front on the other. But Champneys, with all his big effects, has nothing as animated as Jackson's ornament over the bay windows. Jackson's gateway is asymmetrical in the same proportion as the Founder's Tower of Magdalen: three bays on one side, five on the other. The flank of All Saints is unhappily short, and thus there is only one block left to Carfax—with the Market with its homely overweighted pediment, and then a few plastered fronts.

7. The Victorian circus by Carfax is the appropriate end of this tour — fun and games on northwest and northeast, and more genteel neo-Tudor on southwest and southeast. Mr. [Stephan Salter's] crazy Lloyd's Bank is more persistent in its claims on one's attention, but [Henry Hare]'s Midland Bank has more character and a subtle originality.[16] What matters more than these individual differences is, however, that the High ends with as conscious a denial of uniformity as it has shown in the course of its curved development from east to west.

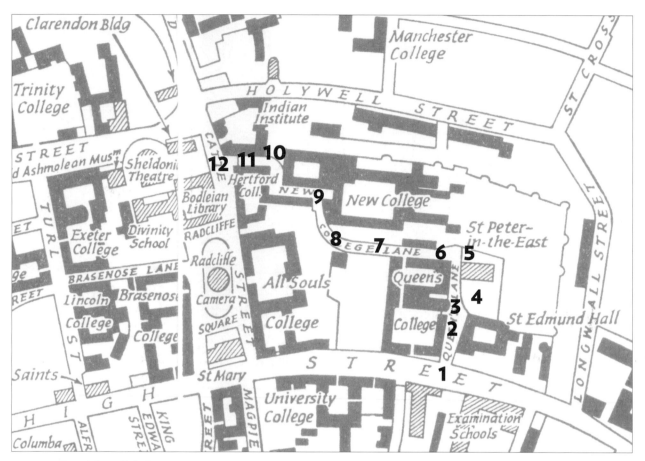

Queen's Lane, Oxford.

Key to 1–12

1. Turn off the High into any side-street, and you have the same character on a more intimate scale. Here you are in the shade between the tall, severe side of Queen's and a few private houses in the then-typical Great Western chocolate-and-cream paint. The front of St. Edmund Hall is just opposite [the] apse of Queen's Chapel.

2. And the apse, in its roundness and smoothness, contrasts with St. Peter's[17] standing at the end of the vista, square and rough, and with trees and bushes around, whereas Queen's is wholly man-shaped with no vegetation intruding anywhere.

3. By the church the lane narrows and starts twisting.

4. The church tower faces a late-Stuart front with a more pronounced and lively relief $[12]$ than Wren or Aldrich or Hawksmoor would have tolerated. The rhythm sets off the bluntness of the tower.

5. A sharp turn, and we enter a stretch of no other than accidental picturesque affect. The flaking-off stones of Queen's and the garden wall behind, and the forbidding black wall of the back buildings of New College.

6. A gentle bend, and behind the leafage of Queen's we get a glimpse of Hawksmoor's Gothick and Gibbs's Roman-Baroque dome, and then a lower Gothick gable comes into the field of vision.

7. It is the gable of the Codrington Library of All Souls, an odd frontage to an Italian room, and shown up to perfection by Sir Thomas G. Jackson's companion-piece, the [Chapel][18] of Hertford College—a master work of design in the spirit of variety. It is worth following in detail the similarities and the differences between the two, with their triplet windows and their gables of moderate pitch. They appear as on a stage, too; for the lane seems to widen here, as the buildings of New College recede on the right and give place to a strip of orchard.

8. After this flash of lively picturesque interest, of display and breadth, the scene shrinks again. Another turn, and we are in the back street of a small market-town. The bridge drives us on. A bridge across a street is always the greatest temptation to explore beyond.

9. And there is indeed surprise behind it, though no pleasant surprise. The next stretch, after another turn of ninety degrees, is between prison walls. The entrance to New College we don't see; it is behind us, and in front is not much promise of an escape. The chimney appears asymmetrical on the wall between the windows, though it isn't.

10. Yet another turn, the fourth, and we experience an almost irritating change of atmosphere. There in front of us, below laburnum, stands a brick house in its garden, prim and comfortable. It [12a] might be at St. Albans or Warwick or anywhere. The lane turns back to its prior direction almost immediately and returns us to the Oxford scene. Hertford College walls left and right, and Jackson's brilliant Bridge connecting them.

11. It is fine in section and in detail; that is seen in dark shadow or clear light, and what comes out beyond it is worth so sumptuous a frame.

12. An Oxford forum with the Bodleian, square and pinnacled on the left; the Clarendon Building, massive in block-shape and detail on the right; and the oddly unbalanced side-view of Wren's Sheldonian in the front. The view, framed as it now appears, is an epitome of Oxford planning: monumental in its elements, but full of contrasts in their arrangement or the way they have grown together.

[————]¹⁹*

This peculiar collegiate pattern, with its variety and intricacy, is not confined to Oxford.²⁰* It can be studied in London as well, and first and foremost in that belt between the cities of London and Westminster, which were the domain of the jurists and their colleges. The Inns of Court convey to the perambulating visitor sensations very similar to those we have tried to re-evoke at Oxford. When Clements Inn, Serjeant's Inn, Clifford's Inn, and Furnival's Inn still were there, and when the Temple, Staple Inn, and Gray's Inn had not yet been lacerated by fire and explosives, the belt was all but complete from the River to Theobald's Road. Today, Lincoln's Inn is the only one to show in unbroken sequence the space-and-time sensations which, we maintain, are a prerequisite of England: in wandering through the Inn from the Tudor Gatehouse in Chancery Lane, through the first court by the passage through the [O]ld [H]all, to the gardens, the [N]ew [H]all and [L]ibrary [13] and New Square on the left, and then back by Stone Buildings and New Stone Buildings.²¹

[————]²²*

LINCOLN'S INN

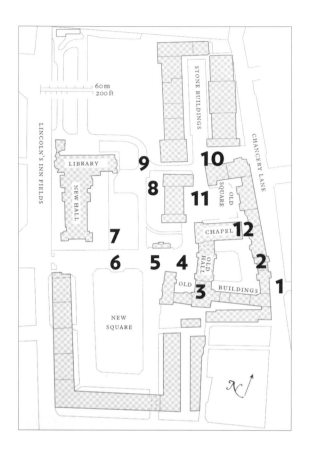

Lincoln's Inn, London.
Key to 1–12

1. Into Lincoln's Inn from Chancery Lane, out of the long, sunny street into the tall, dark Tudor arch of 15[18][23] with its blackened brickwork.

2. Old Square[24]—a comfortably sized quad with lawn and a few trees, rather menacing Tudor chambers on the left, —— lower Old Hall in front, brick again, but with the characteristic trellis of vitrified headers.

3. Through another, lower passage by the Old Hall, and we emerge into another age: turn your eyes sharp right and you have Sir George Gilbert Scott's New Stone Buildings, —— screened by plane trees.

4. Half right instead of sharp right—you see it better by walking on a little to the west—a first glimpse of the Lincoln's Inn Gardens can be gained with Hardwick's[25] prominently picturesque New Hall and Library of 18[43],[26] perhaps the last buildings of any size in London of that early phase of revivalism which was not yet afraid of fantasy—closer in spirit still to Strawberry Hill and Fonthill than to the Law Courts and the Prudential.[27]

5. Further west still, and you see where Hardwick's pretty gate joins the New Square of a sedate and comfortably William-and-Mary character. All appears wide and open from the spot where you stand. Now first turn left and then right.

6. On the left, New Square is large and symmetrical, though with the total absence of a dominant motif of no demonstrative formality. A slightly misty day shows it at its best. You don't need to see the repeated detail all the way through. It is planning in broad groups—nothing pretentious.

7. Opposite New Square, there is the wide garden with not many, but magnificently spreading plane trees and well-kept lawn. Hardwick's buildings suddenly appear hearty and a little vulgar when [14] faced by Sir Robert Taylor's Stone Buildings, a City Palladian style, just a little ——, but carefully keeping up its best behaviour. The fatuous little lodge in front of the south pavilion is a foretaste of what follows.

8. You approach it and see behind it—to its right, as we look at the picture—a charm between Georgian ashlar stone, with beautiful —— tooling, and Victorian brick.

9. Enter and cross it now, another sensation of contraction after expansion, but this time not a vaulted passage but an open gangway.

10. At its end, you have on your left the back court of Stone Buildings. Picturesque architecture is more at ease, where, for reasons of cost, full dress is out of the question. Classical architecture in negligé looks *negligé* indeed, neglected, or, [as] you may see, behind the scenes.

11. Opposite is one of the most charming spot[s] of the Inn, a small square courtyard just large enough for one plane tree's generously outstretched branches, tall Victorian brick all around except for the grey, over-buttressed wall of Inigo Jones's chapel with its undogmatic and very collegiate semi-gothic detail.

12. Through behind the chapel or, better still, under the chapel, with its stumpy columns and low vaults, like a town-hall's, and we are back where we started, in Old Square.[28] The gaunt and towering chambers are now in front; the Tudor gatehouse is on our left.

[————]29*

That the sensations are then very much as here described no-one will deny.[30]* But it may well be said that they can neither in Oxford nor in Lincoln's Inn be taken as a fair example of English planning, because they were not planned in the way we see them now. They are the outcome of growth, and usually growth on a pre-determined site. What we appreciate as a little drama of pleasant or piquant surprises in many scenes may only be due to the fact that architects could not plan as they liked. When Hawksmoor was free, the symmetry of the Queen's College appeared. Had Wren been free, [16]31 would not Trinity College, Cambridge, have had a courtyard in an all-round uniform harmony with his Library? Would we, in fact, have been given colleges as formal and balanced as those very "factories of learning" on the Continent which Pugin so scornfully sets against our colleges?32*

The strongest argument in favour of such an attribution to accident of English informal grouping is Wren's plan for London.[33]* He had been in Paris in 1665 and, not satisfied with as close a study of French architecture and decoration as was possible to him, he must also have been impressed with that new technique of large-scale planning with rond-points and straight radiating streets, which during the seventeenth century became a great French specialty. Much was yet only laid out, when Wren was there, but he was quick in the observation of the effects of grandeur and clarity that could thus be obtained, and so when the chance of his life as an architect came with the Fire of London in 1666, he submitted his design

Fig. 2

Fig. 2. Edward Rooker (ca. 1712–74), after John Gwynn (English, 1713–86). *A Plan for Rebuilding the City of London, after the Great Fire in 1666; Design'd by That Great Architect Sr. Christopher Wren...,* 1749, engraving, 27 × 39 cm (10⅝ × 15⅜ in.). New Haven, Yale Center for British Art

for an improved London almost immediately. So did John Evelyn (another leading Francophile), Hooke, and others.

Wren's plan is wholly French, dominated by the rond-point-radiating-streets principle. The only concession to the City and its peculiar character is that in the centre of the largest square there is not a Royal Palace but the Exchange. The plan had, as far as we can see, never the slightest chance of being accepted—we have not far to seek for reasons. There are three especially, belonging to these different [plans]. At shortest term such a sweeping re-distribution of property to make way for new streets and squares could, by no King or city council, be advocated immediately after a conflagration. The life of the city had to be brought back to normal as quickly as possible, and so there was no time for planning—a sad and illuminating lesson for the twentieth century. Then, secondly, to carry out so bold a scheme at any time would require somebody's overriding powers against "vested interests," that is, individual at the expense of communal advantages. Such powers were in the hands of the French Kings. The seventeenth and eighteenth centur[ies] in France [were] centuries of absolutism. The Stuart Kings, although they coveted [these powers], never possessed them. Wren's London would have been a monument to absolutism, alien in its pattern—besides being a monument to the rational, and systematic, spirit of the age.

Wren himself—it can be argued—recognised how foreign his scheme had been when his [17] growing architectural experience enabled him to appreciate the character of Oxford, Cambridge, and the City of London. For how could it

Fig. 3. The towers and steeples of Wren's city churches. Left to right: St. Stephen Walbrook, Christchurch, St. Mary-le-Bow, St. Bride, St. Martin Ludgate, and St. Dunstan-in-the-East

otherwise be explained that for his church steeples, the one contribution he found himself able to make to the appearance of London as a whole, he decided on the greatest possible variety of shapes and even styles? I know of no other architect **Fig. 3** of the seventeenth century who would so readily have abandoned the unity of personal self-expression to a diversity close to incongruity: the Baroque classicism of St. Mary-le-Bow, turned into Italian complexity at St. Stephen's Walbrook and with a severity reminiscent of the Palladian eighteenth century at Christ Church, Newgate Street, the wholly original telescoping of St. Brides's, the Dutch jollity of St. Martin's Ludgate, the playful revivalism of St. Dunstan's-in-the-East.[34]*

Here for the first time, with the work of the greatest English architect of his century, can we say that variety as against uniformity appears as a principle and not as an accident. Still, the case is unusual and only to a limited degree valid from the point of view of the usual town-planning history which works with maps rather than visually.

It is therefore all the more important that this same principle of individual design for small units, instead of sweeping sameness over a large area, can also be discovered in the one significant English contribution to seventeenth- and early-eighteenth-century town-planning in the accepted sense. This contribution, not so far sufficiently brought out in the literature (including Professor Lavedan) is the square.

England did not invent the planned square. Its history goes back to the fifteenth and sixteenth centuries in Italy and then to French work of the sixteenth and seventeenth. But only England made of the square the hallmark of planning to the extent to which the [W]est [E]nd of London shows it, and especially

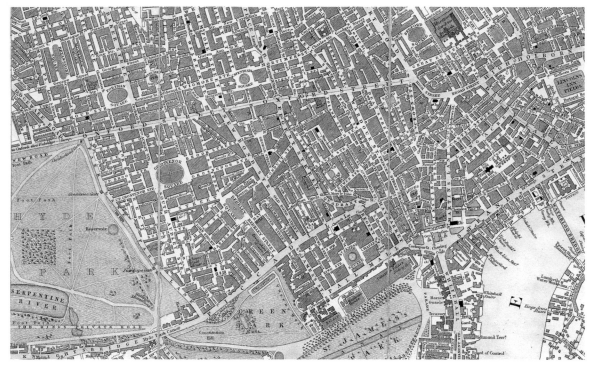

Fig. 4. The squares of London's West End: Plan of Mayfair

Fig. 5. Bloomsbury Square, London: Formal squares surrounded by irregular houses

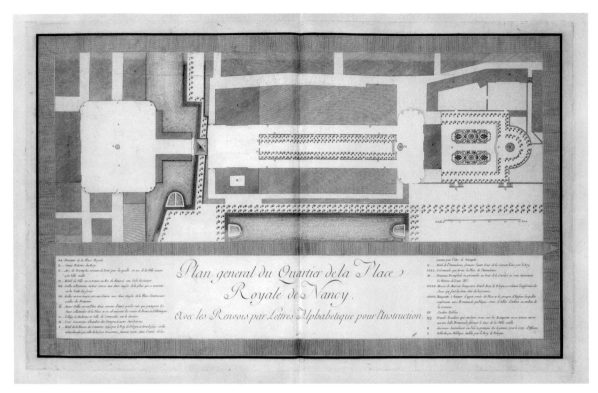

Fig. 6. General plan of the quarter of the Place Royale, Nancy

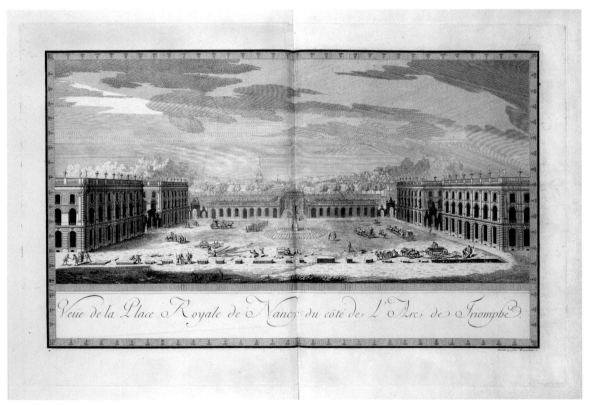

Fig. 7. View of the Place Royale, Nancy, near the Arc de Triomphe

Bloomsbury.[35]* In Italy and France, the square was either the centre or subcentre Fig. 4
of a whole district or it remained an individual composition unrelated to its surroundings, as for instance the [18] Place Royale in Paris. Only in England do
we find whole systems of squares, each planned on its own and not axially connected with the next, as is the case in Paris; and only in England is the rule that
the houses surrounding a square have no uniformity of appearance. The first
of London squares, it is true, Inigo Jones's Covent Garden of about 1685, was
intended to have all houses of the same design, and the Londoners rightly gave
it the outlandish name Piazza. But after that, for nearly a century no square was
designed in that way, and this century, chiefly its second half, was the heyday of
square-making in London.

The development of the West [E]nd since the Restoration was indeed car-
ried on under the sign of the square. St. James's Square was started in 1661,
Bloomsbury Square in 1665, Soho Square in 1681, Red Lion Square in the [1680s]
and [1690s], Golden Square in the [1690s], Queen's Square about 1705, Hanover
Square and Cavendish Square about 1715–20, Grosvenor Square in the [1720s],
Berkeley Square in the [1730s] and [1740s].

Now wandering through the West End of London, one experiences, though in
a somewhat subdued form, the same contrasts of effect between first [the] square,
[the] planned approach-road to it, [the] unplanned or less planned streets connecting the area of one district plan with another, [the] planned approach-road to
the second square, and so on.[36]* Take Berkeley Street and Berkeley Square [and] Fig. 5
then Davies Street, leaving the square at an odd angle, and the system of streets
framing Grosvenor Square. Or leave Berkeley Square by Bruton Street, walk on,
and find yourself suddenly at the south end of [St.] George Street with the straight
Hanover Square–Cavendish Square perspective in front of you. Or remember the
pleasant little shock when out of the intricacies of Soho you emerge into the Soho
Square system.

However, even the validity of this example might be doubted. It could well be
said that each ground landlord did as much as he could to create his own little
French plan, and only because his ground was limited and co-ordination with
neighbouring estate could only rarely be obtained, do we find various schemes
and no-man's-lands in between. [19] I would argue that if the wish for uniformity and the French kind of rational city pattern had been strong, agreement
could have been reached; but I would perhaps not be so confident, if it [were] not
for at least one example of the first magnitude, England's greatest town-planning
achievement, which proves beyond doubt that what I am trying to show as a conscious or subconscious principle was indeed a principle: Bath.

Bath is the work of Beau Nash and the two John Woods. The conversion of a
green into a designed form began in 1726. There was all the freedom architects
could wish for—no powerful ground landlords, no opposed vested interests. So
here was a chance to display the splendours of Nancy, the unforgettable feeling
of spatial crescendo from the Town Hall across the Place Stanislas through the
triumphal arch into the Carriére and into the elliptical forecourt of the Palace.[37]*
Instead of that, what are the sensations of the spectator on a tour through Bath? Figs. 6, 7
They must be gone through in some detail.

[38]*

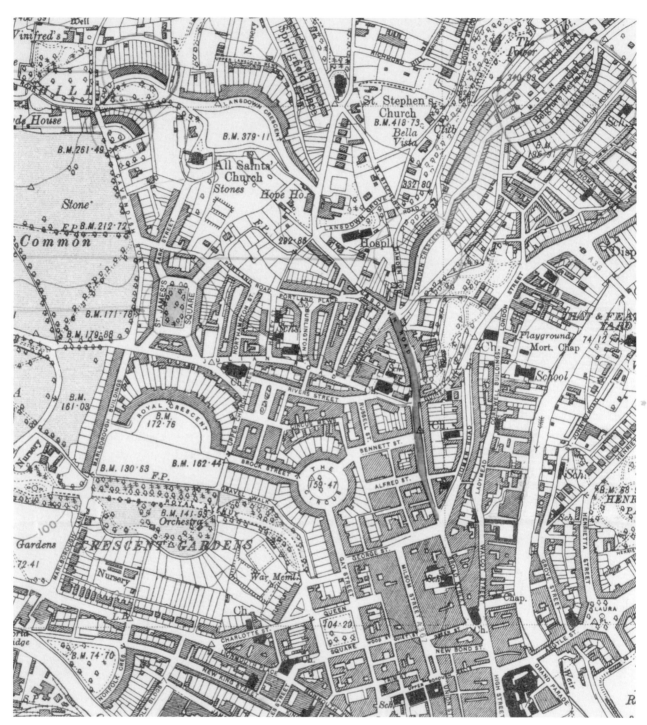

Bath. Key to 1–4

1. To cover the chief stations of the Wood plan, we must start at Queen's Square. The lease of the ground belonged to John Wood, and he laid the foundations of the first houses on December 10, 1728. The last houses were completed in 1735. The square itself had, of course, no tall trees and no picturesque layout. It had a basin in the centre with an obelisk erected in 1738. From the centre, eight straight gravel paths radiated towards the four corners and the centres of the four sides. A low stone balustrade enclosed the square. The houses around the square were equally formal, each side a set pattern concealing the fact that they were not palaces but terraces of houses to be let to the summer guests of Bath. Not since Inigo Jones had so monumental a square been designed. It matches in uniformity and formality [20] the Place Vendôme of some twenty-five years earlier. But as the Paris of Louis XIV had its circular Place des Victoires as well as its rectangular Place Vendôme, so Wood also wished to add to Queen's Square a second, round centre—the Circus. Now it was left to him, entirely, as far as we can see, where he would place the Circus and how he would connect the two. But which did he do? He ran Barton Street up into the Circus, [which] spoiled any axial connection that might have been possible. Instead of a carefully worked-up gradual crescendo—surprise: a strong accent where it cannot be expected.

2. And between Circus and Royal Crescent the same deliberately non-axial relation is established. Yet the architecture of the three centres is clearly designed to be seen as part of one programme: the giant pilasters of Queen's Square, the three super-imposed orders of the Circus, and the giant attached columns of the Royal Crescent. There is also a magnificent crescendo of scale between Circus and Royal Crescent. Yet instead of doing what academic conventions would have recommended and carrying on the Queen's Square–Circus axis straight towards the centre of the Crescent, Wood allows it to run against a wall so that, having reached the Circus, the spectator feels at the end of his tour. The two streets leading out of the Circus hold out no promises of new visual adventures. Neither leads to any *point de vue*. Yet following the one to the left, [Brock] Street,[39] we are at its end suddenly faced with the most spectacular of vistas.

3. The long expanse of the Royal Crescent enters, again not seen pat from the front, as the photograph shows it, but from the right-hand end, so that the act of development of the half ellipse itself is a thrilling spatial experience. The planting which appears at the front of the picture belongs to a later generation. In Wood's time there was only sloping lawn [21] to respond to the splendid sweep of the Crescent.

4.[40] Nor did Wood's successors depart from his principles when, towards the end of the eighteenth century and early in the nineteenth, more squares, crescents, and other set pieces of town-planning were designed.[41] To reach [St. James's] Square, [Cavendish] Crescent, and the elegant double curve of Lansdown Crescent, the Royal Crescent has to be left at its other end and a similarly meandering promenade to be gone through. And it is the same on the other side of [Lansdown Road][42] with [Camden] Crescent and [Belgrave] Crescent.

[43]*

In Bath, at last we get the full proof of informal planning as a principle. The effects of surprise, intricacy, and seeming impropriety are here all developed with supreme adroitness and achieve a visual drama just as delightful as, but fundamentally different from, Nancy. Can this one example of untrammeled town-planning be taken as corroborative evidence in favour of conscious attempts on the same lines at Oxford and Cambridge, and in the Inns of Court and the West [E]nd squares of London? One thing at least is certain. Where London made its most ambitious effort towards co-ordinated planning in the early nineteenth century, the principles were again the same, and even if John Nash in laying out Regent Street was originally limited by conditions of ownership, he turned these difficulties to advantage so deftly as only an English planner could do.[44]* To the French observer, Regent Street from where Carlton House used to stand at its south end to the Regents Park in the north is a travesty of Rue de Rivoli and Champs Elysées—no sustained logic, no grandeur of manner.[45]

Figs. 8, 9

Yet with the experience, Bath fresh in one's eyes and feet, it is clear that the sudden end of the first stage of Regent Street [22] by Piccadilly Circus and the equally sudden turn with the one piece of grand unified-facade architecture, the Quadrant, is a deliberate effect of surprise—or was, as long as the old facades were in existence. It is one of the many major crimes of Londoners against their own traditions that, for no valid reason whatever, they pulled down the whole of the best example of English town-planning they possessed—and pulled it down as late as the [1920s]. Only a few bits survive towards its southern end (Suffolk Street). Apart from the Quadrant there was no uniformity of architecture. Each block and sometimes each half block was designed on its own. So the street

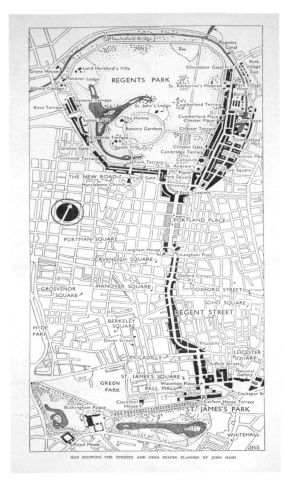

Fig. 8. Map showing the streets and open spaces planned by John Nash

Fig. 9. The Quadrant, and Part of Regent Street

VISUAL PLANNING, PART I

Fig. 10. East Side of Park Crescent

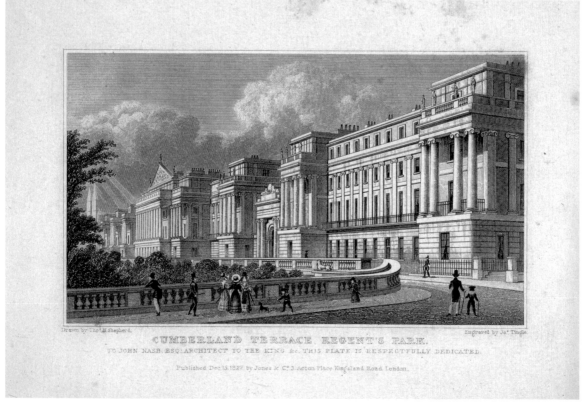

Fig. 11. Cumberland Terrace, Regent's Park

Fig. 12. The Holme, Regent's Park

Fig. 13. Park Village East, Regent's Park

ambled on northward until by Langham Place another short change of direction had to be forced to connect the new street with the existing Portland Place. Here again Nash made a positive effect out of a snag in plan. The circular tower and spire of the little church of All Saints acts as a *point de vue* from south as well as north. Only a circular piece could achieve that.

A last, equally convincing motif marks the north end of the street. The wide opening of Park Crescent[46*]—another part of Nash's going to school with the Woods—connects the long, comparatively narrow street with the wide expanse of the park.

Fig. 10

But the Nash epic is not complete without the park, and the park is not complete without its nine terraces, its dotted-about villas, and its two picturesque villages on the north-eastern outskirts.[47*] The composition in stone finds its final climax in a composition in foliage and stone. The contrasts of facades and of directions culminate in the contrast between architecture and nature. Here again Nash was not the creator of a new principle but only the most skilful of epigones. Landscape as an essential part of planning had been established in England several generations before him.

Figs. 11–13

[48*]

NOTES

1. At this point, Pevsner indicated the insertion of two paragraphs from page 2 of the manuscript.

2*. The text returns to the bottom of page 3. **<AR Aug. 1949.>** Note for insertion of text from Pevsner's article "Reassessment 4: Three Oxford Colleges," *AR* 106 (1949): 119–24. The inserted text comprises the remainder of this section, with the manuscript text resuming again at "High Street," the next section heading.

Beginning on page 3 of the manuscript, the title "Christ Church" is crossed out, as are the subsequent passages of text from the last third of page 3 and all of page 4. The original pages following page 4 are missing from the file, presumably taken for the *AR* article. Although Pevsner originally intended his tour of Oxford to encompass four colleges, the bulk of the *AR* article was concerned with Christ Church, Corpus Christi, and, to a lesser extent, St. Edmund Hall Colleges. Magdalen College is not discussed in the article and the bulk of the original manuscript is missing, with the exception of the caption to the last illustration, number six. The six images of Magdalen College that Pevsner had selected for publication are kept in the folder "Oxford Illustrations," found in box 25 of the Nikolaus Pevsner papers, Getty Research Institute, Los Angeles, acc. no. 840209; hereafter the Nikolaus Pevsner papers. The manuscript text begins again on page 8. The following commentary and illustrations are taken from the "Reassessment 4" article.

3. Cardinal Thomas Wolsey (1470/71–1530), the founder of the first college on this site.

4. James Wyatt (1746–1813).

5. James Gibbs (1682–1754).

6. This marks the end of the inserted article; pagination returns to that of the manuscript.

7. This section on Oxford's High Street has many similarities to the tour of the same street published in Thomas Sharp, *Oxford Replanned* (London: Architectural, 1948). Six of the illustrations are identical; see pp. 21–26. The idea for the tour appears

to stem from Raymond Unwin and a similar tour of Oxford's High Street. See Raymond Unwin, *Town Planning in Practice: An Introduction to the Art of Designing Cities and Suburbs* (London: Adelphi, 1909), 265–75. Pevsner tacitly acknowledges this in a tribute to Unwin in 1963, writing, "there is in [Unwin's] book already an illustration of the plan of the Oxford High and a sequence of shots to illustrate how the various vistas follow each other—in fact the Sharp device of his *Oxford Replanned* of 1948"; see Nikolaus Pevsner, "History: Unwin Centenary," *AR* 134 (1963): 207. Jennifer Sherwood and Pevsner's *Oxfordshire* (in *The Buildings of England* series) also contains a tour within the "Perambulations" section, which is the reverse of the one printed here: beginning at Carfax and ending at Magdalen Bridge; see Jennifer Sherwood and Nikolaus Pevsner, *Oxfordshire* (Harmondsworth: Penguin, 1974), 306–11. These "Perambulations" were an integral feature of *The Buildings of England* series, appearing first in Pevsner's *Nottinghamshire* (1951) and later in *London: Except the Cities of London and Westminster* (1952). As such, the tour published here predated those used in Pevsner's guidebooks.

8. Space left by Pevsner for the species of tree.

9. Sherwood and Pevsner, *Oxfordshire* (note 7), 153, points out that the architects of Saint Swithun's Buildings were George Frederick Bodley and Thomas Garner.

10. Sir Arthur Blomfield (1829–99). The building Pevsner refers to as Magdalen School Hall is also known as Magdalen College School, built from 1893 to 1894.

11. Pevsner had selected two images, labeled "4a" and "4b," for this illustration; see Nikolaus Pevsner papers, box 25, folder "Illustrations: Oxford." The reverse side of 4b has a handwritten note stating "perhaps 4a instead," which has provided the basis for the current selection. Curiously, both photographs were published in Sharp's *Oxford Replanned* (note 7), 23–24. Image 4b carries the stamp of the photographers Dell and Wainwright, suggesting Pevsner was working from original prints; 4a is printed on glossy paper and contains no attribution but was presumably from Dell and Wainwright, as acknowledged in Sharp's book (p. 10).

12. Pevsner is most likely referring to Sir Charles Barry's New Building (1842). See Sherwood and Pevsner, *Oxfordshire* (note 7), 211.

13. Pevsner names Henry Aldrich as the designer of All Saints and Dean of Christ Church College. However, Sherwood and Pevsner, *Oxfordshire* (note 7), 287–88, is equivocal on the subject, admitting the possibility that Nicholas Hawksmoor was its designer. Woolley notes that the spire was the work of Hawksmoor; see Alfred Russell Woolley, *The Clarendon Guide to Oxford,* 2nd ed. (London: Oxford Univ. Press, 1972), 94.

14. Pevsner refers to Basil Champneys's Rhodes Building (1908–11). See Sherwood and Pevsner, *Oxfordshire* (note 7), 180.

15. Sir Thomas G. Jackson, and his New Quad begun in 1886. See Sherwood and Pevsner, *Oxfordshire* (note 7), 108.

16. Here Pevsner did not know the architects of Lloyd's Bank or the Midland Bank at Carfax and left their names blank. Sherwood and Pevsner's *Oxfordshire* (note 7), 306–7, names Stephen Salter with R. C. Davey as Lloyd's architects and Henry Hare for the Midland Bank.

17. The full name of the church on Queen's Lane, Oxford, is Saint Peter-in-the-East; see Sherwood and Pevsner, *Oxfordshire* (note 7), 295–97.

18. Pevsner did not name this building. Sherwood and Pevsner, *Oxfordshire* (note 7), 140, refers to the building on the southern range of the Quad as a "Chapel," built in 1908, and of which they stated, "The [East] window, undeniably, is a splendid sight from New College Lane."

19*. {**Back to the large Text.**} Pevsner's note to return to running text.

20*. **<Also Camb[ridge]—though perhaps less.>** Note in pencil.

21. This tour later formed the basis of Nikolaus Pevsner, *London, I: The Cities of London and Westminster* (Harmondsworth: Penguin, 1957). Aspects of Pevsner's views on Lincoln's Inn were also published in the *AR*'s special issue of June 1945, which put forward precinctual and collegiate planning principles as the hallmark of English planning and as the method for reconstructing the City of London; see "A Programme for the City of London," special issue, *AR* 97 (1945): 157–96. This issue shows a plan of the Temple in London (p. 180), a view of Lincoln's Inn (p. 181), and a plan (p. 187). The accompanying caption—although published anonymously—resembles Pevsner's style and syntax. It reads,

> 11. the visual coherence of collegiate layout. In the few surviving urban precincts like the Temple, for instance, or the Tower, there exists the proof that the elements of the London scene can be combined in a manner that does not do violence to its character. In these groups of buildings with planting, street furniture, narrow passages and intimate courts there is a visual concord, which makes a direct human appeal and does not chill the heart like the extraneous forms of visual order practised not far away in Kingsway. This special kind of beauty cannot be codified, for unlike the classical order it is not built of standardised elements nor does it obey any obvious rules of composition. The types of buildings it uses always vary; they may be mediaeval, classical, or both, and yet are joined with ease in an informal order. Generally the collegiate pattern is cultivated to-day by those who want to insulate themselves from active life. But this is a modern misuse of the practice. The argument here is that collegiate layout is particularly applicable to City needs and has been used throughout its history. (p. 181)

Pevsner's earlier edition on London carries a similar treatment of the Inns; see Nikolaus Pevsner, *London: Except the Cities of London and Westminster* (Harmondsworth: Penguin, 1952), 212–14:

> Gray's Inn is the northernmost of the London Inns of Justice or colleges of lawyers. These colleges, similar in architectural character to a certain extent to the colleges of Oxford and Cambridge, extend as a belt to the [west] of the City of London, starting in the [south], by the River, with the Temple.... The many contrasts between heights and sizes of open spaces should be specially studied: narrow paved spaces, wide turfed spaces, and finally the long expanse of the gardens. It is English visual planning at its best.

22*. {**Here Lincoln's Inn 1–12 as follows, but only as captions, not as running commentary, as is the case of Oxford. That is, the text runs on unbroken—the pictures are with their captions[,] only a strip accompanying the previous paragraph.**} Pevsner's instructions for the layout of the section on Lincoln's Inn.

23. This date was left blank by Pevsner. In Pevsner, *London* [1957] (note 21), 276–79, Pevsner not only recounts much of the following text but also points out that the Gatehouse was begun in 1518.

24. The quad to which Pevsner refers is not Old Square, which is further to the north, but that of Old Buildings; see Pevsner, *London* [1957] (note 21), 276–77.

25. Phillip Hardwick; see Pevsner, *London* [1957] (note 21), 278–79.

26. Date left blank by Pevsner. New Hall and Library, begun in 1843; see Pevsner, *London* [1957] (note 21), 278–79.

27. Pevsner is referring to the Prudential Assurance building by Alfred Waterhouse, built in 1879; see Pevsner, *London* [1957] (note 21), 309.

28. Once again, this appears to be a mistake on Pevsner's behalf; see note 24 above.

29*. {**On in the text.**} Note regarding the layout.

30*. **<cf. Gabriel.>** Note in pencil, presumably indicating that Jacques-Ange Gabriel (1698–1782) might have disagreed with Pevsner's opinions. **<Or is all this only because of incremental growth? Did [England], when there was a chance of unhampered large scale planning behave in the French way and plan in the grand manner? The most famous of all [English] city plans seem to bear that out: Wren's for London.>** Note in pencil.

31. There is no page 15 in the manuscript; however, the text flows seamlessly from page 14 to 16.

32*. {*True Principles,* **p. 54.**} Augustus Welby Northmore Pugin, *The True Principles of Pointed or Christian Architecture* (London: John Weale, 1841), 54.

33*. **<Doubtful / In [Rome] they would wait until money then to pull down / In [England] ready for mixture / —— case of Wren not quite so clear / Plan of [London]. / French[,] but spires all variety.>** Note in pencil.

34*. **<Ill. Steeples X Church Newgate St. / St. Bride's / St. Dunstan's i.t. East / St. Martin's Ludgate / St. M-le-Bow / St. Steph. Walbrook.>** An indication of what Pevsner had in mind can be found in the illustrations in Pevsner, *London* [1957] (note 21), 69. An early discussion and illustrations of the variety of Wren's spires are found in the *AR*'s special issue "A Programme for the City of London" (note 21), 170–90.

35*. {**Ill. Mayfair Plan.**} Note for illustration.

36*. {**Ill. Engraving of one square with variety of house facades.**} Note for illustration.

37*. {**Ill. Nancy Engravings.**} Note for illustration.

38*. {**Now back to illustrations and captions. First Nancy: Plan and engravings from Mariette or Blondel? Brief captions which I can write later. Then.**} Note for layout and presentation of illustrations. Here Pevsner is referring to Jean Mariette, *L'architecture françoise...,* 5. vols. (Paris: Jean Mariette, 1727–38); and Jacques-François Blondel, *Architecture françoise...,* 4 vols. (Paris: Charles-Antoine Jombert, 1752–56). Neither contains illustrations of Nancy. Thanks to Jean-François Bédard for this information. Instead, the figures have been taken from Emmanuel Héré, *Plans et élévations de la Place royale de Nancy et des autres édifices...* (Paris: Ches François, Graveur Ordinaire de Sa Majesté..., 1753).

39. Pevsner left the name of the street blank.

40. The back of this image is marked with green ink, indicating that it is keyed to the large plan contained in Nikolaus Pevsner papers, box 25, folder "Illustrations: Bath," and reproduced here as the key to figures 1 through 4.

41. Pevsner left the name of this square blank, as with all others in the following passage. Theses names have been interpolated from the key to Bath.

42. This field was originally listed as "—— Street." An analysis of the map mentioned in note 40 shows this to be most likely Lansdown Road.

43*. {**Back to Text.**} Note for layout.

44*. {**Plan of Regent St + ill. from Metropolitan Improvements.**} Note for illustrations. This refers to the plan of Nash's work in John Summerson, *John Nash,*

Architect to King George IV (London: Allen & Unwin, 1935); and illustrations from James Elmes and Thomas Shepherd, *Metropolitan Improvements; or, London in the Nineteenth Century: Displayed in a Series of Engravings…from Original Drawings,…by Mr. Thos. H. Shepherd:…with Historical, Topographical, and Critical Illustrations by James Elmes* (London: Jones, 1827).

45. See Pevsner, *London* [1957] (note 21), 559–62. With regard to Regent Street, Pevsner stated,

> But whatever the reason for his employment, [Nash's] plan was certainly a work of genius. A straight avenue in the Parisian sense was out of the question. […] Nash—referring in his memorandum explicitly to so paramount an example of picturesque growth as the High Street at Oxford—made this Quadrant his chief display piece, with sweeps of colonnades […] leading you round. It was a way of making the most ingenious use of that principle of picturesque planning: surprise" (p. 560).

To this passage, Pevsner inserted a note: "Prince Pückler-Muskau, that enthusiastic German anglophile who made one of the most extensive and famous landscape gardens in Germany on the English pattern, appreciated this point. He wrote from London in 1826: 'It is a peculiar beauty of the new street that, though broad, it does not run in straight lines, but makes occasional curves which break its uniformity'" (p. 560, unnumbered note).

46*. {**plates Park Crescent.**} Note for illustrations.

47*. {**Photos Terraces.**} Note for illustrations. Here, engravings from Elmes and Shepherd, *Metropolitan Improvements* (note 47), have been employed instead.

48*. **<On to my discovery.>** Note in pencil.

PART II,
mostly presented in quotations

I must now for a moment go back to a personal experience. Having seen and enjoyed Oxford and Cambridge and Bath and Edinburgh and the shadow of Regent Street as re-evoked by the *Metropolitan Improvements* and Mr. Summerson,[2] I began to ask myself whether the qualities revealed had not a counterpart in an English-planning literature or philosophy, preferably contemporary with the buildings themselves. I could find nothing, and was ready to resign myself to the acceptance of yet another case of English pragmatism without underlying formulated systems, when I hit on the first of the English landscape books of the eighteenth century. I forget which it was; as one led to the other, and in the end the whole philosophy of planning with contours and trees and lakes and footpaths was revealed. It was only one step from there to the application of the principles then established from landscape to townscape. The step, however, was taken only rarely by the eighteenth- and nineteenth-century writers.

The subject of the following pages is to show the evolution of English planning principles in terms of landscape between 1700 and 1800. I propose to do this mainly in a series of quotations in chronological order. Quotations will be chosen with a view to their relevance to the particular subject of this book rather than to the particular character of the author; no attempt will be made to provide another history of the Picturesque after Mr. Hussey's fascinating and comprehensive book of 1927 and the many more recent and more detailed studies.[3]*

[2] Gardens and Parks: Stage One

FRANCIS BACON, 1597 AND SIR HENRY WOTTON, 1624

In spite of the seemingly revolutionary first sentence of [Bacon's] *Essay of Buildings*—"Houses are built to live in, and not to look on; therefore, let use be preferred before uniformity, except when both may be had,"[4] the princely palace which he goes on to describe is grand and symmetrical, and the garden, which in the following *Essay of Gardens* is described, is equally formal. It consists of a Green close to the house, with "a fair alley in the midst," a main garden with a high surrounding hedge trimmed at intervals into the shape of pyramids, columns, and the like, a central mount covered by a banqueting house, and side alleys, and only at a distance "a heath, or desert" "to be framed as much as may be to a natural wildness."[5]

There is all the difference between this admission of the irregular in a place away from house and trimmed gardens—wilderness of this kind became an accepted part even of the gardens of the age of Louis XIV—and Sir Henry Wotton's remarkable suggestion to make gardens entirely irregular.

> First, I must note a certaine contrarietie between *building* and *gardening:* For as Fabriques should bee *regular,* so Gardens should bee *irregular,* or at least cast into a very wilde *Regularitie.* To exemplifie my conceit; I have seene a *Garden* (for the maner perchance incomparable) into which the first Accesse was a high walke like a *Tarrace,* from whence might bee taken a generall view of the whole *Plott* below but rather in a delightful confusion, then with any plaine distinction of the pieces. From this the *Beholder* descending many steps, was afterwards conveyed again, by severall *mountings* and *valings,* to various entertainments of his *sent,* and *sight;* which I shall not neede to describe.[6]*

Wotton was a friend of Bacon's—he wrote Bacon's epitaph for the monument in St. Michael's at St. Albans—and also a friend of Inigo Jones's and one of England's first virtuosi. For nearly fifteen years he lived in Venice, and nothing in his life and writings prepares one for so heretical a view on the art of gardening. It does not seem to have found any successors for at least two generations.

SIR WILLIAM TEMPLE, 1685 (PUBLISHED IN 1695)

In his *Gardens of Epicurus* Temple describes Moor Park near Farnham in Surrey as his ideal garden.[7] This is completely regular, with a terrace in front of the house, a gravel walk even with it, a parterre divided into quarters, symmetrically disposed summer houses, and a lower garden with fruit trees. But to this description Temple adds the following paragraph:

> What I have said of the best forms in Gardens, is meant only of such as are in some sort regular; for there may be other forms wholly irregular, that may, for ought I know, have more beauty than any of the others; but they must owe it to some extraordinary dispositions of nature in the seat, or some great race of fancy or judgment in the contrivance, which may produce many disagreeing parts into some figure, which shall yet upon the whole, be very agreeable. Something of this I have seen in some places, but heard more of it from others, who have lived much among the Chinese; a people whose way of thinking seems to lie as wide of ours in Europe, as their country does. Among us, the beauty of building and planting is placed chiefly in some certain proportions, symmetries, or uniformities; our walk and our trees ranged so, as to answer one another, and at exact distances. The Chinese scorn this way of planting, and say a boy that can tell an hundred, may plant walks of trees in straight lines, and over against one another, and to what length and extent he pleases. But their greatest reach of imagination, is employed in contriving figures where the beauty shall be great, and strike the eye, but without any order or disposition of parts, that shall be commonly or easily observed. And though we have hardly any notion of this sort of beauty, yet they have a particular word to express it; and where they find it hit their eye at first sight, they say the Sharawaggi is fine or is admirable, or any such expression of esteem. And whoever observes the work upon the best Indian gowns, or the painting upon their best screens or purcellans, will find their beauty is all of this kind (that is) without order. But I should hardly advise any of these attempts in the figure of gardens among us; they are adventures of too hard achievement for any common hands; and though there may be more honour if they succeed well, yet there is more dishonour if they fail, and 'tis twenty to one they will; whereas in regular figures, 'tis hard to make any great and remarkable faults.[8]*

[3] The reference to China is interesting, and must be understood with the light of much information on the Far East which had reached England, Holland, and France during Temple's life-time,[9]* but what is more interesting is that here, for the first time, a possible principle of irregular beauty is envisaged and that at once the dangers inherent in its application are stated.

LORD SHAFTESBURY, 1709–13[10]*

Shaftesbury's philosophy is certainly one of rationalism. His aesthetics are an integral part of his philosophy. In its centre stands the concept of a "universal concord" of beauty, truth, and goodness: "[W]hat is Beautiful is harmonious and proportionable; what is *harmonious* and *proportionable,* is True; and what is at once *beautiful* and *true,* is, of consequence, *agreeable* and Good."[11]*

Shaftesbury presents this philosophy with elegance. He detested the pedants and insisted that truth must "stand up to Raillery," that "good humour" is the best foundation of true religion, and that scepticism is "the prettiest, agreeablest, roving exercise of the mind."[12]* Any show of enthusiasm disagreed so much with him that he wrote a whole paper against it. This attitude determined his taste. Beauty to him depends on "symmetry and order,"[13]* [Insertion A][14]* and what he meant by that comes out clearly in a passage in which he states as a matter of course that "'Tis enough if we consider the simplest of figures; as either a round *ball,* a *cube,* or *dye.* Why is even an infant pleas'd with the first view of these proportions? Why is the *sphere* or *globe,* the *cylinder* and *obelisk* prefer'd; and the irregular figures, in respect of these, rejected and despis'd?"[15]*

This determines his judgements on architecture. Christopher Wren he disliked, partly, it is true, for political reasons, but partly also for what he called a "false and counterfeit... magnificence."[16]* He evidently wanted something more restrained, something, one guesses, Palladian, though some years before Palladianism re-emerged in England under the patronage of Lord Burlington. The most interesting passage is this:

> Nothing surely is more strongly imprinted on our minds, or more closely
> interwoven with our souls, than the idea or sense of *order* and *proportion.*
> Hence all the force of *numbers* ... What a [3] difference ... between the regular
> and uniform pile of some noble architect, and a heap of sand and stones![17]*

[4] But whereas the heap of sand and stones is to him a symbol of the chaotic, the tree and the animal are included in his categories of order and proportion. Nature indeed Shaftesbury loved first of all as an expression of universal orderliness. The microscope on the one hand and Newton's physics on the other had taught the seventeenth century to identify nature with reason. The result in Shaftesbury is curious. *The Moralists* is called "a Philosophical Rhapsody." The book is a rhapsody on nature, written with that very enthusiasm which he otherwise deprecated so much. He insisted in his *Letter [C]oncerning Enthusiasm* that any such "romantick ranting" should be measured by "reason and sound sense,"[18] and he could only afford now to rant himself because what he praises in praising nature is that very firmness of initial order.

> Nor can we judg less favourably of that consummate art exhibited thro all
> the works of nature, since our weak eyes, help'd by mechanick art, discover
> in these works a hidden scene of wonders; worlds within worlds, of infinite
> minuteness.[19]*

This original nature Shaftesbury holds against the "folly and perverseness" of Man,[20]* and the theme of his moralizing is that very contrast between man and the world, "this *mansion*-Globe, this *man*-container":[21]*

> O Glorious *nature!* supremely fair and sovereignly good! All-loving, and all-
> lovely, all-divine! Whose looks are so becoming, and of such infinite grace;
> whose study brings such wisdom, and whose contemplation such delight.[22]*

So far, Shaftesbury's system seems consistent. But at that stage an odd and very English thing happened to him. In his Dorset countryside, nature meant to him more than the divine order; it meant

> [t]he verdure of the field, the distant prospects, the gilded horizon, and purple sky, form'd by a setting sun.[23]*

That is the visual experience of ever-varied charms, not of an order established under "the force of numbers." And so nature in the pages of *The Moralists* imperceptibly changes to something quite different, —— Philocles explains,

> I shall no longer resist the passion in me for things of a *natural* kind; where neither *art,* nor the *conceit* or *caprice* [5] of man has spoil'd their *genuine order,* by breaking in upon that *primitive state*. Even the nude *rocks,* the mossy *caverns,* the irregular unwrought *grotto*[s], and broken *falls* of waters, with all the horrid graces of the *wilderness* it-self, as representing Nature more, will be more engaging, and appear with a magnificence beyond the formal mockery of princely gardens.[24]

In the particular context of this book few things remain from this passage, the —— visual delight in the irregular, be it of the gentle country scene or of the horrid graces of a regular nature, and the contrasting of nature unspoilt and nature trimmed into formal gardens. Both were to have an immediate effect on younger writers, poets, and philosophers.

JOSEPH ADDISON, 1712

The chief tenet which Addison held in two letters in *The Spectator* is the same as Shaftesbury's. But expressed in a much more commonsensical way, it popularized what had so far only been seen by the few who read Shaftesbury's *Moralists.* Moreover, Addison went beyond Shaftesbury in one or two respects which are of importance to the future:

> [T]here is generally in nature something more grand and august, than what we meet with in the curiosities of art. When, therefore, we see this imitated in any measure, it gives us a nobler and more exalted kind of pleasure than what we receive from the nicer and more accurate productions of art. On this account our English gardens are not so entertaining to the fancy as those in France and Italy, where we see a large extent of ground covered over with an agreeable mixture of garden and forest, which represent everywhere an artificial rudeness much more charming than that neatness and elegancy which we meet with in those of our own country. It might indeed be of ill consequence to the public, as well as unprofitable to private persons, to alienate so much ground from pasturage and the plough, in many parts of a country that is so well peopled, and cultivated to a far greater advantage. But why may not a whole estate be thrown into a kind of garden by frequent plantations, that may turn as much to the profit as the pleasure of the owner? A marsh overgrown with willows, or a mountain shaded with oaks, are not only more beautiful but more beneficial than when they lie bare and unadorned. Fields of corn make a pleasant prospect; and if the walks were a little taken care of that lie between them; if the natural embroidery of the meadows were helped and improved by some small additions of art, and

the several rows of hedges set off by trees and flowers that the soil was capable of receiving, a man might make a pretty landskip of his own possessions.

Writers who have given us an account of China, tell us the inhabitants of that country laugh at the plantations of our Europeans, which are laid out by the rule and line; because, they say, any one may place trees in equal rows and uniform figures. They choose rather to show a genius in works of this nature; and therefore always conceal the art by which they direct themselves. They have a word, it seems, in their language, by which they express the particular beauty of a plantation that thus strikes the imagination at first sight, without discovering what it is that has so agreeable an effect. Our British gardeners, on the contrary, instead of humouring nature, love to deviate from it as much as possible. Our trees rise in cones, globes and pyramids. We see the marks of the scissors upon every plant and bush. I do not know whether I am singular in my opinion; but, for my own part, I would rather look upon a tree in all its luxuriancy and diffusion of boughs and branches, than when it is thus cut and trimmed into a mathematical figure; and cannot but fancy that an orchard in flower looks infinitely more delightful, than all the little labyrinths of the most finished parterre. [25 June]

I have several acres about my house, which I call my garden, and which a skilful gardener would not know what to call. It is a confusion of kitchen and parterre, orchard and flower garden, which lie so mixt and interwoven with one another, that if a foreigner, who had seen nothing of our country, should be conveyed into my garden at his first landing, he would look upon it as a natural wilderness, and one of the uncultivated parts of our country...There is the same irregularity in my plantations, which run into as great a wilderness as their nature will permit. I take in none that do not naturally rejoice in the soil, and am pleased when I am walking in a labyrinth of my own raising, not to know whether the next tree I shall meet with is an apple, or an oak, an elm, or a pear-tree...I must not omit, that there is a fountain rising in the upper part of my garden, which forms a little wandering rill, and administers to the pleasure as well as the plenty of the place. I have so conducted it, that it visits most of my plantations; and have taken particular care to let it run in the same manner as it would do in an open field; so that it generally passes through banks of violets and primroses, plats of willows, or other plants that seem to be of its own producing. [6 September]25*

From this passage and some others by Addison in *The Spectator* the following can be gathered as of use to the problem of visual planning: Like Shaftesbury, Addison contrasts the trimmed garden—to him a Dutch vision with plenty of topiary rather than Shaftesbury's grand Versaillean vision—with nature in her natural state. Like Shaftesbury, he sees nature in the form of "rough careless strokes"26* and "a huge heap of mountains, high rocks and precipices"27* as well as of the "orchard in flower." But Addison is the first to draw a practical conclusion from this widening of visual pleasures. He suggests the principles of irregularity and the imitation of seemingly unspoilt rural nature as principles of landscape [6] planning. It is characteristic that he introduces the word *landscape* in this context, a word which had appeared in the English language in the sixteenth or early seventeenth century to denote painted scenery but was already used in Milton's *Allegro* {1632} for real scenery of an appeal similar to that of a picture. Here Addison heralds the later theory of the Picturesque.

The same is true of an introductory passage in his first letter in *The Spectator* {June 23} in which he tried to establish—casually, it is true—a distinction of aesthetic categories:

> I shall first consider those pleasures of the imagination which arise from the actual view and survey of outward objects: and these, I think, all proceed from the sight of . . . *greatness, novelty* or *beauty*.[28]

Greatness and Beauty are then defined, in no specially novel way. But on the Uncommon Addison has some remarkable things to say:

> Every thing that is *new* or *uncommon* raises a pleasure in the imagination, because it fills the soul with an agreeable surprise, gratifies its curiosity, and . . . serves us for a kind of refreshment . . . It is this that recommends Variety, [and] . . . improves what is great or beautiful.[29]

The effect of this passage on Pope, on Hogarth, on Price will be followed later.

ALEXANDER POPE, 1713, 1728-44[30]

In the history of the two kinds of gardening suggested by Addison—for they are two kinds: one with the stress on irregularity, the other on naturalness—Pope stands in a pioneer position. For not only did he write in Addison's *Guardian* in 1713 confirming Addison's views, but he also was one of the first actually to lay out a garden on the lines tread by Shaftesbury and *The Spectator*. His garden at Twickenham, the work of the years 1719–c. 1725, is known to us from an engraved plan. From this it certainly does not seem specially "natural." It has still all its main axes straight, and between them elaborately twisted paths, a highly artificial grotto {still in existence}, and a ruin of "various sorts of Stones thrown promiscuously together."[31]*

With all these qualities, it belongs to the Rococo—the European style created [7] in France, Italy, and Germany just at that moment, between 1715 and 1720. But Pope's theories point beyond the Rococo in many ways. First there is Nature, again from whose golden teachings we must never deviate:

> First follow Nature, and your judgment frame
> By her just standard, which is still the same...
> Unerring Nature . . . must to all impart,
> At once the source, and end, and test of art.[32]*

But in that way, Nature had already been preached by the French rationalists of the seventeenth century, nature as identical with original order and as sanctioning a similarly rigid order in man's productions, such as buildings and gardens. It sounds as if Pope followed the French there, too:

> Those rules of old, discover'd, not devis'd,
> Are nature still, but nature mechaniz'd.[33]*

But when it comes to actual theories of layout, Pope appears on the side of Addison:

A tree is a nobler object than a prince in his coronation robes.[34]*

> In all, let Nature never be forgot;
> But treat the Goddess like a modest fair,
> Nor overdress, nor leave her wholly bare.
> Let not each beauty everywhere be spied,
> When half the skill is decently to hide.
> He gains all points, who pleasingly confounds,
> Surprises, varies, and conceals the bounds.[35]*

Here are plenty of principles laid down: [n]o over-decorating, but a consistent use of surprise, variety, and concealment—the qualities belonging to Addison's category of Novelty. Later on in the same poem Timon is blamed for laying out his ground all symmetrical without intricacy and artificial roughness:

> No pleasing intricacies intervene,
> No artful wilderness to perplex the scene;
> Grove nods at grove, each alley has a brother,
> And half the platform just reflects the other.[36]

Moreover, Pope does not recommend intricacy for its own sake, as a Rococo ornament—in the way he himself tried to use it at Twickenham, but wishes it adopted to the particular *genius loci* of each estate to be improved.

> In laying out a garden, the first thing to be considered is the genius of the place.[37]*

[INSERT to p. 7.][38] However, in dealing with Pope we have to be careful. Just as his garden is visually less advanced than his theories might let us believe, so this reference to the *genius loci* is not meant as romantically as it sounds. It would be wrong to assume that Pope recommends to abandon one's own initiative to nature. To the passage quoted he adds as an example,

> [T]hus at Riskins [. . .] Lord Bathurst should have raised two or three mounts; because his situation is all a plain, and nothing can please without variety.[39]

So while the *genius loci,* we would think, is plain and calls for a skilful development of this natural theme, Pope wants the planner for set-principles' sake to create a new *genius loci* and then follow it.

There appears from Spence's *Anecdotes* one more important principle to have been in Pope's mind: [t]he process of composing actual scenery is almost identical [to] the process of composing a landscape painting—in general and in detail.

> All gardening is landscape painting.[40]*

> Those clumps of trees are like the groups in pictures [. . .] You may distance things . . . by narrowing the plantation more and more towards the end, in the same manner as they do in painting, and as 'tis executed in the little cypress walk to that obelisk.[41]

But here again Pope only threw out a brilliant suggestion, without following it up in theory and practice. Moreover, most of the passages from Pope here quoted [7] are out of the chronological order which we follow. The *Anecdotes* were begun in 1728 and go on to Pope's death in 1744, and the Epistle to Lord Burlington belongs to 1731. Had any progress been made [8][42] towards or beyond Pope during the years between 1713 and about 1740?

BRIDGMAN AND KENT, C. 1720-45

In gardening itself, certainly; for now Bridgman and Kent began to follow the new principles in earnest. Bridgman seems to have invented the ha-ha, that is, the sunken fence which conceals the boundary between dressed gardens and fields kept trim by sheep. By this he broke down the border lines between the worlds of art and of nature, between beauty consciously made and beauty happening by accident. And of Kent, Horace Walpole wrote in 1771,

> He leaped the fence, and saw that all nature was a garden. He felt the delicious contrast of hill and valley changing imperceptibly into each other, tasted the beauty of the gentle swell, or concave scoop, and remarked how loose groves crowned an easy eminence with happy ornament, and while they called in the distant view between their graceful stems, removed and extended the perspective by delusive comparison.
>
> Thus the pencil of his imagination bestowed all the arts of landscape on the scenes he handled. The great principles on which he worked were perspective, and light and shade. Groups of trees broke too uniform or too extensive a lawn; evergreens and woods were opposed to the glare of the champain, and where the view was less fortunate, or so much exposed as to be beheld at once, he blotted out some parts by thick shades, to divide it into variety, or to make the richest scene more enchanting by reserving it to a farther advance of the spectator's step. Thus selecting favourite objects, and veiling deformities by screens of plantation; sometimes allowing the rudest waste to add its foil to the richest theatre, he realised the compositions of the greatest masters in painting. Where objects were wanting to animate his horizon, his taste as an architect could bestow immediate termination. His buildings, his seats, his temples, were more the works of his pencil than of his compass. We owe the restoration of Greece and the diffusion of architecture to his skill in landscape.[43]*

So the serpentine lake and the clump were familiar to Kent, although at least in his earlier gardens the main axes were still formal. Of his chief works, Claremont for the Duke of Newcastle, Esher Place for Henry Pelham, Gunnersbury, Rousham, Holkham, Stanstead Park Sussex are known, and Kensington Gardens {where he is reported to have planted a dead tree}. At Stowe for Lord Cobham he replaced Bridgman. Lord Burlington's Chiswick is doubtful between Kent, Bridgman, and Lord Burlington himself who certainly designed the first piece of Palladian furnishing in the garden: the Bagnio. This was done as early as 1715, and so Lord Burlington's garden, completed before 1736, must be assigned the earliest in the new style in England. Others are: ——[44]* Neither of them left any theoretical writings on gardening. [8] Of [g]arden theory, between 1713 and the [1730s] less can be reported.

STEPHEN SWITZER, 1718

Switzer was a professional gardener and nursery man. So his repetition in *Ichnographia Rustica* of the principles laid down by such amateurs as Addison and Pope proves their early acceptance by practical men—on the strength, he says, of an acceptance earlier still by "gentlemen of very good Genius." But Switzer in his designs sticks to the Twickenham scheme of irregularity introduced only away from the main axes.

[9] Gentlemen of very good Genius's, and Dispositions...esteem {the traditional "fine Sett Gardening"} as too stiff and formal, and...not capable of giving so great satisfaction to the Eye...as the more beautiful, tho' less elaborate Works of Nature.[45]*

Variety is the greatest and most distinguishing Characteristick in any Country-Seat or Garden.[46]*

The natural Gardener {is he who will make} his Design submit to Nature, and not Nature to his Design.[47]*

A whole estate may appear as one great Garden.[48]*

In truth the loose Tresses of a Tree...easily fann'd by every gentle Breeze of Air, and the natural tho' unpolish'd dress of a beautiful Field, Lawn or Meadow {a little trimm'd, and...retrench'd, cut off, and redress'd...} are much more entertaining than the utmost exactitude of the most finish'd Parterre.[49]*

The Middle and Side Walk, and a very few Diagonals {are necessary in straight avenues, but if your grounds have} Hills and Dales,...almost all compos'd of Irregularities, 'tis there one should...follow those little shelvings and natural turns and Meanders {and adorn them with} little Gardens, Caves, little natural Cascades and Grottos of Water.[50]*

BATTY LANGLEY, 1728

Langley was another professional gardener. He was a busybody and an opportunist as well. There are no new thoughts in his *Principles of Gardening,* but the book proves even more clearly than Switzer's *Ichnographia* that in the fifteen years since *Spectator* and *Guardian*[51] the ideas there advocated had become common property. Langley also admits straight principle avenues and regular parterres,

[b]ut afterwards...all the remaining Parts should consist of *regular Irregularities.*[52]*

{Nothing is} more ridiculous, and forbidding, than a Garden which is regular.[53]*

{Between the avenues introduce} small Inclosures of Corn...with the rural Enrichments of Hay-Stacks, Wood-Piles, etc. [...] small rivulets and purling Streams[54]* [...] [l]ittle Walks...in Meadows, [10] and through Corn-Fields, Thickets, etc.[55]*

The underlying principles are again naturalness and variety.

> [W]hen we come to *copy,* or *imitate* Nature, we should trace her Steps with the greatest Accuracy that can be.[56]*

> [T]he Pleasure of a Garden depends on the variety of its Parts.[57]*

[INSERT p. 10][58]*
ROBERT CASTELL, 1728

Robert Castell's *Villas of the Ancients* was financed by Lord Burlington.[59] Mr. H. F. Clark has been the first to introduce it into the history of the Picturesque.[60]* It plays indeed an important part, for it provided the blessings of Roman tradition for the irregularity of the new style in gardening. The relevant passages are these: Roman gardens are of three types: laid out "by Rule and Line" {the words come from Addison—see above}, irregular, and of a beauty consisting "in a close imitation of nature, where, though the parts are disposed with the greatest art, the irregularity is still preserved."[61] In Pliny's villa all three types appeared. The main garden was regular, but the *Pratulum* displayed "Nature in her plainest and most simple dress" and the *Imitatio Ruris* had "hills, rocks, cascades, rivulets, woods and buildings . . . thrown into such an agreeable disorder as to have pleased the eye from several views, like so many beautiful landskips."[62]

So the Romans were proved to have imitated in their gardens rural as well as horrific nature, and the results of this, seen gradually, have shown to be comparable to the works of the landscape painter. The passage is reminiscent of Vanbrugh's pleading with the Duchess of Marlborough for the preservation of the ruin of the old Woodstock Palace in the grounds of Blenheim, because, amongst other things, the ruins "make one of the Most Agreeable Objects that the best of Landskip Painters can invent."[63]* In both cases, for real scenery to look like pictures—that is, as we shall see later, picturesque—was claimed as an asset.

[10]
JAMES THOMSON, 1736

Pope's *Epistle* had taken us as far as 1731. Thomson's *Seasons,* it has been rightly pointed out, are proof of a closer observation of nature than had been within the power of the seventeenth century and Pope. As to matters of principle, Thomson need only be quoted for his emphasis on the connection of formal gardens with Tyranny—a conceit developed, of course, from Shaftesbury's "mockery of princely gardens." [Insert B.][64]* In the tyrant's country what you see are "disgraceful Piles of [Wood and] Stone";

> Those Parks and Gardens, where, his Haunts be-trimm'd,
> And *Nature* by presumptuous *Art* oppress'd,
> The *woodland Genius* mourns.[65]*

But in the Britain [10] of the future no-one will any longer be "Of pompous Tyrants, and of dreaming Monks, [t]he gaudy Tools, and Prisoners";[66] there will be "the Blooms of *Genius, Science, Art*"[67] and "Numerous Domes"[68]* in the texts of Lord Burlington, and there will be

Sylvan Scenes, where *Art* alone pretends
To dress her *Mistress,* and disclose her Charms;
Such as a Pope in Miniature has shown;
A Bathurst o'er the widening Forest spreads;
And such as form a Richmond, Chiswick, Stowe.[69]

Pope's Twickenham, Bathurst's Cirencester, and Richmond, Chiswick, Stowe have been mentioned a few pages ago. Thomson spent his last years on an ever more famous landscaped estate, Lord Lyttelton's at Hagley, one of the show pieces of early picturesque gardening. He paid his first visit in 1743 and was delighted with its

> great variety of at once beautiful and grand, extensive prospects, . . . its sweet, embowered retirements, . . . a winding dale . . . over hung with woods, and enlivened by a stream, that, now gushing from mossy rocks, now falling in cascades, and now spreading into a calm length of water, forms the most natural and pleasing scene imaginable.[70]*

But this scene belongs to the second stage in the evolution of English eighteenth-century gardening.

Gardens and Parks: Stage Two

In landscape planning, this second stage, the stage of, say, 1740 to 1760, is characterized by the laying out of plenty of picturesque parks and gardens with the motifs introduced by Bridgman and Kent and on the principles of Shaftesbury, Addison, [11] and Pope. It is a phase of diffusion more than creation. The leading garden designers, if you can call them that, were amateurs. We know from Mason, Whately, Walpole, and others which gardens were by contemporaries regarded as exemplary. They are Mr Philip Southcote's Wooburn Farm near Chertsey in Surrey; the Hon. Charles Hamilton's Pains Hill near Esher in Surrey; the elder Pitt's South Lodge Enfield Chase north of London; Shenstone's The Leasowes, close to Halesowen, and then Hagley; General Conway's Park Place, Henley-on-Thames; Sir Henry Englefield's White Knights near Reading; the Earl of Stamford's Envil near [Hagley in Staffordshire];[71] Henry Hoare's Stourhead in Wiltshire; the Earl of Mount Edgcumbe's Mount Edgcumbe; [Valentine Morris]'s[72] Persfield on the Wye; and several others. Pains Hill still exists and is described in Mr. Tunnard's *Gardens in the Modern Landscape.*[73] The best recent description of Stourhead is [by Sirén in his *China and Gardens of Europe of the Eighteenth Century*].[74]* Wooburn Farm and Pains Hill were begun about 1740, Hagley it seems also in the [1940s], Enfield immediately afterwards.[75] The Leasowes about 1745, Stourhead after 1741. Mount Edgcumbe was praised by Walpole in a letter of 1756; Pains Hill, Hagley, The Leasowes, Persfield, Wooburn, and Stourhead by Joseph Warton in the same year. Walpole, in his *History,*[76] makes Wooburn the first example of the *ferme ornée,*[77]* and Pains Hill the example of "savage alpine . . . grand . . . wild and uncultivated" scenes. Of Charles Hamilton we are indeed told that he designed a cascade for Bowood as a copy of a motif from a Salvator Rosa painting.[78]

For Salvator was the ever-present prototype of rude scenery with fir trees, caves, and cascades in gardens, as Claude Lorraine was that of gentle and Gaspar

Dughet or Poussin that of noble, heroic scenery. The three are bracketed together in plenty of passages referring to landscape beauty, from Richardson's *Theory of Painting* of 1715,[79] in which we find that in "the other branches of Painting," i.e., in what is neither history, mythology, allegory, and so on, nor portrait,

> some few...have been excellent in them: as...Salvator Rosa, Claude Lorrain, and Gasper Poussin for Landscapes....[80]*

to Thomson's famous

> Whate'er *Lorrain* light-touch'd with softening hue,
> Or savage *Rosa* dash'd, or learned *Poussin* drew....[81]*

and on to Reynolds's *Discourses* and to Uvedale Price.

To planning theory this phase has not contributed much. The two main books are Gilpin's first publication on matters connected with aesthetics, [12] the *Dialogues...upon the Gardens at Stowe* of 1748,[82] only by recent research restored to its real author,[83]* and Shenstone's *Unconnected Thoughts on Gardening* published posthumously in 1764.[84]

WILLIAM GILPIN, 1748

Of Gilpin little need be said at this stage. *À propos* Stowe he writes, for instance,

> Regularity and Exactness excites no manner of Pleasure in the Imagination, unless they are made to contrast with something of an opposite kind.... The Fancy is struck by Nature alone.[85]*

> [T]ho' I can allow {Nature} to have an excellent Fancy, I do not think she has the best *Judgement*.[86]*

> Villages, Works of Husbandry, Groups of Cattle, Herds of Deer, and a Variety of other beautiful Objects, are brought into the Garden, and make a Part of the Plan. Even to the *nicest* Taste these rural Scenes are highly delightful.[87]*

> [A] regular building perhaps gives us very little pleasure; and yet a fine Rock, beautifully set off in Claro-obscuro, and garnished with flourishing Bushes, Ivy, and dead Branches, may afford us a great deal; and a ragged Ruin, with venerable old Oaks, and Pines nodding over it, may perhaps please the Fancy yet more than either of the other two Objects.[88]*

> There is something so vastly picturesque, and pleasing to the Imagination in {Ruins}.[89]*

> The Shrubs half-concealing the ragged View...raise very romantic Ideas in my Head.[90]*

What appears predominant in this is the emphasis on sentimental associations, as it comes out so strongly in the cult of the ruin. Appreciation of ruins appears already in Vanbrugh's plea of 1709 for the preservation of the old building at Blenheim,[91]* which, in another context, has already been quoted, and Vanbrugh put forward arguments both visual and associational. Ruins

> make One of the most Agreeable Objects that the best of Landskip Painters can invent...

{and}

> move even lively and pleasing Reflections...On the Person who has Inhabited them, On the Remarkable things which have been transacted in them, Or the extraordinary Occasions of Erecting them.[92]*

However, what distinguishes Vanbrugh's from Gilpin's and Shenstone's associations is that those of the early eighteenth century were still wholly unsentimental, whereas by 1740 or so romantic overtones appear. Their appearance in literature needs no emphasis. The name[s] Gray, Blair, Young, and Warton have often been mentioned in conjunction with the coming of the romantic passion for the Middle Ages.

The first artificial ruin actually built is, according to Sir Kenneth Clark's *Gothic Revival,* that at Edgehill by Sanderson Miller.[93] Its date is given as 1746. However, not only had both Wooburn and Pains Hill their ruins, and these may easily have been contemporary with, or a little earlier than, Edgehill, but Serle tells us of the moment in Pope's garden at Twickenham, consisting of odd stones thrown together "in imitation of an old Ruine."[94]*

After Edgehill, artificial ruins became at once extremely popular. Sanderson Miller built seven more, e.g., at Wimpole, and the grounds of the other many houses are still graced with them. They were all built for sentimental as much as visual reasons. If corroboration of this is needed, it can be found in Shenstone.

[13]
WILLIAM SHENSTONE, C. 1745–1760

Shenstone's *Unconnected Thoughts on Gardening* were published posthumously in 1764.[95] He started laying out The Leasowes, his little estate close to Hagley, about 1745. The *Unconnected Thoughts* are as a declaration of principles of far greater value than Gilpin's youthful and conventional *Dialogue.*

The associational aspect of planning stands right at its beginning and is stressed more than once:

> [L]andskip, or picturesque gardening...consists in pleasing the imagination by scenes of grandeur, beauty, or variety.[96]*

> Objects should...be less calculated to strike the immediate eye, than the judgement or well-formed imagination; as in painting.[97]*

This attitude, never before proclaimed so clearly, tinges Shenstone's conceptions also where at first they seem identical with those of his forerunners of the first stage.

For instance, in the case of ruins, he says,

> Ruinated structures appear to derive their power of pleasing, from the irregularity of surface; which is variety,

but he adds at once,

> and the latitude they afford the imagination . . . to recollect any events or circumstances appertaining to their pristine grandeur.[98]*

Again concerning the *Genius Loci* we read,

> Ground should first be considered with an eye to its peculiar character: whether it be the grand, the savage, the sprightly, the melancholy, the horrid, or the beautifull. As one or other of these characters prevail, one may somewhat strengthen its effects, by allowing every part some denomination, and then supporting its title by suitable appendages.[99]*

The *Genius Loci,* then, is not to be interpreted visually, but associationally. And so the Lovers' Walks and Virgil's Groves and all the rest are coming in, and The Leasowes fairly bristled with appendages. In Dodsley's description of the Leasowes, published in the *Works,*[100]* we get no end of urns, memorial seats, little temples, root houses, and so on. Here again Shenstone was not the first, and Stowe, of course, had both more and grander appendages than he could afford. But his possessed the more concentrated sentimental impact. Inscriptions appear everywhere, such as "Ingenio et amicitiae Gulielmi Somerville," "P. Vergilio Maroni," "Celeberrimo poetae Jacobo Thomson Prope fontes illi non fastiditos G. S. Sedem hanc ornavit."[101] Another is for Pope, yet another to Spence of the *Anecdotes,* and so on.

All this, needless to say, is as unnatural as the Rococo paths of the first stage, but while there the actual forms were artificial, these now attempt to be artless, and art enters only into their self-conscious interpretation. In fact, [14] Shenstone's is very firm about the division between the worlds of art and of nature. To the one belongs building; to the other, gardening.

> Art should never be allowed to set a foot in the province of nature, otherwise than clandestinely and by night.[102]*

> [I]n regard to gardens, the shape of ground, the disposition of trees, and the figure of water, must be sacred to nature; and no forms must be allowed that make a discovery of art.[103]*

Two more points need emphasis. It will have been noticed that Shenstone in the first passages quoted refers to painting and to variety. We have read of both in Pope. Concerning painting, Shenstone does not go beyond Pope:

> [T]he landskip painter is the gardener's best designer.[104]*

> [I]n pursuance of our present taste in gardening, every good painter of landskip appears to me the most proper designer.[105]*

But when it comes to variety and the closely connected qualities of irregularity, surprise, novelty, a new note can be faintly heard—the note which developed into the leading tune at the end of the century.

> Variety appears to me to derive a good part of its effect from novelty.[106]*

> Are there not broken rocks and rugged grounds, to which we can hardly attribute either beauty or grandeur, and yet when introduced near an extent of lawn, impart a pleasure equal to more shapely scenes? Thus a series of lawn, though ever so beautiful, may satiate and cloy, unless the eye passes to them from wilder scenes; and then they acquire the grace of novelty.[107]*

> Variety is the principal ingredient in beauty; and simplicity is essential to grandeur.[108]*

In all this Shenstone appears groping for those definitions which during the eighteenth century helped found aesthetics as an independent branch of philosophy. Burke's *Sublime and Beautiful* had come out in 1756,[109] and Uvedale Price was to add the Picturesque as [15] a third category in 1794. Shenstone, following of course Addison,[110]* at least in one passage helped to prepare for that last stage, the fourth in the history of the picturesque movement. It is this:

> Perhaps the division of the pleasures of imagination, according as they are struck by the great, the various, and the beautiful, may be accurate enough for my present purpose.[111]*

Gardens and Parks: Stage Three

The third stage, roughly covering the years between 1750 and 1790, is in practice that of Capability Brown, that is, of a large-scale conversion of the English countryside by professional garden and park designers into the landscape character, which to us has become that of indigenous nature herself. Amateurs {such as Horace Walpole}, of course, went on doing improvements to their own designs, but the hallmark of the later eighteenth century remains landscape gardening by landscape gardeners of a higher social status than that enjoyed by Switzer and Langley.

Capability Brown {1716–83} began his career as an architect and landscape gardener about 1750. It brought him enough prosperity to enable him to send his sons to Eton and buy himself the manor of Fenstanton in Huntingdonshire. The style of Brown gardens differs considerably and characteristically from that of Pope, Kent, and their generation. Rococo twists disappeared and are disapproved of. Already in 1750 Walpole wrote in an essay {*The World*}, "There is not a citizen who does not take more pains to torture his acre and a half into irregularities, than he formerly would have employed to make it as formed as his cravat."[112] And Uvedale Price, hostile as he was to Brown's style, granted him that before his time "improvers…could hardly make too many turns" so that in the end in walking along those "zig-zag, corkscrew" path[s] one "might put one foot upon zig, and the other upon zag."[113] Now instead, long undulating lines appeared everywhere, as gentle as those in Gainsborough's or Greuze's pictures. A small scale was replaced by a large, and liveliness by a tender sentimentality. Lawns now reach right up to the house, and this arrangement, as well as the grouping of trees in clumps, the manifold buildings, widenings and narrowings of rivers and lakes, and the shrubberies concealing the boundary between the estate and the land around it, all combine to conceal the art of the gardener and make the result of his endeavour appear the work of Dame Nature herself.[114]*

As for theoretical writing, the dearth of 1735 to 1750 changes into a flood of books and pamphlets on aesthetics and gardening. Concerning aesthetics in general, Hogarth's *Analysis of Beauty* belongs to 1753, Burke's *Sublime and Beautiful* to 1756, Gerard's *Essay on Taste* to 1759, and Lord Kames *Elements of Criticism* to 1761.[115] The latter has a special chapter on Gardening and Architecture and thus stands at the beginning of the gardening literature of the third stage. What followed was Thomas Whately's *Observations on Modern Gardening* written in 1765 and published in 1770, George Mason's *Essay on Design in Gardening* of 1768, Walpole's *History of the Modern Taste in Gardening* of 1771, William Mason's *The English Garden* of 1772–1780, and Sir William Chamber's *Dissertation on Oriental Gardening* also of 1772.[116] Most of Gilpin's Picturesque Tours belong to this phase too {Wye 1770, Lakeland 1772, Sussex and Kent 1774, Scottish Highland 1776, etc.}, although he did not allow the first of his *Observations* on them to be printed until 1782.[117]

[16] How far can this spate of publications help to develop our conception of picturesque planning?[118]* First of all, in so far as these writers agree explicitly or implicitly that England in its landscape gardening possesses an art of a very high order:

> [G]ardening is now improved into a fine art.[119]*

> [O]ur country is a *school of landscape.*[120]*

> We have given the true model of gardening to the world.[121]*

To these three publications may be added two from other contemporary writers:

> …this enchanting art of modern gardening, in which this kingdom claims a preference over every nation in Europe.[122]*

> The only proof of our original talent in matters of pleasure is our skill in gardening and the laying out of grounds.[123]*

So much of British pride in landscaping. It is no wonder that it should have grown so fast and to such an extent during those particular years. Capability more than anyone must be given credit for this conversion of gardening into a fine art.

[17] As to the character and the few innovations of the third phase, it may be best to concentrate on one writer, the one who made the best use of his eyes, and introduce the others only as secondary supporters or opponents. For with the accumulation of gardening literature during this third phase, quarrels between writers over individual points become frequent, although on fundamentals there still was fairly universal agreement.

THOMAS WHATELY {1765, 1770}, HORACE WALPOLE {1771}, AND OTHERS

Neither Whately nor any of the other writers of the third stage were conscious innovators. Such conceptions as variety and contrast Whately takes from Stage One:

> [V]ariety wants not this recommendation; it is always desirable where it can be properly introduced.[124]*

But he adds—which is conspicuously in the style of 1760 as against that of Twickenham,

> Whether...a mixture of contrarieties would for a length of time be engaging, can be known only to those who are habituated to the spot.[125]*

> [W]himsical wonders...lose their effect when represented in a picture, or mimicked in ground artificially laid.[126]*

The same reservation appears in Lord Kames, in Walpole's *History,* and in George Mason:

> [E]verything trivial or whimsical ought to be avoided.[127]*

> The more we exact novelty, the sooner our taste will be vitiated.[128]*

> Independency has been as strongly asserted in matters of taste, as in religion and government; it has produced more motley appearances, than perhaps a whole series of ages can parallel. Yet to this whimsical exercise of caprice the modern improvements in gardening may chiefly be attributed.[129]*

In these reservations the vision of landscape as favoured by the men of Stage Three comes out most clearly.

> The living landscape was chastened and polished, not transformed.[130]*

> Let...our taste...reign here on its verdant throne, original by its elegant simplicity, and proud of no other art than that of softening nature's harshnesses.[131]*

Soft, chaste, polished, simple, elegant—these are indeed the terms which one would apply to surviving mid- and late-eighteenth-century gardens, [18] and especially those laid out by Brown. Hence Walpole had the greatest respect for Brown. "A very able master" on the same footing as Kent he called him in the *History*[132]* and "Dame Nature's second husband" in a letter of 1783.[133]* Not that he was not critical of Brown, too, where he thought manner interfered with nature. Just as he had objected to the style of Twickenham as "twisted and twirled"[134]* so he blamed Brown at More Park for undulating "the horizon in so many artificial molehills, that it is full as unnatural as if it was drawn with a rule and compasses."[135]* Mason went further and called Brown—evidently for the same reason—an "egregious mannerist,"[136]* and Whately must have felt the same when he expressed himself against regularly drawn serpentines.

In Whately the best attitude of this stage comes out, that of watching patiently real nature before trying to imitate her. A few larger quotations are necessary to bring out this point which is of importance, because Whately was the first to take Pope's appeal to the *Genius Loci* seriously.

> Trees and shrubs are of different *shapes, greens* and *growths....* Some {are} thick with branches and foliage have almost an *appearance of solidity,* as the beech and the elm, the lilac and feringa. Others{,} thin of boughs and of leaves{,} seem *light and airy* as the ash and the arbele, the common arbor vitae and the tamarisk.... {Trees} may again be divided into those whose *branches begin from the ground,* and those which *shoot up in a stem before their branches begin....* Of those whose branches begin from the ground, some rise in a *conical figure,* as the larch, the cedar of Lebanon, and the holly: some *swell out in the middle of their growth, and diminish at both ends,* as the Weymouth pine, the mountain ash, and the lilac: and some are *irregular and bushy* from the top to the bottom, as the evergreen oak, the Virginian cedar, and Guelder rose.... {Then there is a kind of tree whose} *base is very large,* and another *whose base is very small,* in proportion to its height: the cedar of Lebanon, and the cypress, are instances of this difference;... The heads... *slender cones,* as of many firs;... *broad cones,* as of the horse chestnut;... *round,* as of the stone pine, and most sorts of fruit trees; and sometimes *irregular,* as of the elm.... branches [grow] *horizontally,* as of the oak... *tend upwards,* as in the almond... *fall,* as in the lime and the acacia;... *incline obliquely,* as in many of the firs; in some they *hang directly down,* as in the weeping willow[;]... *dark green,* as the horse chestnut, and the yew; some of a *light green,* as the lime, and the laurel; some of a *green tinged with brown,* as the Virginian cedar; some of a *green tinged with white,* as the arbele, and the sage tree: and some of a *green tinged with yellow,* as the ashen-leaved maple, and the chinese arbor vitae.[137]*

> {Water} is the most interesting object in a landscape, and the happiest circumstance in a retired recess; [it] captivates the eye at a distance; [it] invites approach, and is delightful when near; it refreshes an open exposure; it animates a shade; cheers the dreariness of a waste, and enriches the most crowded view: in form, in style, and in extent, may be made equal to the greatest compositions, or adapted to the least; it may spread in a calm expanse to soothe the tranquillity of a peaceful scene; or hurrying along a devious course, [it] add[s] splendour to a gay, and extravagance to a romantic, situation. So various are the characters which water can assume, that there is scarcely an idea in which it may not concur, or an impression which it cannot enforce: a deep stagnated pool, dank and dark with shades which it dimly reflects, befits the seat of melancholy; even a river, if it be sunk between two dismal banks, and dull both in motion and colour, is like a hollow eye which deadens the countenance; and over a sluggard, silent stream, creeping heavily along all together, hangs a gloom, which no art can dissipate, nor even the sunshine disperse. A gently murmuring rill, clear and shallow, just gurgling, just dimpling, imposes silence, suits with solitude, and leads to meditation: a brisker current, which wantons in little eddies over a bright sandy bottom, or babbles among pebbles, spreads cheerfulness all around: a greater rapidity, and more agitation, to a certain degree are animating; but in excess, instead

of wakening, they alarm the senses: the roar and the rage of a torrent, its force, its violence, its impetuosity, tend to inspire terror; that terror, which, whether as cause or effect, is so nearly allied to sublimity.[138]*

The *style* also of every part must be accommodated to the character of the whole: for every piece of ground is distinguished by certain properties: it is either tame or bold; gentle or rude; continued or broken; and if any variety, inconsistent with those properties, be obtruded, it has no other effect than to weaken one idea without raising another.[139]*

[A] character of greatness belongs to some scenes, which is not measured by their extent, but raised by other properties, sometimes only by the proportional largeness of their parts. On the contrary, where elegance characterises the spot, the parts should not only be small, but diversified besides with subordinate inequalities, and little delicate touches every where scattered about them.[140]*

Character, then, is the word which Whately uses instead of Pope's *Genius Loci*. Character comprises both visual and emotional qualities. The emphasis on the Emotional and Associational comes from Stage Two, from Shenstone and Gilpin, and appears in Lord Kames as well as in Whately.

Architecture and gardening cannot otherwise entertain the mind, but by raising certain agreeable emotions or feelings.[141]*

[19] Gardening...can raise emotions of grandeur, of sweetness, of gayety, of melancholy, of wildness, and even of surprise and wonder.[142]*

Gardening...possesses one advantage, never to be equalled in the other art: in various scenes, it can raise successively all the different emotions above mentioned.[143]*

[S]uch is the constitution of the human mind, that if once it is agitated, the emotion often spreads far beyond the occasion; [. . .] we may be led by thought above thought, widely differing in degree, but still corresponding in character, till we rise from familiar subjects up to the sublimest conceptions, and are rapt in the contemplation of whatever is great or beautiful, which we see in nature, feel in man, or attribute to divinity.[144]*

Thus Whately is as delighted with ruins, real or sham, as Shenstone:

[T]hey are a class by themselves, beautiful as objects, expressive as characters, and peculiarly calculated to connect, with their appendages, into elegant groupes.[145]*

Whatever building we see in decay, we naturally contrast its present to its former state, and delight to ruminate on the comparison....[S]uch effects properly belong to real ruins; they are, however, produced in a certain degree by those which are fictitious; the impressions are not so strong, but they are exactly similar.[146]*

In other ways, however, Whately and his contemporaries represent a decidedly [more] mature attitude to emotional connotations of landscape than Shenstone. The naïve directions with which Shenstone, by inscriptions and the like, imposed precise and detailed associations on those who wandered in his grounds [are] no longer admitted. Emotions must be roused by other means. To scatter about statues, urns, and inscriptions in the way it was done at The Leasowes, Whately calls

> puerilities, under pretence of propriety,[147]*

and Mason is almost as sceptical about them.

> Shenstone says, "a rural scene to me is never perfect without some kind of building."[148]*

Walpole went even further and doubted the possibility altogether of connecting in perpetuity one particular vista with one particular emotion:

> It is almost comic to set aside a quarter of one's garden to be melancholy in.[149]*

The same maturity dictates Whately's remarks on sham buildings, cascades, and the like. He is much more sceptical than Shenstone about their effects. He insists that nearly all of them can too easily be detected, and in that case they are ridiculous. But as he agrees with Shenstone that art should not appear in gardening; he recommends artificial devices if well enough executed:

> [I]t may be sometimes expedient to begin the descent {of a cascade} out of sight; for the beginning is the difficulty; if that be concealed, the subsequent falls seem but a consequence of the agitation which characterises the water at its first appearance; and the imagination is at the same time let loose to give ideal extent to the cascades: . . . {S}ometimes a low broad bridge may furnish the occasion; a little fall hid under the arch will create a disorder, in consequence of which, a greater cascade below will appear very natural.[150]*

The point which needs special emphasis in a book today is that he did not object to sham structures as such. Nor did, for instance, Walpole as the following passage shows:

> If . . . deceptions, as a feigned steeple of a distant church, or an unreal bridge to disguise the termination of water, were intended only to surprise, they were indeed tricks that would not bear repetition; but being intended to repair the landscape, are no more to be condemned . . . than they would be if employed by a painter in the composition of a landscape.[151]*

[20] All Art, the argument implies, is a make-believe. If a visual deception comes off, why refuse to use it? The improver is as much an artist as the painter, and no-one would refuse the painter the right to deceive, that is, to create illusion. The comparison between improver and painter is familiar from the first and second stages. It appears again in the third, for instance, where Lord Kames *à propos* Kent

speaks of painting "in the gardening way"[152]* and Walpole of "the pencil of his {i.e., Kent's} imagination" and "the great principles of perspective, and light and shade" on which he worked.[153]* Only Whately saw deeper. Just as associational effects are a highly complex matter, so are the aesthetic relations between painting and landscaping:

> The works … of a great master are fine exhibitions of nature, and an excellent school wherein to form a taste for beauty; but still their authority is not absolute; they must be used only as studies, not as models; for a picture and a scene in nature, though they agree in many, yet differ in some particulars. … In their *dimensions* the distinction is obvious.[154]*

Whately exemplifies this by referring to the different dimensions in which painter and gardener work, and then by referring to colour:

> [A] gardener … is not debarred from a view down the sides of a hill, or a prospect where the horizon is lower than the station, because he never saw them in a picture. […] [M]any beautiful tints denote disagreeable circumstances; the hue of a barren heath is often finely diversified…[155]*

[With] his emphasis on the differences between painting and gardening Whately was —— out by Reynolds who said, in his *Thirteenth Discourse,* i.e., in 1786,

> Even though we define {gardening as} "Nature to advantage dress'd," … it is [however], when so dressed, no longer a subject for the pencil of a Landscape-Painter, as all Landscape-Painters know, who love to have recourse to Nature herself, and to dress her according to the principles of their own Art; which are far different from those of Gardening, … and such as a Landscape-Painter himself would adopt in the disposition of his own grounds.[156]*

And Reynolds went on to draw the necessary conclusion from this—in reply to Shenstone's "Art should never be allowed to set a foot in the presence of Nature":

> Gardening, as far as Gardening is an Art, … is a deviation from nature; for if the true taste consists, as many hold, in banishing every appearance of Art, … it would be no longer a Garden.[157]*

[21][158] Amongst contemporary writers on gardening the one to make this point most strongly was Reynolds'[s] friend and fellow academician Chambers:

> Without a little assistance from art, nature is seldom tolerable.[159]*

> Nature produces nothing either boiled, roasted or stewed; and yet we do not eat raw meat.[160]

> The scenery of a Garden should differ as much from common nature, as an heroic poem doth from a prose relation.[161]*

But Chambers in more than one way goes decidedly beyond the boundaries of Stage Three.

Gardens and Parks: Stage Four

THE FORERUNNERS: SIR WILLIAM CHAMBERS, 1772

Chambers had been in China as a supercargo on [a] Swedish ship between the ages of sixteen and eighteen. He published a book on the *Designs of Chinese Buildings* in 1757[162] and was made Architect to the King in 1760. His *Dissertation on Oriental Gardening* pretended to be nothing but a report compiled "from my own observations in China, from conversations with their artists, and remarks transmitted to me by travellers."[163]* In fact, it is full of the most personal and original ideas, playfully disguised under the cloak of Oriental views and customs which Montesquieu's *Lettres persanes*[164] and Voltaire's *Zadig* and *Babouc* had made popular.[165] In the first half of [22] the book, Chambers keeps to descriptions of supposed Chinese gardens; in the second, he all but lifts his mark. For this *Explanatory Discourse* is alleged to have been delivered by one Tan Chet-Qua of Quang-Chew-fu, Gent. F. R. S. S., M. R. A. A. P., also MIAAF, TRA, CGHMW, and ATTQ. And while Chambers himself, according to the rules of his game, can in the first part only report what he insists to have seen or heard, Tan Chet-Qua in the second can say, "Our style of gardening may be adopted amongst you, even to its whole extent."[166]

This whole extent goes very far into the reign of unbridled fancy. Chambers was wholly against Brown's sweet simplicity—so much so that Walpole in a letter {May 25, 1772} said the whole book was written "in wild revenge against Brown."[167]

[23][168]* In England where ... a ... manner is universally adopted, in which no appearance of art is tolerated, our gardens differ very little from common fields, so closely is vulgar nature copied in most of them; there is generally so little variety, and so much want of judgement, in the choice of the objects, such a poverty of imagination in the contrivance, and of art in the arrangement, that these compositions rather appear the offspring of chance than design; and a stranger is often at a loss to know whether he be walking in a common meadow, or in a pleasure ground, made and kept at a very considerable expense: he finds nothing either to delight or to amuse him; nothing to keep up his attention, or excite his curiosity; little to flatter the senses, and less to touch the passions, or gratify the understanding. At his first entrance, he sees a large green field, scattered over with a few straggling trees, and verged with a confused border of little shrubs and flowers; on farther inspection, he finds a little serpentine path, twisting in regular esses amongst the shrubs of the border, upon which he is to go round, to look on one side at what he has already seen, the large green field; and on the other side at the boundary, which is never more than a few yards from him, and always obtruding upon his sight. From time to time he perceives a little seat or temple stuck up against the wall ... Sometimes ... you are treated with a serpentine river; that is, a stripe of stagnant water, waving, in semi-circles, as far as it will reach, and finishing in a pretty little orderly step cascade, that never runs but when it rains. The banks of these curious rivers are every where uniform, parallel, level, smooth and green, as a billiard-table; and the whole composition bears a great resemblance to the barge-canals of Holland: the only difference being that the Dutch ditches are regularly straight, whilst ours are regularly crooked. Of the two, ours

are certainly the most formal and affected, they are by no means the most picturesque.[169]*

[22] What Chambers sets against the "eternal, uniform, undulating lines"[170] of the gardens of his day is a grandeur, a sense of drama unheard of:

> Convert a whole province into a garden.[171]*

> {Create} quick successions of opposite and violent emotions.[172]

For in his belief in the "efficacy {of Gardening} in moving the passions,"[173]* Chambers is at one with Shenstone, Whately, and the others. But when he says passions, he means passions. The emotions roused by gardens should not be pleasing only; they should also be "terrible and surprizing."[174]* The technique of garden art he pleads for is a Shock technique:

> ...from limited prospects to extensive views; from places of horror to scenes of delight; from lakes and rivers to woods and lawns; and from the simplest arrangements of nature to the most complicated production of art.[175]*

For Chambers does not believe in "nature unadorned" and in dressing her "like a modest fair":[176]

> Nature and simplicity...are the constant cry of every half-witted dabbler.[177]*

> Excessive simplicity can only please the ignorant or weak, whose comprehensions are slow, and whose powers of combination are confused.[178]*

All this was immensely novel and courageous. After having read it we are not surprised to find Chambers appreciates the formality of French gardens {"they are all affectation; yet it is an affectation often delightful, and an absurdity generally overflowing with taste and fancy"}[179]* and the "elevation of style" of Italian gardens, the grand avenues of the sixteenth and seventeenth centuries [24], and their terraces and statues:

> In "grounds that immediately surround elegant structures...order and symmetry are absolutely necessary."[180]*

> For "little enclosures...nicety of dress, and excessive decoration are in character."[181]*

But the f[a]rther you go away from the house, the wilder your scenery ought to be. And it is in the parks proper that Chambers gives free rein to his fancy. It is here that the scenes of horror and surprise are unfolded, which infuriated Walpole so much. It is here that Chambers merrily places tigers and jackals, and scantily dressed odalisques, the instruments of torture, gibbets, "foundries, lime-kilns, and glass-works because of their volcano-like smoke,"[182]* "repeated shocks of electrical impulse"[183]* rustic bridges "laid upon large roots of trees,"[184]* "showers of artificial rain," windgusts, explosions, cries, serpents, wondrous birds,[185]* "miserable cottages and half-famished animals,"[186]* "most accomplished concubines,"[187]* echoes and halls with crystal ceilings below lakes.[188]*

Chambers cannot have believed that much or any of this would ever be carried out by garden lovers in England or anywhere. Yet he seems to have been more serious in these fanciful visions than may at first appear. He advises gardeners

> always boldly {to} look up to the sun, and copy as much of its lustre as they can.[189]*

And he admonishes them to

> humour the ground, hide its defects, improve or set off its advantages.[190]*

In fact, his shock-technique is probably a deliberate attempt at reintroducing vigour into visual planning.

> A cabbage-planter may reveal a Claude, and a clown out-twine a Poussin... But wherever a better style is adopted...Gardeners must be men of genius, of experience and judgement; quick in perception, rich in expedients, fertile in imagination, and thoroughly versed in all the emotions of the human mind.[191]*

In all the passages quoted here, and in his valiant defense of "the most magnificent confusion imaginable,"[192]* Chambers anticipates the great theories of the fourth stage. This has so far to my knowledge not been sufficiently recognized in the literature on the [25] Picturesque Movement. Nor has it yet been adequately summed up to what extent Gilpin's *Picturesque Tours and Essays* forms in this respect a parallel to Chambers.[193]*

[26] SIR UVEDALE PRICE, 1794, 1798[194]

Nothing can here be said of Price's life and character, of his youthful travels in Italy with Charles James Fox, his social life in London, his quiet years and —— improvements at Foxley near Hereford, his old age still "all life and spirits, as active in ranging about his woods as a setter dog," and his controversies with Richard Payne Knight and Humphry Repton. He lives on as the most comprehensive and most inspired of writers on the Picturesque. The first volume of his *Essay on the Picturesque* came out in 1794, when he was already forty-seven years of age, the second in 1798, and the final edition in three volumes in 1810.[195]

Many, or indeed most of the individual points made and arguments put forward in the *Essay* are not new. What gives the *Essay* its quite exceptional value and vitality is the way in which Price makes out his case and the vigorous and sensitive style in which he writes.

His aim, to establish The Picturesque as a third basic aesthetic quality besides Burke's Sublime and Beautiful, was more than is usually realised a direct development from Addison, Shenstone, and especially Gilpin. Addison's Greatness, Beauty and Novelty and Shenstone's Grand, Beautiful, and Various had been taken up and amplified in Gilpin's *Three Essays on Picturesque Beauty,* which came out in 1782.[196] The book made his fame and induced him, at last, to publish his tours to the Wye Valley, the Lakes District, the English coasts, the Highlands of Scotland, and so on, which had been written as early as 1769–1776. In the first of the three Essays Gilpin wrote this:

Disputes about beauty might perhaps be involved in less confusion, if a distinction were established, which certainly exists, between such objects as are *beautiful,* and such as are *picturesque.*[197]*

[R]*oughness* forms the most essential point of difference between the *beautiful,* and the *picturesque.*[198]*

A piece of Palladian architecture may be elegant in the last degree. . . . Should we wish to give it picturesque beauty, we must use the mallet, instead of the chisel: we must beat down one half of it, deface the other, and throw the mutilated members around in heaps.[199]*

[W]hy does an elegant piece of garden-ground make no figure on canvas? The shape is pleasing; the combination of the objects, harmonious; and the widening of the walk in the very line of beauty. All this is true; but the *smoothness* of the whole, tho right, and as it should be in nature, offends in picture. Turn the lawn into a piece of broken ground: plant rugged oaks instead of flowering shrubs: break the edges of the walk: give it the rudeness of a road: mark it with wheel-tracks; and scatter around a few stones, and brush-wood; in a word, instead of making the whole *smooth,* make it *rough;* and you make it also *picturesque.*[200]*

We admire the horse, as a *real object;* the elegance of his form; the stateliness of his tread; the spirit of all his motions; and the glossiness of his coat. We admire him also in *representation.* But as an object of picturesque beauty, we admire more the worn out cart-horse, the cow, the goat, or the ass.[201]*

The connection here established between picturesqueness and roughness, ruggedness and decay will be found again in Price. Whether The Picturesque or indeed The Sublime and The Beautiful can be accepted as valid aesthetic categories need not concern us here. Price's friend and later opponent Richard Payne Knight [27] denied it. He defined picturesque as "that kind of beauty which belongs exclusively to the sense of vision,"[202]* and proceeded from this definition to very interesting and novel distinction[s] between what is really visually pleasing and what, although we may think it appeals to the eye, does in fact appeal to the mind by means of associations. I come back to this later.[203]* This psychological approach of Knight allowed him to reject such [qualities] as [Beauty], [Sublime], and [Picturesque] altogether, because [they are] said to be inherent in objects, whereas in fact such qualities depend on our perception of and reaction to objects.

The whole of Price's first essay is dedicated to an analysis of the Picturesque. Most of the qualities discussed go straight back to the beginning of the movement in the early eighteenth century, and especially to Pope:

[I]ntricacy in landscape might be defined, *that disposition of objects, which, by a partial and uncertain concealment, excites and nourishes curiosity.*[204]*

[T]he effect of the picturesque is curiosity.[205]*

Any winding road, indeed, especially where there are banks, must necessarily have some degree of intricacy; but in a dressed lane every effort of art seems directed against that disposition of the ground: the sides are so regularly sloped, so regularly planted, and the space, when there is any, between them and the road, so uniformly levelled; the sweeps of the road so plainly artificial, the verges of grass that bound it so nicely edged; the whole, in short, has such an appearance of having been made by a receipt, that curiosity, that most active principle of pleasure, is almost extinguished.[206]*

While these general principles of Price's *Essay* coincide with those of Pope, further examples show him to share Gilpin's taste in roughness.

[T]he two opposite qualities of roughness, and of sudden variation, joined to that of irregularity, are the most efficient causes of the picturesque.[207]*

[A]lthough smoothness be the ground-work of beauty, yet...roughness is its fringe and ornament, and that which preserves it from insipidity....One principal charm of smoothness, whether in literal or a metaphorical sense, is, that it conveys the idea of repose; roughness, on the contrary, conveys that of irritation, but at the same time of animation, spirit, and variety.[208]*

Now irritation is a new category, and Price insists on it. It becomes indeed more and more patent, as one goes on reading him, that his own taste was for effects more lively and even violent than had up to his time been appreciated by anyone but Chambers:

Repose is always used in a good sense; as a state, if not of positive pleasure, at least as one of freedom from all pain and uneasiness: irritation, almost always in an opposite sense, and yet, contradictory as it may appear, we must acknowledge it to be the source of our most active and lively pleasures.[209]*

[I]f I were obliged to determine between insipid congruity, and incongruity which produces grand and striking effects, I should not hesitate in preferring the latter.[210]*

Just as in the case of Chambers, such statements were a reaction against the universally accepted style of Capability Brown. Price makes no secret of this:

It is very unfortunate that {the famous Mr. Brown,} this great legislator of our national taste, whose laws still remain in force, should not have received from nature, or have acquired by education, more enlarged ideas.[211]*

What Price blames him for is the very thing for which Brown's generation {in Walpole's writings for instance} blamed the early picturesque gardeners, and for which they blamed the garden designers in the Dutch and French styles: artificiality and lack of [28] naturalness:

What appears to me the great defect of modern gardening in the confined sense, is exactly what has given them their greatest reputation; an affectation of ... nature.[212]*

Mr. Brown has upon system, and in almost all cases, very studiously destroyed symmetry, while he has in many instances preserved, and even increased formality.[213]*

> Formerly, every thing was in squares and parallellograms; now every thing is in segments of circles, and ellipses: the formality still remains; the character of that formality alone is changed. The old canal, for instance, has lost, indeed, its straitness and its angles; but it is become regularly serpentine, and the edges remain as naked and as uniform as before: avenues, vistas, and strait ridings through woods, are exchanged, for clumps, belts, and circular roads and plantations of every kind: strait alleys in gardens, and the platform of the old terrace, for the curves of the gravel walk. The intention of the new improvers was certainly meritorious; for they meant to banish formality, and to restore nature; but it must be remembered, that strongly marked, distinct, and regular curves, unbroken and undisguised, are hardly less unnatural or formal, though much less grand and simple, than strait lines.[214]*

So once again it is in the cause of nature that Price sets his new spicier brand of picturesqueness against the "*unnaturalness* of modern gardening."[215]*

It is now time to look at some of Price's examples of the Picturesque: The ass, the shaggy goat, and the worn-out cart horse he could take over from Gilpin.[216]* So he could the ruin.[217]* He added gypsies and beggars, "old mills" and "hovels,"[218]* and—a specially telling instance of his keenly observant eye—"a building with scaffolding."[219]*

The case he tries to make is that these objects are not beautiful in any accepted sense and yet please the eye. Anything, indeed, that has character cannot be ugly, even if devoid of beauty. Ugliness Price defines very sensitively as

> that *want* of form, that unshapen lumpish appearance, which, perhaps, no one word exactly expresses.[220]*

And again,

> The *ugliest* forms of hills, if my ideas be just, are those which are lumpish, and, as it were, unformed; such, for instance, as from one of the ugliest and most shapeless animals are called pigbacked.[221]*

> An ugly man or woman, with an aquiline nose, high cheek bones, beetle brows, and lines in every part of the face, is, from these picturesque circumstances, which might all be taken away without destroying ugliness, much more *strikingly* ugly, than a man with no more features than an oyster.[222]*

Although after all this there can be no doubt as to what kind of visual pleasures appealed to Price, he was sensible and fair enough to admit that picturequeness alone is not enough in landscape planning. The passages referring to this point are specially interesting:

> The great point...is to mix according to circumstances, what is striking, with what is simply pleasing.[223]*

> If the improver, as it usually happens, attend [*sic*] solely to verdure,

smoothness, undulation of ground, and flowing lines, the whole will be insipid. If the opposite, and much rarer taste should prevail; should an improver, by way of being picturesque, make broken ground, pits, and quarries all about his place; encourage nothing but furze, briars, and thistles; heap quantities of rude stones on his banks; or, to crown all, like Mr. Kent, plant dead trees—the deformity of such a place would, I believe, be very generally allowed, though the insipidity of the other might not be so readily confessed.... It can hardly be doubted, that what answers to the beautiful in the sense of tasting, has smoothness and sweetness for its basis, with such a degree of stimulus as enlivens, but does not overbalance those qualities; such, for instance, as in the most delicious fruits and liquors. Take away the stimulus, they become insipid; increase it so as to overbalance those qualities, they then gain a peculiarity of flavour, are eagerly sought after by those who have acquired a relish for them, but are less adapted to the general palate. This corresponds exactly with the picturesque; but if the stimulus be encreased beyond that point, none but depraved and vitiated palates will endure, what would be so justly termed deformity in objects of sight.[224]*

Two more points need brief comments. The use of the word *picturesque* leads Price, as it had led his predecessors, into thoughts on the relation between the painting of pictures of landscape and the planning of real landscape. Price defines the relation between the two in an unusually stimulating way. He says,

[W]ith respect to the art of improving, we may look upon pictures as a set of experiments of the different ways in which trees, buildings, water, &c. may be disposed, grouped, and accompanied, in the most beautiful and striking manner, and in every style, from the most simple and rural, to the grandest and most ornamental.[225]*

[M]any connoisseurs consider pictures merely with a reference to other pictures, as a school in which they may learn the routine of connoisseurship;...[T]hey rarely look upon them in that point of view in which alone they can produce any real advantage—as a school in which we may learn to enlarge, refine, and correct our ideas of nature.[226]*

[29] So it is not the painter who should lay out gardens but the connoisseur who has acquired from a close study of pictures a sufficient sensibility in visual matters. It must have been primarily that emphasis on amateur as against professional which incensed Humphry Repton against him and made him write an answer to the first *Essay* in the very year in which it had come out. Repton, who after Brown's death had become the most successful garden designer in England—he was the first to call himself a landscape gardener—also objected to Price's taste for roughness.[227]* But the differences between the two men, and indeed between either of them and a second amateur improver, Richard Payne Knight, hardly concerns us here. They were discussed in public forward and backward [between] the years 1794 and 1805. Many of them seem to us insignificant after a hundred and fifty years. In essentials they often appear certainly at one. One such case must here be mentioned as an illustration of a last point of importance in Price's *Essays*.

It is the point which, Price himself foretells, might by his adversaries of the Brown-school be called "a counter-revolution . . . to restore the *ancien regime*."[228]*

Price defends—influenced probably by Chambers—"neatness, and a dressed appearance,"[229]* near the house, in conscious contrast to picturesqueness in the grounds. But while Repton's argument in favour of this {put forward actually before Price},[230]* was the client's convenience, Price even near the house is pining for some drama. So his recommendation is the terraced and balustraded gardens of Italy, with the rich and magnificent effects of their fountains and statuary, pines and cypresses.

The principle established here was to have further-reaching effects than could at first be seen. It is the principle of the use of two different styles of landscape for two different purposes, "the habitation of man, and that of sheep."[231]*

> [30] In forming a general comparison of the two styles of gardening, it seems to me that what constitutes the chief excellence of the old garden, is richness of decoration and of effect, and an agreement with the same qualities in architecture; its defects, stiffness, and formality. The excellencies of the modern garden, are verdure, undulation of ground, diversity of plants, and a more varied and natural disposition of them than had hitherto been practised: its defects, when considered as accompanying architecture,—a uniformity of character too nearly approaching to common nature.[232]*

RICHARD PAYNE KNIGHT[233]

Knight is perhaps [a] more interesting man than Price, though [a] less loveable character. His achievement is more varied than Price's. He wrote many books on many subjects; Price was a one-book man. But as we are here only concerned with visual planning, Knight's importance shrinks. His contribution to the theory of landscape is negligible. It is contained in a mediocre poem called *The Landscape*, which came out in the same year as Price's first essay, 1794, and is both dedicated to Price and clearly inspired by him. It contains nothing beyond Price.

Its point of departure, as Price's, is dislike of Capability Brown, whom he calls "Thin, meagre genius of the bare and bald,"[234]* whose scenery he describes as "one dull, vapid, smooth and tranquil scene."[235]* Against this dullness he conjures up with approval "the moss-grown terraces"[236]* of Italian formal gardens and a more dramatic nature, the disused quarry "o'ergrown with thorns,"[237]* "rough uneven ground,"*[238] the river-bank "with moss and fern o'ergrown,"[239]* the avenue of "ductile yew,"[240]* the "retired and antiquated cot; Its roof with weeds and mosses covered o'er, And Honeysuckle climbing round the door,"[241]* and, what is more, he illustrated the kind of nature he liked. Thomas Hearne[242] drew—in the form of the cautionary tale as Pugin's *Contrasts*[243]—a parallel of a Brown garden with a Palladian mansion, and a rough Dutch —— piece of —— with an Elizabethan mansion. The significance of this extremely early profession of faith in the Elizabethan style is not our business in this book, but the etching gives a fair picture of the kind of planning Price and Knight recommended. It made it easy for the more reasonable Repton to reply and re-instate common sense in gardening.

But Knight was not really as much interested in gardening and landscaping as Price. His chief concern, as he grew older, became more and more aesthetics as a much more general subject. His *Analytical Enquiry into the Principles of Taste* came out in 1805.[244] It was no doubt originally inspired by that controversy with Price which had found preliminary expression in the Preface to the second edition

[of] *The Landscape*.[245]* Knight, in the first place, objected to the introduction of the term *Picturesque* in addition to Burke's accepted terms *Sublime* and *Beautiful,* and, in the second, to all terms by which aesthetic qualities are made to appear inherent in objects, while in fact they "only exist in the modes [31] and habits of viewing and considering them."[246]* In this thesis Knight obviously follows Hume.[247]* But he is original where he proposes a new definition of the word *picturesque* and draws conclusions from this. He says that picturesque is "after the manner of painting,"[248]* and that "painting, as it imitates only the visible qualities of bodies, separates those qualities from all others."[249]*

The distinction here established forms Knight's ever-recurrent theme. Burke, for instance, equates smooth with beautiful. But what seems smooth to the touch, such as [an] undulating line without breaks, may be harsh to the eye. Knight's example is the bank of a canal treated in Brown's way, with lawn reaching right down to the water.[250]* Or the carcass of an ox, as painted by Rembrandt, can be beautiful to the eye, even if in reality it is nauseating.[251] Conversely, a man may think he admires the heavenly form of a "lovely bosom." But take a mould from it and "cast a plum pudding in it {an object by no means disgusting to most men's appetites} and ... he will no longer be in raptures with the form."[252]*

[This] all goes to show that in our consideration and valuation of beauty associative values play a much greater part than we are usually ready to admit. The town-planning implications of this wholly new trend of thought are of significance to this day.

And now that landscape-planning has been examined to the year 1800 and a little beyond, it is time to return to town-planning and to architectural matters altogether. The first question must be this: how far do the same writing[s] which have been consulted with reference to gardening contain evidence on buildings and town-planning?

[32] Picturesque Building and Town-Planning, 1700–1800

The ruling taste in England from about 1720 was Palladian; in gardening it was picturesque. How this seeming contrast between regular building and irregular gardening could be bridged appears with precision already in a passage in Shaftesbury which has been quoted before:

> Nothing surely is more strongly imprinted on our minds, or more closely interwoven with our souls, than the idea or sense of *order* and *proportion*. Hence all the force of *numbers,* and those powerful *arts* founded on their management and use. What a difference ... between the regular and uniform pile of some noble architect, and a heap of sand or stones![253]*

So architecture must be regular because of a sense of order inborn in us, the sense whose justification, as we have seen, is the regularity of the Universe. John Dennis wrote in 1704 {of poetry} [that]

> The work of every reasonable creature must derive its beauty from regularity, for Reason is rule and order, and nothing can be irregular ... any further than it swerves from rules, that is from Reason ... The works of man must needs be the more perfect, the more they resemble his Maker's. Now the works of God,

though infinitely various, are extremely regular. The Universe is regular in all its parts, and it is to this exact regularity that it owes its admirable beauty.[254]*

Now Nature and the Universe may in one sense be considered identical, and in another, narrower sense Nature must at least be accepted as part of the Universe. Hence the seventeenth century—Boileau, for instance—and part of the eighteenth century arrived at an equation of nature and regularity.[255]

This equation worked —— in theory, but when it came to looking at an individual project in nature—for instance, a tree—as Addison was the first to do, then it was clearly not the regularity of its parts which one admired but the inexhaustible irregularity of its whole, and so gradually, in the course of the eighteenth century, the conception of nature changed from one of the ordered Universe to one of infinite variety and intricacy.

So the contrast between the building and its setting became established in England. [33] It exists already in Pope who, as we have seen, made a happy Sharawaggi of his garden, but gave this piece of advice to architects:

> [A]ll the rules of architecture would be reducible to three or four heads. The justness of the openings, bearings upon bearings, and the regularity of the pillars.[256]*

Similarly Lord Kames, in spite of his views on gardening, wrote on architecture,

> Regularity and proportion are essential in buildings...because they produce intrinsic beauty.[257]*

And so porticoed mansions with symmetrical plans went on rising all over England, some noble, some ——, some of the size of Royal palaces on the Continent, some were suburban villas, but all set in the lush Green and between the majestic trees of landscape gardens and parks.

The ways in which houses might, at least on their fringe, participate in the irregularity of their surroundings were only considered towards the end of the century. Price gives the most sensitive advice, starting [out] characteristically from the lessons of landscape painting:

> In the pictures of Claude, the character of which is beauty and cheerfulness, detached architecture, as far as I have observed, is seldom unaccompanied with trees.[258]*

> But the number of trees which an inhabitant of Holland, without fear of inconvenience, plants close to his house, is by no means necessary to picturesque composition: a very few, even a single tree, may make such a break, such a division in the general view, as may answer that end.[259]*

> The accompaniments of beautiful pieces of architecture, may in some respects, be compared to the dress of beautiful women. The addition of what is no less foreign to them than trees are to architecture, varies and adorns the charms even of those, who, like Phryne, might throw off every concealment, and challenge the critic eyes of all Athens assembled.[260]*

How many buildings have I seen, which, with their trees, attract and please
every eye! But deprive one of them of those accompaniments, what a solitary
deserted object would remain![261]*

So much of trees. An even closer alliance between house and nature can be established by creepers.

[T]hough trees and shrubs of every kind have a peculiar and distinguished
effect, in consequence of accompanying, and being accompanied by the
houses of a village, there is another tribe of plants which gains still more by
such a situation, and which indeed no other can shew to such advantage; I
mean the various sorts of climbing plants.[262]*

Humphry Repton incidentally, in spite of his quarrels with Price[,] followed him
in this without qualification:

[N]o building can appear truly picturesque, unless, in its outline, the *design* be
enriched by vegetation.[263]*

There are few situations in which any buildings, whether of rude materials or
highly finished architecture, can be properly introduced without some trees
near it.[264]*

So far, in none of these passages [has] any doubt been expressed as to the [34]
necessity of making houses regular. In fact, both Knight and Price affirm this
more than once. Knight wrote,

Man, both from his natural and social habits, is so accustomed to respect
order and regularity, that it may properly be considered both physically and
morally, as a principle of his existence. All our limbs and organs serve us
in pairs, and by mutual co-operation with each other: whence the habitual
association of ideas has taught us to consider this uniformity as indispensable to the beauty and perfection of the animal form. There is no reason to
be deduced from any abstract consideration of the nature of things why an
animal should be more ugly and disgusting for having only one eye, or one
ear, than for having only one nose or one mouth: yet if we were to meet with
a beast with one eye, or two noses or mouths, in any part of the world, we
should without inquiry, decide it to be a monster, and turn from it with
abhorrence: neither is there any reason, in the nature of things, why a strict
parity, or relative equality, in the correspondent limbs and features of a man
or a horse, should be absolutely destructive of it in the roots and branches of
a tree. But, nevertheless, the Creator having formed the one regular, and the
other irregular, we habitually associate ideas of regularity to the perfection of
the one, and ideas of irregularity to the perfection of the other; and this habit
has been so unvaried, as to have become natural.[265]*

But that refers primarily to the contrast of man and nature, not of his buildings
and nature. However, there also Knight is quite explicit:

Are not, therefore, new buildings beautiful? Unquestionably they are; and peculiarly so: for neatness, freshness, lightness, symmetry, regularity, uniformity, and propriety are undoubtedly beauties of the highest class.[266]*

This passage at once conjures up visions of the —— brick houses of Georgian England, red, with hipped roofs and nicely proportioned and disposed windows. Price evidently felt less comfortable about these houses. In one place he actually went out of his way to denounce them:

> The ugliest buildings are those which have no feature, no character; those, in short, which most nearly approach to the shape, "if shape it may be called," of a clamp of brick, the ugliness of which no one will dispute. It is melancholy to reflect on the number of houses in this kingdom that seem to have been built on that model.[267]*

But even he admits that "straight lines" belong to the "very essence" of architecture and that "any attempt to avoid them, must in general appear unnatural, or affected."[268]*

Yet at the time when Price and Knight wrote, there had already been others who had faced the problem of picturesque architecture as against picturesque landscaping—both in theory and practice. Picturesque buildings, however, are not necessarily asymmetrical buildings, and the two men who are foremost in recommending architectural picturesqueness did not suggest anywhere that symmetry ought to be abandoned. They are both unexpected allies: Robert Adam, in spite of his antiquarian interest in the architecture of Imperial Rome, and Sir Joshua Reynolds, in spite of his sustained plea for the grand manner.

> Movement is meant to express the rise and fall, the advance and recess with other diversity of form, in the different parts of a building, so as to add greatly to the picturesqueness of the composition, for the rising and falling, advancing and receding, with the convexity and concavity and other forms of the great parts, have the same effect in architecture that hill and dale, foreground and distance, swelling and sinking, have in landscape; that is, they serve to produce an agreeable and diversified contour that groups and contrasts like a picture, and creates a variety of light and shade which gives great spirit, beauty and effect to the composition.[269]*

Reynolds's pronouncement comes in to his *Thirteenth Discourse,* delivered in 1786. He said to the students of the Royal Academy:

> [35] It may not be amiss for the Architect to take advantage *sometimes* of that which I am sure the Painter ought always to have his eyes open, I mean the use of accidents: to follow when they lead, and to improve them, rather than always to trust to a regular plan. It often happens that additions have been made to houses, at various times, for use or pleasure. As such buildings depart from regularity, they now and then acquire something of scenery by this accident, which I should think might not unsuccessfully be adopted by an Architect, in an original plan, if it does not too much interfere with convenience. Variety and intricacy is a beauty and excellence in every other of the arts which address the imagination; and why not in Architecture?[270]*

It is difficult to imagine what kind of architecture Reynolds was thinking of in this passage, and one's surprise on the independence and originality of his views rises if another passage is looked up in which he warmly recommends the architecture of Sir John Vanbrugh, least popular architect amongst the Palladians. Yet Reynolds in the same discourse said,[271]*

> [T]he buildings of Vanbrugh, who was a poet as well as an Architect, there is a greater display of imagination, than we shall perhaps find in any other, and this is the ground of the effect we feel in many of his works, notwithstanding the faults with which many of them are justly charged. For this purpose, Vanbrugh appears to have had recourse to some of the principles of the Gothick Architecture: which, though not so ancient as the Grecian, is more so to our imagination, with which the Artist is more concerned than with absolute truth.[272]

> I can pretend to no skill in the detail of Architecture. I judge now of the art, merely as a Painter. When I speak of Vanbrugh, I mean to speak of him in the language of our art. To speak then of Vanbrugh in the language of a Painter, he had originality of invention, he understood light and shadow, and had great skill in composition. To support his principal object, he produced his second and third groups or masses; he perfectly understood in his Art what is the most difficult in ours, the conduct of the back-ground; by which the design and invention is set off to the greatest advantage. What the back-ground is in Painting, in Architecture is the real ground on which the building is erected; and no Architect took greater care than he that his work should not appear crude and hard: that is, it did not abruptly start out of the ground without expectation or preparation.[273]

Appreciation of Vanbrugh might well be taken as a —— test of appreciation of the Picturesque, and so—in spite of the contrast between his own *delicatesse* and Vanbrugh's "masculine show"—Robert Adam also is found in the camp of the Vanbrugh admirers.

> Sir John Vanbrugh's genius was of the first class, and in particular of movement, novelty and ingenuity his works have not been exceeded by anything in modern {i.e., since classic} times.

> In the hands of the ingenious artist, who knows how to polish and refine and bring them into use, we have always regarded his productions as rough jewels of inestimable value.[274]*

Add to these sentences those written in praise of Vanbrugh by Price[275]* and Knight,[276]* and you have the complete array of the combatants for picturesque architecture.

But Vanbrugh himself went much further than any of them. It is in fact due to him that the first asymmetrical house in Europe since the Renaissance was built, the house which characteristically enough he had designed for himself: Vanbrugh Castle at Blackheath near London. The date is 1717–25. That Vanbrugh Castle in addition is also one of the first houses designed in a neo-medieval style, reminiscent of a castle, or, as Vanbrugh once wrote, with "something of a Castle Air," is

Fig. 14

Fig. 14. South front of Vanbrugh Castle, designed by John Vanbrugh

Fig. 15. Sham Castle, Edgehill, Warwickshire, designed by Sanderson Miller

Fig. 16. Strawberry Hill, Twickenham, designed by Horace Walpole, 4th Earl of Orford

Fig. 17. Downton Castle, near Ludlow, designed by Richard Payne Knight

equally characteristic, but does not immediately concern us here. Informal planning and medieval revival joined forces from the beginning.

No-one followed Vanbrugh for several decades, at least, if we exclude some few impossible ——, or evocative structures in gardens and grounds, such as Sanderson Miller's cottage at Edgehill. The next picturesque building of some consequence was again neo-medieval: Horace Walpole's Strawberry Hill, on which he began work in 1750.[277] Between that date and 1776, a cottage of no pretence grew into a fancy castle with a round tower, a cloister arcade, a Long Gallery complete with white and gold Gothic fretwork and fan-vaults, and so on. The house in its first state was not the result of accidental growth. Walpole knew from the beginning what he was up to. In a letter of 25 Feb. 1750 he wrote,

Fig. 15
Fig. 16

> I am almost as fond of the *Sharawaggi,* or Chinese want of symmetry in
> buildings, as in grounds or gardens.[278]

[36] So here, in 1750, an architectural application of the new principle of picturesque landscaping was attempted for the first time. But Walpole again was not immediately followed in this. The Gothic style, it is true, soon became a craze for mansions and villas in England and abroad. But they, at least up to 1800, were, with only few exceptions, symmetrical—that is, Palladian under a veil of Gothic ornament. The most notable exception is specially significant in our context: Richard Payne Knight's country house Downton Castle in Shropshire which he built in 1774–78 in the likeness of one of those vaguely medieval, vaguely Roman fortified apparitions in the background of Claude Lorraine's pictures.[279]*

Fig. 17

Considering the boldness of this design of Knight's, it is doubly surprising to find that as a writer he nowhere explicitly recommends to put up buildings such as his own. All he does is to praise them when they appear in Claude or in reality; because where they do appear in reality they belong to the past and have grown into irregularity by the action of time:

> [In] the pictures of Claude and Gaspar, we perpetually see a mixture of
> Grecian and Gothic architecture employed with the happiest effect in the
> same building; and no critic has ever yet objected to the incongruity of it: for,
> as the temples, tombs, and palaces of the Greeks and Romans in Italy were
> fortified with towers and battlements by the Goths and Lombards in the
> middle ages, such combinations have been naturalized in that country; and
> are, therefore, perfectly in harmony with the scenery; and so far from interrupting the chain of ideas, that they lead on and extend it, in the pleasantest
> manner, through different ages, and successive revolutions in tastes, arts, and
> sciences.[280]*

> [T]he fortresses of our ancestors, which, in the course of the two last centuries, were transformed into Italianized villas, and decked with the porticos,
> balustrades, and terraces of Jones and Palladio, affording, in many instances,
> the most beautiful compositions; especially when mellowed by time and
> neglect, and harmonized and united by ivy, mosses, lichens, &c.[281]*

Similarly, Price recognized the picturesque value of Gothic buildings without suggesting that it should be emulated. "Gothic architecture," he writes, is … more picturesque, though less beautiful than Grecian, {because} in Gothic buildings, the outline of the summit presents such a variety of forms, of turrets and pinnacles, some open, some fretted and variously enriched.[282]*

But are there no indications at all, then, in Price and Knight of a sympathy with the type of house that Strawberry Hill and Downton Castle represent? It seems almost unbelievable. Yet the indications which can be found are both rare and faint. Here they are, complete as far as I can see. One comes from Price, two from Knight:

> [A] number of common houses become picturesque … because they are built of various heights, in various directions, and because those variations are sudden and irregular.[283]*

> In many productions of art, symmetry is still more apparently the result of arbitrary convention.[284]*

[37]

> [S]trict historical unity of plan and design is only felt by the learned.[285]*

———

This search for evidence in eighteenth-century literature of an appreciation of picturesque architecture has brought us but a meagre harvest. Even more disappointing is a search for any appreciation of the problem of visual planning in towns. What can here be quoted does not exceed some four or five passages, and not one of them is Knight's or Price's.[286] Price[,] in fact, right at the beginning of his one architectural essay, *Architecture and Buildings, as Connected with Scenery* {Vol. II, that is 1798}, states that he is only concerned with buildings in the country; for,

> Architecture in towns, may be said to be principal and independent; {only} in the country, it is in some degree subordinate and dependent on the surrounding objects. … In a street, or a square, hardly anything but the front is considered, for little else is seen; and even where the building is insulated, it is generally more connected with other buildings, than with what may be called landscape.[287]*

So, buildings in relation to buildings are not landscape. This is disappointing; for the most helpful lessons can be derived the one for the other. [There is] [j]ust one example to illustrate this. Whately, in his *Observations* of 1765, warns quite in general against designs,

> by which an object, which ought to be part of the whole, is reduced to a mere individual.[288]*

And [he] considers the many ways in which buildings "as objects" can be made,

> to *distinguish,* or to *break,* or to *adorn,* the scenes to which they are applied.[289]*

It is this attitude which we shall have to follow through the nineteenth century and into the twentieth in the next part of this book—an attitude which can consider building as objects in a scene. Our writers of the eighteenth century hardly ever did so, and I can indeed [38] contribute no more than two passages in which townscape is looked at according to the newly established principles of landscape. The first comes once more from Reynolds's *Thirteenth Discourse,* the second from Repton. This is what Reynolds said in 1786:

> The forms and turnings of the streets of London, and other old towns, are produced by accident, without any original plan or design; but they are not always the less pleasant to the walker or spectator, on that account. On the contrary, if the city had been built on the regular plan of Sir Christopher Wren, the effect might have been, as we know it in some new parts of the town, rather unpleasing; the uniformity might have produced weariness, and a slight degree of disgust.[290]*

Repton is even more surprising:

> [I]t is commonly observed by those who have seen both St. Peter's, at Rome, and St. Paul's, at London, that the latter appeared the largest at the first glance, till they became aware of the relative proportion of the surrounding space; and I doubt whether the dignity of St. Paul's would not suffer if the area round the building were increased, since the great west portico is in exact proportion to the distance from whence it can now be viewed, ... but if the whole church could be viewed at once, like St. Peter's, the dome would over-power the portico, as it does in a geometrical view of the west front.[291]*

Repton wrote this in 1803.[292]*

NOTES

1. Although unnumbered, this page has been nominated as page 1. Pevsner began a new pagination for Part II of the manuscript.

2. This refers to James Elmes and Thomas Shepherd, *Metropolitan Improvements; or, London in the Nineteenth Century: Displayed in a Series of Engravings...from Original Drawings,...by Mr. Thos. H. Shepherd:...with Historical, Topographical, and Critical Illustrations by James Elmes* (London: Jones, 1827); and possibly John Summerson, *John Nash, Architect to King George IV* (London: Allen & Unwin, 1935); and John Summerson, *Georgian London* (London: Pleiades, 1945).

3.* Pevsner refers to Christopher Hussey, *The Picturesque: Studies in a Point of View* (London: Putnam, 1927). Additionally, Pevsner listed the other relevant studies: **<C. Tunnard / H. F. Clark: AR / H. F. Clark: Warbg / H. F. Clark: Book / O. Sirén / ——Chase / ——Templeman / N. Pevsner: Genesis, Price, Knight, Repton / Sp Allen?>** These refer to the following works: Christopher Tunnard, *Gardens in the Modern Landscape* (London: Architectural, 1938); H. F. Clark, "Lord Burlington's Bijou, or Sharawaggi at Chiswick," *AR* 95 (1944): 125–29; H. F. Clark, "Eighteenth Century Elysiums: The Rôle of 'Association' in the Landscape Movement," *Journal of the Warburg and Courtauld Institutes* 6 (1943): 165–89; H. F. Clark, *The English Landscape Garden* (London: Pleiades, 1948); Osvald Sirén, *China and Gardens of Europe of the Eighteenth Century* (New York: Ronald, 1950); Isabel Wakelin Urban Chase, *Horace Walpole, Gardenist: An Edition of Walpole's "The History of the Modern Taste in Gardening" with an "Estimate of Walpole's Contribution to Landscape Architecture"*

(Princeton: Princeton Univ. Press for the University of Cincinnati, 1943); William D. Templeman, *The Life and Work of William Gilpin (1724–1804), Master of the Picturesque and Vicar of Boldre* (Urbana: Univ. of Illinois Press, 1939); [Nikolaus Pevsner,] "Price on Picturesque Planning," *AR* 95 (1944): 47–50; Nikolaus Pevsner, "The Genesis of the Picturesque," *AR* 96 (1944): 139–46; Nikolaus Pevsner, "Humphrey Repton: A Florilegium," *AR* 103 (1948): 53–59; Nikolaus Pevsner, "Richard Payne Knight," *Art Bulletin* 31 (1949): 293–320; and Beverly Sprague Allen, *Tides in English Taste (1619–1800): A Background for the Study of Literature* (Cambridge: Harvard Univ. Press, 1937).

4. Francis Bacon, *The Essays; or, Councels, Civil and Moral: and the Wisdom of the Ancients* (Boston: Little, Brown, 1856), 207.

5. Bacon, *The Essays* (note 4), 215, 218.

6*. **<First, I must note a certaine...{A}...describe.>** Note for insertion of text. The quotation is taken from Henry Wotton, *Elements of Architecture* (London: printed by John Bill, 1624), 109, and is found in a typewritten letter addressed to Pevsner and signed "Marcus," which is contiguous with page 2. This is presumably Marcus Whiffen, assistant literary editor of *Architectural Review* in the 1940s and 1950s. Appended to the typewritten page are handwritten notes from Pevsner titled "Wotton 1568-1639," which set out a chronology of Wotton's life and work that Pevsner draws on in this passage.

7. William Temple, *Miscellanea, the Second Part...II. Upon the Gardens of Epicurus...* (London: printed by T. M. for Ri. & Ra. Simpson, 1690). Pevsner cites the following edition: William Temple, *Sir William Temple upon the Gardens of Epicurus, with other XVIIth Century Garden Essays,* ed. Albert Forbes Sieveking, (London: Chatto & Windus, 1908).

8*. **<What I have said...AR 1944 II. 140...remarkable faults.>** Note for insertion of a quotation cited in Pevsner, "Genesis of the Picturesque" (note 3), 140. The quotation is from Temple, *Gardens of Epicurus* [1908] (note 7), 50–54.

9*. **{FOOTNOTE: See S. Lang and N. Pevsner: Sir William Temple and Sharawaggi, *The Architectural Review*, vol. 106, 1949.}** Susan Lang and Nikolaus Pevsner, "Sir William Temple and Sharawaggi," *AR* 106 (1949): 391–93.

10*. **<Date? / Charact? / L. on Design?>** Note in pencil regarding the dating of Shaftesbury's books *Characteristicks* and *A Letter Concerning Design,* which are introduced later.

11*. **{*Characteristicks*, ed. 1758, vol. III, p. 113–28.}** Anthony Ashley Cooper, earl of Shaftesbury, *Characteristicks,* 4 vols. (London: n.p., 1758), 3:124–25. These quotations are drawn from Pevsner's notes on Shaftesbury; see Nikolaus Pevsner papers, box 26. Pevsner's quotations from Shaftesbury have been made consistent with the 1758 edition.

12*. **{*Characteristicks*, vol. I, Enthusiasm, p-_____, *The Moralists*, ed. 1732, vol. II, p. 206.}** The first quotation is from the 1723 edition of Shaftesbury's *Characteristicks.* The second is drawn from Shaftesbury's *A Letter Concerning Enthusiasm,* republished in Shaftesbury, *Characteristicks* [1758] (note 11), 1:16. See Shaftesbury, *Characteristicks* [1758] (note 11), 2:135.

13*. **{*Characteristicks*, vol. III, p. 120?}** Incorrect citation; see Shaftesbury, *Characteristicks* [1758] (note 11), 3:123.

14*. **<Insertion A.>** This refers to a handwritten addendum titled "Insertion A p. 3."

15*. **{*Moralists*, p. 414.}** **<Check exact text.>** Note in pencil. Pevsner's quotation in the manuscript ran thus: "it is in our nature to prefer globe, cylinder, sphere, ball, dye {etc} to irregular forms." The full quotation has been corrected to match that in Shaftesbury, *Characteristicks* [1758] (note 11), 2:268.

16*. {*A Letter concerning Design,* ed. 1737, vol. III, p. 402.} Anthony Ashley Cooper, earl of Shaftesbury, *Characteristicks of Men, Manners, Opinions, and Times,* 3 vols. ([London]: n.p., 1737–38), 3:402. Shaftesbury, *Characteristicks* [1758] (note 11), 4:41.

17*. {*Moralists,* p. 285.} Shaftesbury, *Characteristicks* [1758] (note 11), 2:185. This and several of the passages that follow are also quoted in Pevsner, "Genesis of the Picturesque" (note 3), 140–41.

18. No such quotations have been found in the 1758 edition of Shaftesbury's *A Letter Concerning Enthusiasm.*

19*. {*Moralists,* p. 367.} Shaftesbury, *Characteristicks* [1758] (note 11), 2:238.

20*. {*Moralists,* p. 201.} Shaftesbury, *Characteristicks* [1758] (note 11), 2:132.

21*. {ib., p. 373.} Shaftesbury, *Characteristicks* [1758] (note 11), 2:242.

22*. {ib., p. 345.} Shaftesbury, *Characteristicks* [1758] (note 11), 2:224.

23*. {ib., p. 193.} Shaftesbury, *Characteristicks* [1758] (note 11), 2:127.

24. Shaftesbury, *Characteristicks* [1758] (note 11), 2:255.

25*. <There is generally…AR, p. 141, col. 2…own producing.> {June 26 and Sep. 6.} Note for insertion of a quotation cited in Pevsner, "Genesis of the Picturesque" (note 3), 141. The following quotations from Addison are drawn to Pevsner's instructions, but from the 1790 compendium of Addison's works: Joseph Addison, *The Papers of Joseph Addison, Esq. in the Tatler, Spectator, Guardian, and Freeholder, Together with his Treatise on the Christian Religion, to Which Are Prefixed Tickell's Life of the Author, and Extracts from Dr. Johnson's Remarks…in Four Volumes* (Edinburgh: printed for William Creech, 1790), 3:257–59, 3:378–79.

26*. {*Spectator,* June 25.} Addison, *Papers* (note 25), 3:255.

27*. {ib., June 23.} Addison, *Papers* (note 25), 3:246.

28. Addison, *Papers* (note 25), 3:245–46.

29. Addison, *Papers* (note 25), 3:247.

30. In Pevsner, "Genesis of the Picturesque" (note 3), 142, he heads the section on Pope thus: "1713 The Guardian, 29 September (Alexander Pope)." In the article, he pointed out that Pope's writings in *The Guardian* were eventually reworked for inclusion in his *Essay on Man* (1733) and *Epistle to Lord Burlington* (1731). Presumably, it is this reference to *The Guardian* that Pevsner points to in his discussion of Batty Langley later in Part II.

31*. {J. Serle: A Plan of Mr Pope's Garden, 1745.} John Serle, *A Plan of Mr. Pope's Garden, as It Was Left at His Death: With a Plan and Perspective View of the Grotto; All Taken by J. Serle, His Gardener; with an Account of All the Gems, Minerals, Spars, and Ores of Which It Is Composed,…to Which Is Added, a Character of All His Writings* (London: printed for R. Dodsley & sold by M. Cooper, 1745), 5.

32*. {*Essay on Criticism,* 1711, pt. I.} The edition cited by Pevsner has not been consulted. Quotations have been taken from Pevsner, "Genesis of the Picturesque" (note 3), 143.

33*. {ib.} Pevsner, "Genesis of the Picturesque" (note 3), 143.

34*. {Spence's *Anecdotes,* 1745, ed. S. W. Singer, 1858, p. 9.} Joseph Spence, *Anecdotes, Observations, and Characters of Books and Men; Collected from the Conversation of Mr. Pope, and Other Eminent Persons of His Time; with Notes, and a Life of the Author, by Samuel Weller Singer,* ed. Samuel Weller Singer, 2nd ed. (London: John Russell Smith, 1858), 9.

35*. {*Essay on Man;* Epistle IV To Richard Boyle, Earl of Burlington; 1731.} Pevsner, "Genesis of the Picturesque" (note 3), 143.

36. Pevsner, "Genesis of the Picturesque" (note 3), 143.

37*. {Spence's *Anecdotes* p. 9.} Spence, *Anecdotes* (note 34), 9.

38. <INSERT to p. 7.> Note for insertion of smaller piece of adjacent text.

39. Spence, *Anecdotes* (note 34), 9.

40*. {p. 109.} Spence, *Anecdotes* (note 34), 109.

41. Spence, *Anecdotes* (note 34), 158.

42. The erratic nature of Pevsner's addenda for manuscript pages 7 through 13 has resulted in a slightly confusing page order in what follows.

43*. <He leaped the fence / Quote from Chase p——.> Note for insertion of text. See Urban Chase, *Horace Walpole, Gardenist* (note 3), 25–26. Unlike other notes for insertions, which contain markers for the end of the passage, this quotation did not. It has been selected based on content, along with the amount of space left by Pevsner for the purpose. In this space, Pevsner made around eight lines of notes, which he later crossed out. These consist largely of names, places and dates, which he goes on to discuss later in Part II.

44*. <Pains Hill, Charles Hamilton / Sherborne, Robert Digby / Richmond Lodge, —— Pope, Bridgman / Marble Hill, Twickenham, Pope, Bridgman / Down Hall, Essex, Earl of Oxford, Pope / Stowe and Kent / Delville 1743 —— / Gubbins, Bridgman / Amesbury, Bridgman / Cirencester, Allen IV Earl of Bathurst / Claremont Vanbrugh 1715–1718? / —— / End Bridgman—1711, Kent in 1748.> Notes in pencil listing significant people and estates. <AR p. 145 Kip etc.> Note referring to Pevsner, "Genesis of the Picturesque" (note 3), 145.

45*. {Vol. III, 2.} Stephen Switzer, *Ichnographia Rustica; or, The Nobleman, Gentleman, and Gardener's Recreation* (London: D. Browne, 1718). The text of this quotation and those that follow, as well as their page citations, are taken from Pevsner, "Genesis of the Picturesque" (note 3). Page citations to Switzer's *Ichnographia Rustica* are likewise taken from Pevsner's article.

46*. {II, 196.} Switzer, *Ichnographia Rustica* (note 45), 196.

47*. {II, 200.} Pevsner, "Genesis of the Picturesque" (note 3), 145.

48*. {III, VI.} Pevsner, "Genesis of the Picturesque" (note 3), 145.

49*. {III, 2–3.} Parts of this quotation are also published in Pevsner, "Genesis of the Picturesque" (note 3), 145.

50*. {II. 197–201.} Switzer, *Ichnographia Rustica* (note 45), 197–201.

51. This refers to the writings of Pope. See note 30 above.

52*. {Introd.} Batty Langley, *New Principles of Gardening; or, The Laying Out and Planting Parterres, Groves, Wildernesses, Labyrinths, Avenues, Parks, etc. after a More Grand and Rural Manner, Than Has Been Done Before* (London: printed for A. Bettesworth & J. Batley [etc.], 1728), x. Pevsner quotes many of the same passages in Pevsner, "Genesis of the Picturesque" (note 3), 146.

53*. {194.} Langley, *New Principles of Gardening* (note 52), 198.

54*. {198.} Langley, *New Principles of Gardening* (note 52), 198.

55*. {201.} Langley, *New Principles of Gardening* (note 52), 201.

56*. {Introd.} Langley, *New Principles of Gardening* (note 52), x, vi. The pagination of the introduction to Langley's book appears inconsistent. Cf. Pevsner, "Genesis of the Picturesque" (note 3), 146, where Pevsner lists the pagination of this quotation as page v.

57*. {Introd.} Langley, *New Principles of Gardening* (note 52), iii.

58*. <INSERT p. 10.> Note for insertion of text.

59. Robert Castell, *The Villas of the Ancients Illustrated* (London: printed for the author, 1728).

60*. {*The Architectural Review,* **vol. 95, 1944.**} Clark, "Lord Burlington's Bijou" (note 3), 126. **<Warburg.>** Note in pencil referring to Clark, "Eighteenth Century Elysiums" (note 3), in which Clark also discusses Castell.

61. Clark, "Lord Burlington's Bijou" (note 3), 126.

62. Clark, "Lord Burlington's Bijou" (note 3), 126.

63*. {*The Complete Works of Sir John Vanbrugh,* **Nonesuch ed. 1928, vol. 4, p. 30.**} John Vanbrugh, *The Complete Works of Sir John Vanbrugh; the Plays Edited by Bonamy Dobrée; the Letters Edited by Geoffrey Webb,* 4 vols. (London: Nonesuch, 1927–28), 4:30.

64*. **<INSERT B.>** Note for insertion of text.

65*. {**V. 163 etc.**} This quotation is not from Thomson's *Seasons,* as the reader might expect but his *Liberty.* See James Thomson, *The Works of Mr. Thomson; Volume the Second; Containing, Liberty, a Poem, in Five Parts: Sophonisba, a Tragedy* (London: printed [by Henry Woodfall] for A. Millar, 1736), pt. 5, p. 13, lines 163–66. This same quotation is published in Pevsner, "Genesis of the Picturesque" (note 3), 146.

66. Thomson, *Works* (note 65), pt. 5, p. 37, lines 688–89.

67. Thomson, *Works* (note 65), pt. 5, p. 32, line 588.

68*. {**V., 688–90.**} Thomson, *Works* (note 65), pt. 5, p. 37, line 690.

69. Thomson, *Works* (note 65), pt. 5, p. 37, lines 696–700.

70*. {**Letter to Eliz. Young, August 1743.**} Refers to a letter from Thomson to Elizabeth Young, published in Hussey, *The Picturesque* (note 3), 42.

71. This detail was left blank by Pevsner. According to H. F. Clark, Envil is also known as Enfield or Enville and was in Staffordshire, "about nine miles from Hagley." See Clark, "Eighteenth Century Elysiums" (note 3), 174 n. 5.

72. Pevsner left the owner of this garden blank. See Elisabeth Whittle, "'All These Inchanting Scenes': Piercefield in the Wye Valley," *Garden History* 24 (1996): 148.

73. Tunnard, *Gardens* (note 3).

74. **<Sirén.>** Note in pencil referring to Osvald Sirén's description of Stourhead in Sirén, *China and Gardens* (note 3), 47–52.

75. Presumably, Pevsner is referring to the garden he had previously mentioned as "Envil." See note 71 above and Clark's description of Envil.

76. The work Pevsner refers to as *History* appears to be Walpole's "Essay on Modern Gardening." The point that follows, on the first *ferme ornée,* has been cited in Horace Walpole, *Anecdotes of Painting in England; with Some Account of the Principal Artists; and Incidental Notes on Other Arts; Collected by the Late Mr. George Vertue; and Now Digested and Published from His Original MSS by Mr. Horace Walpole,* 2nd ed. (Twickenham: printed by Thomas Kirgate at Strawberry-Hill, 1765–71, 1765–80), 4:145. Pevsner's quotations that follow are slightly different in order from those in the original and appear to be drawn from Clark's discussion of Walpole's impressions and where Walpole is correctly cited. See H. F. Clark, "Eighteenth Century Elysiums" (note 3), 172 n. 2.

77*. **<Note Delany Delville 1743 same name see her letters.>** Note in pencil. For a discussion of Mrs. Delany and the *ferme ornée,* see Hussey, *The Picturesque* (note 3), 133.

78. Both this observation and the order of presentation suggest that Pevsner was working closely from Clark's article. Clark, "Eighteenth Century Elysiums" (note 3), 172.

79. Jonathan Richardson, *An Essay on the Theory of Painting* (London: printed by W. Bowyer for John Churchill, 1715).

80*. {**Works ed. 1792, p. 21.**} Jonathan Richardson, *The Works of Jonathan Richardson: Containing I. The Theory of Painting…A New Edition, Corrected, with the Additions of an Essay on the Knowledge of Prints, and Cautions to Collectors; Ornamented with Portraits* (London: n.p., 1792), 21.

81*. {*Castle of Indolence* **I, No. 38.**} James Thomson, *The Castle of Indolence: An Allegorical Poem; Written in Imitation of Spenser by James Thomson* (London: printed for A. Millar, 1748), 14, line 38. See also Hussey, *The Picturesque* (note 3), 18.

82. William Gilpin, *A Dialogue upon the Gardens of the Right Honourable the Lord Viscount Cobham, at Stow in Buckinghamshire* (London: printed for B. Seeley, in Buckingham, & sold by J. & J. Rivington, in St. Paul's Church-Yard, 1748).

83*. {**W. D. Templeman: William Gilpin. Illinois's Studies…**} Templeman, *Life and Work of William Gilpin* (note 3).

84. Quotations from Shenstone's "Unconnected Thoughts on Gardening" are from William Shenstone, *The Works in Verse and Prose, of William Shenstone, Esq; Most of Which Were Never before Printed; in Two Volumes, with Decorations* (London: printed for R. & J. Dodsley, 1764), 125–47.

85*. {**p. 5.**} Gilpin, *A Dialogue* (note 82), 5–6.

86*. {**p. 26.**} Gilpin, *A Dialogue* (note 82), 25–26.

87*. {**p. 8.**} Gilpin, *A Dialogue* (note 82), 52.

88*. {**p. 6.**} Gilpin, *A Dialogue* (note 82), 6.

89*. {**p. 5.**} Gilpin, *A Dialogue* (note 82), 5.

90*. {**p. IIIa.**} This quotation appears to be drawn from the second and corrected edition of Gilpin's *A Dialogue*, as the first edition, from which the other quotations are drawn, has a different wording. See William Gilpin, *A Dialogue upon the Gardens of the Right Honourable the Lord Viscount Cobham, at Stow in Buckinghamshire*, 2nd ed. (London: printed for B. Seeley; sold by J. & J. Rivington, 1749), 4.

91*. <**Woodstock Pal.**> Note in pencil referring to Woodstock Palace, which Pevsner mentioned above; see p. 117.

92*. {*Letters,* **ed. G. Webb, Nonesuch Press, 1928, p. 29–30.**} Vanbrugh, *The Complete Works* (note 63), 29–30.

93. Kenneth Clark, *The Gothic Revival: An Essay in the History of Taste* (London: Constable, 1928).

94*. {**cf p.…**} Serle, *A Plan* (note 31), 5.

95. Shenstone, *Works* (note 84).

96*. {**Works, 1764, vol. II, p. 94.**} Shenstone, *Works* (note 84), 125.

97*. {**p. 95.**} Shenstone, *Works* (note 84), 126.

98*. {**p. 99.**} Shenstone, *Works* (note 84), 131.

99*. {**p. 96.**} Shenstone, *Works* (note 84), 127.

100*. {**vol. II ____.**} Refers to "Verses by Mr. Dodsley on his first arrival at the Leasowes, 1754"; published in Shenstone, *Works* (note 84), 380–82.

101. These quotations are from an essay titled "A Description of the Leasowes"; published in Shenstone, *Works* (note 84), 331–69. The capitalization is Pevsner's. The quotations appear on pages 340, 363, 364, respectively.

102*. {**p. 102.**} Shenstone, *Works* (note 84), 136.

103*. {**p. 100.**} Shenstone, *Works* (note 84), 134.

104*. {**p. 87.**} Shenstone, *Works* (note 84), 129.

105*. {**p. 104.**} Shenstone, *Works* (note 84), 139.

106*. {**p. 95.**} Shenstone, *Works* (note 84), 127.

107*. {**p. 95.**} Shenstone, *Works* (note 84), 126–27.

108*. {**p. 110.**} Shenstone, *Works* (note 84), 147.

109. Edmund Burke, *A Philosophical Enquiry into the Origin of Our Ideas of the Sublime and Beautiful* (London: printed for R. & J. Dodsley, 1756).

110*. {see p....} In this note, Pevsner intended to compare the relevant passages from the discussion of Addison above. See this volume, pp. 111–13.

111*. {p. 94.} Shenstone, *Works* (note 84), 125.

112. Horace Walpole, *The Works of Horatio Walpole, Earl of Orford, in Five Volumes* (London: G. G. & J. Robinson & J. Edwards, 1798), 1:148. This quotation is from an essay published under the pseudonym "Julio" and titled "The World, by Mr. Adam Fitz-Adam, Number VI Thursday, February 8, 1753, to Mr. Fitz-Adam."

113. Uvedale Price, *Essays on the Picturesque, as Compared with the Sublime and the Beautiful: And, on the Use of Studying Pictures, for the Purpose of Improving Real Landscape*, 3 vols. (London: printed for J. Mawman, 1810), 2:150 (footnote).

114*. **{FOOTNOTE: Other professional gardeners mentioned in contemporary literature are Morris (for Persfield; see G. Mason), Wright and Eames; (see also G. Mason), Research is needed to find out more about these men.}** This note refers to George Mason, *An Essay on Design in Gardening* (London: printed for Benjamin White, 1768).

115. William Hogarth, *The Analysis of Beauty: Written with a View of Fixing the Fluctuating Ideas of Taste* (London: John Reeves, 1753); Burke, *A Philosophical Enquiry* (note 109); Alexander Gerard, *An Essay on Taste, by Alexander Gerard,...with Three Dissertations on the Same Subject, by Mr. de Voltaire, Mr. d'Alembert, F. R. S. Mr. de Montesquieu* (London: printed for A. Millar, A. Kincaid, & J. Bell..., 1759); and Henry Home, Lord Kames, *Elements of Criticism* (Edinburgh: printed for A. Millar, London; & A. Kincaid & J. Bell, Edinburgh, 1762). The edition used for the following quotations from Lord Kames's work is Henry Home, Lord Kames, *Elements of Criticism* (New York: A. S. Barnes & Burr, 1863).

116. For the works referenced here, see Thomas Whately, *Observations on Modern Gardening, Illustrated by Descriptions* (London: printed for T. Payne, 1770); Mason, *Essay on Design* (note 114); Horace Walpole, "History of the Modern Taste in Gardening," in idem, *Anecdotes of Painting in England; with Some Account of the Principal Artists; and Incidental Notes on Other Arts; Collected by the Late Mr. George Vertue; and Now Digested and Published from His Original MSS by Mr. Horace Walpole* (Twickenham: printed by Thomas Kirgate at Strawberry-Hill, 1765–71), 4:117–51; William Mason, *The English Garden: A Poem, Book the First* (London: printed & sold by R. Horsefield [etc.], 1772); and William Chambers, *A Dissertation on Oriental Gardening* (London: printed by W. Griffin [etc.], 1772). The quotations that follow in the main text are in Thomas Whately, *Observations on Modern Gardening, Illustrated by Descriptions*, 5th ed. (London: printed by G. Stafford, for T. Payne [...], 1793).

117. William Gilpin, *Observations on the River Wye, and Several Parts of South Wales...Relative Chiefly to Picturesque Beauty; Made in the Summer of 1770* (London: printed for R. Blamire, sold by B. Law & R. Faulder, 1782).

118*. **<Aesthetics to go in here. See existing note on Hogarth.>** Note in pencil. This suggests that Pevsner intended to extend his treatment of aesthetics in this period. No such note on Hogarth has been located in the manuscript papers.

119*. {Kames, ed. 1865, p. 463.} In contrast to Pevsner's citation here, this quotation, and those that follow, appear to be drawn from the 1863 edition, as the pagination in most cases is identical. See Kames, *Elements of Criticism* [1863] (note 115), 463.

120*. {G. Mason, 2nd ed. of 1795, p. 143.} George Mason, *An Essay on Design in Gardening, First Published in MDCCLXVIII, Now Greatly Augmented; Also a Revisal of Several Later Publications on the Same Subject*, 2nd ed. (London: printed by C.

Roworth for Benjamin & John White, 1795), 143.

121*. {**Walpole, ed. Chase, 35.**} Urban Chase, *Horace Walpole, Gardenist* (note 3), 35.

122*. {**Joseph Warton:** *Essay on the Genius...of Mr. Pope,* **1756, II, 179.**} Joseph Warton, *An Essay on the Genius and Writings of Pope, in Two Volumes,* 4th ed. (London: printed for J. Dodsley, 1782), 2:184–85.

123*. {**Tho's Gray, Sept. 10, 1763.**} The original quotation runs thus: "[T]he only proof of our original talent in matters of pleasure, I mean our skill in gardening, or rather laying our grounds," from "Letter VIII, Mr. Gray to Mr. How, Cambridge, Sept. 10, 1763." Thomas Gray, *The Poems of Mr. Gray, to Which Are Prefixed Memoirs of His Life and Writings by W. Mason, M. A.* (York: printed by A. Ward; sold by J. Dodsley, London, & J. Todd, York, 1775), 386.

124*. {**p. 17.**} <**A Wh p17.**> Note for insertion of text. See Whately, *Observations* [1793] (note 116), 17. The quotations that follow, labeled A through M, comprise a series of typewritten notes held in Nikolaus Pevsner papers, box 26. Pagination refers to the fifth edition of Whately from 1793.

125*. <**B.**> {**p. 22.**} Note for insertion of text. Whately, *Observations* [1793] (note 116), 23.

126*. <**C.**> {**p. 24.**} Note for insertion of text. Whately, *Observations* [1793] (note 116), 24.

127*. {**Kames, e.c., p. 468.**} Kames, *Elements of Criticism* [1863] (note 115), 468.

128*. {**Walpole, ed. Chase, 36.**} Urban Chase, *Horace Walpole, Gardenist* (note 3), 36.

129*. <**AA.**> {**p. 50.**} Note for insertion of text. Mason, *Essay on Design* [1795] (note 120), 50–51.

130*. {**Walpole; ed. Chase, 27.**} Urban Chase, *Horace Walpole, Gardenist* (note 3), 27.

131*. {**Walpole, ib., 35.**} Urban Chase, *Horace Walpole, Gardenist* (note 3), 35.

132*. {**ed. Chase, 37.**} Urban Chase, *Horace Walpole, Gardenist* (note 3), 37.

133*. <**Hussey.**> {**—.**} Pevsner was not certain of the source for this quotation and mentioned Hussey as a possible source; the editor of the present volume has not been able to corroborate this.

134*. {**Letter of June 20, 1760.**} Horace Walpole, *Letters of Horace Walpole, Earl of Orford, to Sir Horace Mann...,* 2nd ed. (London: Richard Bentley, 1833), 3:390 (20 June 1760).

135*. {**Letter of July 4, 1760.**} Horace Walpole, *The Correspondence of Horace Walpole, with George Montagu, Esq., [and Others], 1760–1769* (London: Henry Colburn, 1837), (note 134), 2:18 (4 July 1760).

136*. {**129.**} Mason, *Essay on Design* [1795] (note 120), 129.

137*. <**D.**> {**pp. 26–28.**} Note for insertion of text. <**Perhaps carry on to p. 29 to "arbor vitae."**> Note for the inclusion of further text. Whately, *Observations* [1793] (note 116), 26–29.

138*. <**E.**> {**pp. 63–64.**} Note for insertion of text. Whately, *Observations* [1793] (note 116), 63–64.

139*. <**F.**> {**p. 14.**} Note for insertion of text. Whately, *Observations* [1793] (note 116), 14.

140*. <**G.**> {**p. 15.**} Note for insertion of text. Whately, *Observations* [1793] (note 116), 15–16.

141*. {**Kames, e.c., p. 464.**} <**Kames 1819 / II 318.**> Note in pencil referring to a different edition and pagination. Kames, *Elements of Criticism* [1863] (note 115), 464.

142*. {**Kames, e.c., p. 464.**} Kames, *Elements of Criticism* [1863] (note 115), 464.

143*. {**Kames, e.c., p. 465.**} Kames, *Elements of Criticism* [1863] (note 115), 465.

144*. **<Wh 160.>** Note for insertion of text. Whately, *Observations* [1793] (note 116), 160.

145*. **<H.>** {**p.134.**} Note for insertion of text. Whately, *Observations* [1793] (note 116), 134.

146*. **<I.>** {**p. 135.**} Note for insertion of text. Whately, *Observations* [1793] (note 116), 135.

147*. {**p. 154.**} Whately, *Observations* [1793] (note 116), 154.

148*. **<M. 90.>** {**pp. 90 etc.**} Note for insertion of text. Mason, *Essay on Design* [1795] (note 120), 90.

149*. {***History,* ed. Chase, 34.**} Urban Chase, *Horace Walpole, Gardenist* (note 3), 34.

150*. **<K.>** {**p. 95.**} Note for insertion of text. Whately, *Observations* [1793] (note 116), 95.

151*. {**ed. Chase, 35–36.**} Urban Chase, *Horace Walpole, Gardenist* (note 3), 35–36.

152*. {**ib., II, 323.**} This quotation was not published in Kames, *Elements of Criticism* [1863] (note 115). Refer instead to Lord Kames, Henry Home, *Elements of Criticism, the Third Edition, with Additions and Improvements* (Edinburgh: printed for A. Millar, London; & A. Kincaid & J. Bell, Edinburgh, 1765), 2:432.

153*. {**ed. Chase, 26.**} Urban Chase, *Horace Walpole, Gardenist* (note 3), 26.

154*. **<L.>** {**p. 150.**} Note for insertion of text. Whately, *Observations* [1793] (note 116), 150.

155*. **<M.>** {**p. 152.**} Note for insertion of text. Whately, *Observations* [1793] (note 116), 152.

156*. {***Works,* ed. Malone, 1809, II, 135.**} Joshua Reynolds, *The Works of Sir Joshua Reynolds, to Which Is Prefixed an Account of the Life and Writings of the Author, by Edmond Malone,* 4th ed. (London: T. Cadell & W. Davies, 1809), 2:134–35.

157*. {***Works,* ib., 134.**} Reynolds, *Works* (note 156), 2:134.

158. This page is marked as page 17 but is otherwise consistent in order.

159*. {***Dissertation,* p. 146.**} William Chambers, *A Dissertation on Oriental Gardening: The Second Edition, with Additions, to Which Is Annexed, an Explanatory Discourse, by Tan Chet-Qua, of Quang-Chew-Fu, Gent.* (London: W. Griffin, 1773), 146. The following section on Chambers draws heavily on Pevsner's article on Chambers; see Nikolaus Pevsner, "The Other Chambers," *AR* 101 (1947): 195–98.

160. Chambers, *Dissertation* [1773] (note 159), 20.

161*. {***Dissertation,* pp. 20–21.**} Chambers, *Dissertation* [1773] (note 159), 20–21.

162. William Chambers, *Designs of Chinese Buildings, Furniture, Dresses, Machines, and Utensils. . . . to Which Is Annexed, a Description of Their Temples, Houses, Gardens, etc.* (London: published for the author [etc.], 1757).

163*. {**p. IX.**} Chambers, *Dissertation* [1773] (note 159), ix.

164. Pevsner is referring to the pseudonymous satirical work by Charles de Secondat, baron de Montesquieu, *Lettres persanes* (Amsterdam: Pierre Brunel, 1721).

165. Voltaire's *Zadig; ou, La destinée* was written in 1747 and first published under the title *Memnon: Histoire orientale* ([Amsterdam]: pour la Compagnie, 1747). *Vision de Babouc* was written in 1748.

166. Pevsner did not include page numbers for this quotation, and the editor has been unable to identify its origin.

167. See "Letter to the Rev. William Mason," 25 May 1772; published in *The Letters of Horace Walpole, Earl of Orford,* ed. Peter Cunningham (London: Henry G. Bohn, 1861), 5:389.

168*. **<INSERTION TO P 22.>** Note for insertion of text on page 23.

169*. **{pp. V–VIII.}** Chambers, *Dissertation* [1773] (note 159), v–viii.

170. Chambers, *Dissertation* [1773] (note 159), 55.

171*. **{p. 127.}** Chambers, *Dissertation* [1773] (note 159), 127.

172. Pevsner did not include page numbers for this quotation, and the editor has been unable to identify its origin.

173*. **{p. 13.}** Chambers, *Dissertation* [1773] (note 159), 13.

174*. **{p. 39.}** Chambers, *Dissertation* [1773] (note 159), 39.

175*. **{p. 83.}** Chambers, *Dissertation* [1773] (note 159), 83.

176. This is a reference to Pope's *Epistle to Lord Burlington;* see note 30 above.

177*. **{p. 145.}** Chambers, *Dissertation* [1773] (note 159), 145.

178*. **{p. 147.}** Chambers, *Dissertation* [1773] (note 159), 147.

179*. **{p. 149.}** Chambers, *Dissertation* [1773] (note 159), 149. In contrast to Pevsner's citation here, Pevsner, "The Other Chambers" (note 159), 196, lists the page numbers of the quotation as pp. 151–52.

180*. **{p. 142.}** Chambers, *Dissertation* [1773] (note 159), 142.

181*. **{p. 142.}** Chambers, *Dissertation* [1773] (note 159), 142.

182*. **{p. 41.}** Chambers, *Dissertation* [1773] (note 159), 41.

183*. **{p. 43.}** Chambers, *Dissertation* [1773] (note 159), 43.

184*. **{p. 80.}** Chambers, *Dissertation* [1773] (note 159), 80.

185*. **{p. 43.}** Chambers, *Dissertation* [1773] (note 159), 43.

186*. **{p. 127.}** Chambers, *Dissertation* [1773] (note 159), 127.

187*. **{p. 30.}** Chambers, *Dissertation* [1773] (note 159), 30.

188*. **{p. 73.}** Chambers, *Dissertation* [1773] (note 159), 73.

189*. **{p. 105.}** Chambers, *Dissertation* [1773] (note 159), 105.

190*. **{p. 15.}** Chambers, *Dissertation* [1773] (note 159), 15.

191*. **{p. 107.}** Chambers, *Dissertation* [1773] (note 159), 107. For the first part of this quotation, see also Pevsner, "The Other Chambers" (note 159), 196.

192*. **{p. 83.}** Chambers, *Dissertation* [1773] (note 159), 83.

193*. Although Pevsner intimates that the discussion will address Gilpin immediately, page 25 and the beginning of page 26 were entirely crossed out. They were to be devoted to "The Forerunners II: William Gilpin, 1782." Instead, the discussion moves straight on to Price and later returns to Gilpin.

194. This next section on Price draws heavily from Pevsner, "Price on Picturesque Planning" (note 3).

195. The quotations from Price in this section are taken from the 1810 edition. See Price, *Essays on the Picturesque* (note 113).

196. William Gilpin, *Three Essays: On Picturesque Beauty; On Picturesque Travel; and On Sketching Landscape: To Which Is Added a Poem, On Landscape Painting* (London: printed for R. Blamire, 1792).

197*. **{*Three Essays*, p. 3.}** Gilpin, *Three Essays* (note 196), 3.

198*. **{ibid., p. 6.}** Gilpin, *Three Essays* (note 196), 6.

199*. **{Ibid., p. 7.}** Gilpin, *Three Essays* (note 196), 7.

200*. **{*Three Essays*, p. 8.}** Gilpin, *Three Essays* (note 196), 8.

201*. **{ibid., p. 13.}** Gilpin, *Three Essays* (note 196), 13–14.

202*. **{*The Landscape,* Note to the Second Edition, p. 251.}** Richard Payne Knight, *The Landscape, a Didactic Poem: In Three Books, Addressed to Uvedale Price,*

Esq., 2nd ed. (London: printed by W. Bulmer, 1795), 19.

203*. {do I? —— **Pt. III.**} Note in pencil.

204*. {**p. 2.**} {**Vol. I, pp. 21–22.**} Price, *Essays on the Picturesque* (note 113), 1:22. In this and the following citations to Price, where two sets of page numbers are given, the page number in the first set of parentheses refers to Pevsner's typescript notes on Price, located in the Nikolaus Pevsner papers, box 26; the volume and page number in the second set of parentheses refers to the 1810 edition of Price's *Essays on the Picturesque.*

205*. {**p. 5.**} {**Vol. I, p. 88.**} Price, *Essays on the Picturesque* (note 113), 1:88.

206*. {**p. 3.**} {**Vol. I, p. 24.**} Price, *Essays on the Picturesque* (note 113), 1:24.

207*. {**p. 3.**} {**Vol. I, p. 51.**} Price, *Essays on the Picturesque* (note 113), 1:50–51.

208*. {**p. 6.**} {**Vol. I, p. 115.**} Price, *Essays on the Picturesque* (note 113), 1:115.

209*. {**p. 6.**} {**Vol. I, p. 126–27.**} Price, *Essays on the Picturesque* (note 113), 1:126–27.

210*. {**p. 25.**} {**Vol. II, p. 231.**} Price, *Essays on the Picturesque* (note 113), 2:230–31.

211*. {**p. 12.**} {**Vol. I, p. 242.**} Price, *Essays on the Picturesque* (note 113), 1:243.

212*. {**p. 17.**} {**Vol. II, p. 108.**} Price, *Essays on the Picturesque* (note 113), 2:108–9.

213*. {**p. 21.**} {**Vol. II, p. 159.**} Price, *Essays on the Picturesque* (note 113), 2:159.

214*. {**p. 11.**} {**Vol. I, p. 230.**} Price, *Essays on the Picturesque* (note 113), 1:230–31.

215*. {**Vol. II, p. 9.**} Price, *Essays on the Picturesque* (note 113), 2:9.

216*. {**Vol. I, pp. 57–59.**} Price, *Essays on the Picturesque* (note 113), 1:57–59.

217*. {**Vol. I, p. 54, Vol. II, p. 259.**} Price, *Essays on the Picturesque* (note 113), 1:54; 2:259.

218*. {**Vol I, p. 63.**} Price, *Essays on the Picturesque* (note 113), 1:63.

219*. {**Vol I, p. 55.**} Price, *Essays on the Picturesque* (note 113), 1:55.

220*. {**Vol I, p. 188.**} Price, *Essays on the Picturesque* (note 113), 1:188.

221*. {**Vol. I, p. 192.**} Price, *Essays on the Picturesque* (note 113), 1:192.

222*. {**Vol. I, p. 202–03.**} Price, *Essays on the Picturesque* (note 113), 1:203.

223*. {**p.19.**} {**Vol. II, p. 131.**} Price, *Essays on the Picturesque* (note 113), 2:131.

224*. {**p. 9–10.**} {**Vol. I, pp. 207–09.**} Price, *Essays on the Picturesque* (note 113), 1:207–9.

225*. {**p. 1.**} {**Vol. I, p. 5.**} Price, *Essays on the Picturesque* (note 113), 1:5.

226*. {**p. 1.**} {**Vol. I, p. 11.**} Price, *Essays on the Picturesque* (note 113), 1:11.

227*. {**"your palate certainly requires a degree of 'irritation' rarely to be expected in garden scenery." Price's *Three Essays*, Vol. III, p. 21.**} Price, *Essays on the Picturesque* (note 113), 3:20.

228*. {**Vol. II, p. 144.**} Price, *Essays on the Picturesque* (note 113), 2:144.

229*. {**Vol. III, p. 168.**} Price, *Essays on the Picturesque* (note 113), 3:168.

230*. {**Repton's *Sketches and Hints*, 1794, ed. London 1840, p. 87. Price's Volume II came out in 1798.**} Pevsner refers to John Claudius Loudon's edition of Repton's *Sketches and Hints:* Humphry Repton, *The Landscape Gardening and Landscape Architecture of the Late Humphrey Repton, Esq.: Being His Entire Works on These Subjects,* ed. John Claudius Loudon (London: Longman, 1840), 87.

231*. {**vol. II, p. 126.**} Price, *Essays on the Picturesque* (note 113), 2:126.

232*. {**p. 21.**} {**Vol. II, p. 159.**} Price, *Essays on the Picturesque* (note 113), 2:158–59.

233. In this section, Pevsner's discussion resembles that found in Pevsner, "Richard Payne Knight" (note 3).

234*. {**I, 234.**} Knight, *The Landscape* (note 202), 25, line 298. Pevsner's discussion of Knight here appears to draw in order of presentation and content on Hussey, *The Picturesque* (note 3), 144.

235*. {**I, 272.**} Pevsner appears to have taken on Hussey's wording in his discussion of Knight. See Hussey, *The Picturesque* (note 3), 144. According to the second edition of *The Landscape* from 1795, this line ran thus: "Makes one dull, vapid, smooth, unvaried scene." See Knight, *The Landscape* (note 202), 24, line 286.

236*. {**II, 9.**} Knight, *The Landscape* (note 202), 31, line 9.

237*. {**II, 234.**} Knight, *The Landscape* (note 202), 52, lines 260–61. See also Hussey, *The Picturesque* (note 3), 168.

238*. {**I, 149.**} Knight, *The Landscape* (note 202), 11, line 149.

239*. {**II, 195.**} Knight, *The Landscape* (note 202), 40, line 195. See also Hussey, *The Picturesque* (note 3), 167.

240*. {**II, 11.**} Knight, *The Landscape* (note 202), 31, line 11.

241*. {**II, 263–265.**} Knight, *The Landscape* (note 202), 53–54, lines 289–91. See also Hussey, *The Picturesque* (note 3), 169.

242. Thomas Hearne (1744–1817).

243. Augustus Welby Northmore Pugin, *Contrasts; or, A Parallel between the Noble Edifices of the Fourteenth and Fifteenth Centuries and Similar Buildings of the Present Day; Shewing the Present Decay of Taste* (London: printed for the author & published by him, 1836).

244. In the quotations that follow, Pevsner cites Richard Payne Knight, *An Analytical Inquiry into the Principles of Taste,* 3rd ed. (London: T. Payne, 1806).

245*. {**see p....**} See the "Advertisement," in Richard Payne Knight, *The Landscape, a Didactic Poem: In Three Books, Addressed to Uvedale Price, Esq.,* 2nd ed. (London: printed by W. Bulmer, 1795), iii–xv.

246*. {**3rd ed. 1806, p. 196.**} Knight, *An Analytical Inquiry* (note 244), 197.

247*. {**see p....**} See Knight's discussion of David Hume's ideas in Knight, *An Analytical Inquiry* (note 244), 16.

248*. {**148.**} In fact, this quotation reads, "*pittoresco* must mean, *after the manner of painters.*" Knight, *An Analytical Inquiry* (note 244), 148.

249*. {**69.**} Knight, *An Analytical Inquiry* (note 244), 69.

250*. {**67.**} Knight, *An Analytical Inquiry* (note 244), 67.

251. This observation is from Price and refers to Rembrandt's painting *The Carcase of an Ox.* See Price, *Essays on the Picturesque* (note 113), 3:315–16. The origin of this error appears to come from the seminal, though anonymous, article later attributed to Hastings, in which he wrote, "Payne Knight, it will be remembered, brought up the carcass of an ox as an instance of a revolting object which could provoke painterly delight—could produce, that is to say, a Picturesque effect." The Editor [Hubert de Cronin Hastings,] "Exterior Furnishing or Sharawaggi: The Art of Making Urban Landscape," *AR* 95 (1944): 5.

252*. {**186.**} Knight, *An Analytical Inquiry* (note 244), 186.

253*. <**AR 141.**> Note for insertion of text from Pevsner, "Genesis of the Picturesque" (note 3), 141. The quotation is found in Shaftesbury, *Characteristicks* [1758] (note 11), 2:185.

254*. {**Quoted from A. O. Lovejoy: *Essays in the History of Ideas,* Baltimore 1948, an admirable book which had remained unknown to me while I went on publishing papers on subjects closely connected with Professor Lovejoy's. I wish to apologize here to Professor Lovejoy for occasional belated duplication of results of his and for omission to quote him where readers of my**} papers could have coincidentally benefited by consulting his.} Arthur O. Lovejoy, *Essays in the History of Ideas* (Baltimore: Johns Hopkins, 1948), 99.

255. For Pevsner's discussion of Nicolas Boileau (1636–1711), see Pevsner, "Genesis of the Picturesque" (note 3), 140.

256*. {**Spence, *l.c.*, p. 9 c. 1728–30.**} Spence, *Anecdotes* (note 34), 9.

257*. {**ed. Boyd, p. 474.**} Kames, *Elements of Criticism* [1863] (note 115), 474.

258*. {**Essays, vol. II, p. 185.**} Price, *Essays on the Picturesque* (note 113), 2:185.

259*. {**ib., p. 188.**} Price, *Essays on the Picturesque* (note 113), 2:188.

260*. {**ib, p. 194.**} Price, *Essays on the Picturesque* (note 113), 2:194.

261*. {**ib. p. 195.**} Price, *Essays on the Picturesque* (note 113), 2:195.

262*. {**ib. p. 352.**} Price, *Essays on the Picturesque* (note 113), 2:352.

263*. {***Fragments on the Theory of Landscape Gardening,* 1807, ed. Loudon, p. 428.**} Humphry Repton, *Observations on the Theory and Practice of Landscape Gardening…*, 2nd ed. (London: printed by T. Bensley for J. Taylor, 1805), 428.

264*. {***Theory and Practice of Landscape Gardening,* 1805, ed. Loudon, p. 255.**} Repton, *Landscape Gardening* [1805] (note 263), 255.

265*. {***Enquiry,* p. 199.**} Knight, *An Analytical Inquiry* (note 244), 198–99.

266*. {**ib. p. 157.**} Knight, *An Analytical Inquiry* (note 244), 156–57.

267*. {***Essays,* vol. I, p. 197.**} Price, *Essays on the Picturesque* (note 113), 1:197.

268*. {**ib., vol. II, p. 236.**} Price, *Essays on the Picturesque* (note 113), 2:236.

269*. {***Works of Architecture,* Part I, 1773.**} <**Quote from my Hussey Extract p. 11.**> Note referring to Pevsner's notes from Hussey, *The Picturesque* (note 3), 189–90. This section of the text bears a heavy resemblance to Nikolaus Pevsner's article "The Picturesque in Architecture," *RIBA Journal* 55 (1947): 57.

270*. {***Works,* ed. Malone, 1809, vol. II, p. 139.**} Reynolds, *Works* (note 156), 2:139–40.

271*. <**Reyn on Vanbrugh.**> <**see Malone.**> Notes in pencil. Although Pevsner did not indicate exactly which passages he was referring to, the quotations below are those pertaining to Vanbrugh from Reynolds's *Thirteenth Discourse,* which are also partially cited by Hussey, and which Pevsner himself had transcribed.

272. Reynolds, *Works* (note 156), 2:138.

273. Reynolds, *Works* (note 156), 2:140–41. See also Hussey, *The Picturesque* (note 3), 192–93.

274*. <**genius 1st class…rough jewel.**> Note for insertion of text. <**Quote from Book at RIBA.**> The following quotation is from Hussey, presumably Pevsner's source; see Hussey, *The Picturesque* (note 3), 190.

275*. {***Essays,* vol. II, p. 212–214.**} Price, *Essays on the Picturesque* (note 113), 2:212–14.

276*. {***Enquiry,* pp. 179–180.**} Knight, *An Analytical Inquiry* (note 244), 179–80.

277. Both of these buildings, and indeed much of the text that follows, are discussed comprehensively in "Appendix One" of Pevsner's lengthy article on Richard Payne Knight; see Pevsner, "Richard Payne Knight" (note 3), 311.

278. Although Pevsner offered no citation for this quotation, it can be found in a letter from Walpole published in Stephen Gwynn, *The Life of Horace Walpole* (London: Thorton Butterworth, 1932), 148.

279*. {**See N. Pevsner: Richard Payne Knight, *The Art Bulletin,* ___. This paper has an appendix in which the early history of picturesque buildings is traced in more detail.**} Pevsner, "Richard Payne Knight" (note 3).

280*. <**Quote p. 160.**> Note in pencil. Knight, *An Analytical Inquiry* (note 244), 160.

281*. <Fortresses...mellow by time and neglect, lichens etc.> Note for insertion of text. See Knight, *An Analytical Inquiry* (note 244), 161.

282*. {Essays, vol. I, pp. 52, 54.} Price, *Essays on the Picturesque* (note 113), 1:52, 53.

283*. {Price, vol. II, p. 266.} Price, *Essays on the Picturesque* (note 113), 2:265–66.

284*. <Symmetry...Knight Enq. 172...conventions.> Note in pencil. Knight, *An Analytical Inquiry* (note 244), 172. Pevsner also intended to include a note here, most of which is illegible: <Footnote: —— Really an —— attack on Got Baroque revival —— Then Price piquant = picturesque.>

285*. {ib., p. 162.} Knight, *An Analytical Inquiry* (note 244), 162.

286. As discussed in the introduction to this volume, Pevsner's assessment is not strictly correct, as there are occasions on which Price did write on the subject of village planning. Refer, for example, to Price, *Essays on the Picturesque* (note 113), 2:312–14.

287*. {Vol. II, pp. 172–173.} Price, *Essays on the Picturesque* (note 113), 2:171–72, 173.

288*. {p. 125.} Whately, *Observations* [1793] (note 116), 125.

289*. {p. 121.} Whately, *Observations* [1793] (note 116), 121.

290*. <The forms and turnings...disgust.> Note for insertion of text. {*Works*, ed. Malone, vol II, p. 140.} Reynolds, *Works* (note 156), 2:140.

291*. <It is commonly...front.> Note for insertion of text. {*Theory and Practice*, ed. Loudon, p. 149.} Repton, *Landscape Gardening* [1805] (note 263), 149. <Say how sometime.> Note in pencil following the quotation.

292*. <At exactly the same time Repton was in practice/IV —— that of landscape in town / how that next part begins.> Note in pencil.

Editorial Introduction to Part III

Although Pevsner began work on Part III of *Visual Planning,* it appears that no draft or running text was ever written. What follows is an assemblage of texts based on the consultation and interpretation of Pevsner's notes and published works on the subject of visual planning, the greater context of which is discussed in the introduction to this volume. In this sense, Part III is not a reconstruction, which would be problematic given Pevsner's own equivocation on the exact content for this part. Instead, the text is presented as a florilegium, Pevsner's favored method for Part II and for other articles on the picturesque and its important personalities. This mode of presentation consists entirely of block quotations strung together in sequence, often with a heading to frame the text. Points raised within the text are underscored by a series of illustrations and captions, several of which Pevsner had marked for publication or had published previously within the cited articles. Where available, captions have been quoted verbatim. The following selection of passages, by its very nature, can only approximate what Pevsner may have intended for this part. Although editorial intervention has been kept to a minimum, the lectures, talks, papers, and articles from which the quotations are drawn were originally prepared for a number of purposes and a variety of audiences; as such, the editor has intervened occasionally to reduce repetition and ensure a coherent presentation.

NOTE TO THE READER

Square brackets, [ ], indicate an editorial intervention.

Notes with an asterisk, e.g., [43]*, contain an endnote that accompanied the excerpt in its original published form. Within the endnotes, Pevsner's endnotes appear in bold type, whereas notes by this volume's editor appear in plain type.

Paragraphs set in italic indicate material added by the editor to make the narrative coherent.

Le point géometral est unique, les autres sont infinis en nombre. Donc il faut failte les monuments non en prévision de ce point unique, mais bien en vie de ces points multiples.
— Viollet-le-Duc. *Letters*, published in 1902

Symmetrical arrangement is more ready to the hand of the unskilled than the harmonious arrangement of differences and unlikeness.
— C. F. A. Voysey, "On Town Planning," *AR* 46 (1919)[1]

PART III,

occasionally submitting solutions

History: Gardens and Landscaping

GARDENESQUE[2]

> Consult the genius of the place in all
> That tells the waters or to rise or fall
> Or helps th'ambitious hill the heavens to scale
> Or scoops in circling theatres the vale...
> Calls in the country, catches opening glades,
> Joins willing woods, and varies shades from shades.

These lines [from Alexander Pope] are a programme of improvements typical of what eighteenth-century landowners did to their grounds. They hardly ever extended the principles of their improvements beyond them. There is in addition the occasional eighteenth-century model village, an old village rebuilt because it had been in the way of some picturesque vista, and there are occasional remarks in the books on village design. On the town there is to all intents and purposes nothing.

The Picturesque entered the town not in urban terms. About 1800 the first squares of London were landscaped—exclaves of the country in the town.[3*] They were welcomed as wholesome and attractive, and they took up, in fact, though not consciously, an old and eminently English tradition of the cathedral towns. The English cathedral stands in a close, that is a precinct, originally as a churchyard turfed and tree-planted, and later landscaped.[4*] No greater contrast can be imagined than that[,] say[,] between the surroundings of Strassburg and Salisbury Cathedrals. The landscaped square became the hall-mark of early-nineteenth-century London, and when in 1825 George IV decided to make Buckingham House his London

114 and 115. *Royal Palaces*. The Louvre, wholly urban and with formal parterres, and Buckingham Palace, a country house in its grounds transported into the metropolis. 116 and 117. Even the English cathedral in its precinct has often acquired a landscape setting. John Constable's *Salisbury Cathedral*, 1823, Victoria and Albert Museum, and a photograph of Salisbury Cathedral.

170

171

Fig. 18. Spread from Nikolaus Pevsner, *The Englishness of English Art* (London: Architectural, 1956), 170–71, showing royal palaces. Left: The Louvre, wholly urban and with formal parterres, and Buckingham Palace, a country house in its grounds transported into the metropolis. Even the English cathedral in its precinct has often acquired a landscape setting. Right: John Constable's *Salisbury Cathedral* (1823; Victoria and Albert Museum), and a photograph of Salisbury Cathedral

palace, he (and his architect John Nash) did not build a metropolitan palace like the Louvre or the palaces of Berlin, Rome (the Quirinal), Stockholm (in spite of the water in front), [or] Madrid, but a country house with a spreading facade. The facade known to Londoners is of course an early-twentieth-century addition by Sir Aston Webb and with the *rond-point* in front of it more Parisian than Londonian in spirit. The real front of the Palace faces west, that is[,] faces a spacious lawn, winding paths, and a serpentine lake with an island.

Fig. 18

NINETEENTH-CENTURY LANDSCAPED SQUARES

Pevsner thought that the introduction and proliferation of gardens and the garden aesthetic in urban areas was a significant result of the picturesque on urban sensibilities. His notes reveal section headings intended for Part III with such titles as "Landscaping of Squares" and "The Vict[orian] Age (Pict Arch and Gardenesque Parks)." Here Pevsner listed several areas in London he thought significant in this trend, including St. James's Park, Green Park, Hyde Park, the Victoria Park, Kensington Gardens, along with cemeteries and other public squares, for which he had taken extensive notes from John Claudius Loudon.[5] Pevsner also pointed to the Ladbroke area as a good example of this mixture of landscaping and housing in nineteenth-century London and commissioned numerous photographs to be taken for a tour, much in the manner of those for Part I.[6] Much of the material contained in Pevsner's notes for Part III reveals that he equivocated to a considerable degree not only on the exact content for this part but also on exactly how direct the application of the picturesque as a series of landscape-gardening techniques could be. He noted the application of the ha-ha as a planning device and likened trees in a landscape to spires in a city. Additionally, Pevsner compared the view of a landscape to the skyline and texture of a city.[7]

Fig. 19

Fig. 19. Lansdowne Crescent, Ladbroke Grove, London

GARDENS IN THE CITY[8]

When I first looked at all these things, I was struck by certain principles which seemed to exist behind them. There are two movements in this country, and two only, which have influenced the whole world. One is the picturesque movement, the landscape movement, or the eighteenth century, and the other is the Garden City and Garden Suburb movement of thirty to forty years ago....

All that refers to landscape, but the question is, is it applicable to towns?

[A]bout the year 1800, an attempt was made to apply these tenets or dogmas to the towns, and a hundred years later, about 1900, a second attempt was made. The result of the first attempt was the landscape square. The square was originally a piece of formal planning, but it became, round about 1800, a piece of picturesque, romantic planning. The result of the second attempt to introduce the picturesque into the town was the Garden Suburb and Garden City.

Fig. 20

Both these movements, however, seem to me to be only an escape. The square established, as it were, a hedgehog of picturesque planning inside a town, leaving the town to itself otherwise. The Garden City, in that sense, is worse; it gives up the town as a bad job altogether, and creates model villages or model towns instead; it does not deal with the city problem as such. Bath, however, was on a small scale a city problem and city solution. There is a possibility of applying this informal planning to city problems, but if we want to derive maximum benefit from Price's principles we must apply them as principles, and not take over such actual objects as the picturesque cottage or the landscape square, or at least not excessively.

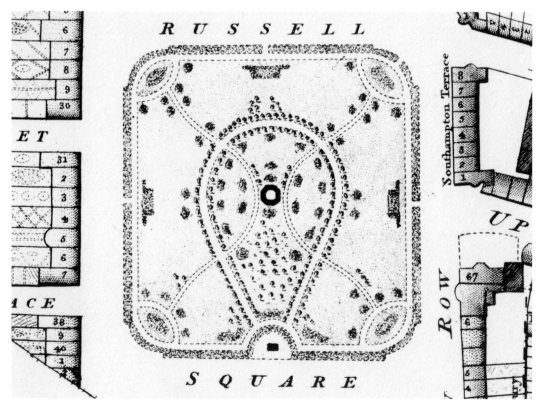

Fig. 20. Russell Square, London. Most likely the landscape design by Humphry Repton, ca. 1800

History: Architecture and Building[9]

NINETEENTH-CENTURY PICTURESQUE BUILDING[10]

With all these [eighteenth-century picturesque] buildings, however, we have stayed in the country. The conquest of the town by picturesque architecture is, I think, a 19th-century contribution. We cannot follow the stages here in detail, but I think we can safely say that when Sir Charles Barry put on paper his preliminary ideas for the Houses of Parliament, we see those criteria which we have so far applied first to landscape and then to building in landscape, applied to what is strictly a problem of building in a town.

Fig. 21

Once that had been achieved, it became the hall-mark of a great deal of Victorian architecture. St. Pancras Station is one of many examples. I mention a Scott example, because Scott, in his book on Domestic Architecture in 1858, suggests that in building houses in a town different from the abominable houses in Gower Street and Baker Street, you should "have a few houses on one scale and a few on another, some higher than others, a group with gabled fronts and another with parapets and dormers, with some little touch of system, though chiefly arranged with a view to varied wants."[11] Two things are interesting there. One is the plea for "some little touch of system," because, thinking in terms of Oxford Street, it would be difficult to admit even that little touch of system. The other is the remark about the arrangement of these fronts "with a view to varied wants"—i.e., function or fitness for purpose.

As the 19th century went on, the picturesque became the accepted idiom for the individual building, but not much beyond that. Individual buildings were in some cases of very subtle composition. I say that unhesitatingly about Philip Webb's Red House, which he built for William Morris in 1859, and which has the qualities of variation, interesting texture, and boldness in the mixing of the motives, all things that belong to the picturesque style, without ever abandoning

NEW PALACE AT WESTMINSTER.

VIEW, FROM THE SOUTH-EAST, OF SIR CHARLES BARRY'S PROPOSED ADDITIONAL BUILDINGS ON THE SITE OF THE PRESENT COURTS OF LAW, AND ENCLOSING NEW PALACE YARD.

Fig. 21. Engraving of the Houses of Parliament, designed by Charles Barry

the needs of the client, William Morris. Again, if you look at the work of Norman Shaw, you will find the deliberate avoidance of symmetry, breaking of the sky-line, variety in the gables, and so on.[12] That kind of subtle grouping the age itself would, I think, have called picturesque. In Eastlake's "Gothic Revival" (1873) he speaks of "that uneven distribution of parts which is at once necessary to convenience and the cause of picturesque composition."[13]

It is very interesting to note how in the course of the 19th century, in the work of Pugin and then of other writers, we find this equation of what we call functional and they called convenience, with the arguments of purely visual quality.[14] That is specially interesting in the light of what happened at the end of the 19th and right on into the 20th century. There was then a tendency, of which the London County Hall is an instance, to abandon what the 19th century had done in terms of picturesque architecture in favour of a return to monumental formality and symmetry. In the case of County Hall this attempt can hardly be called successful. For here we have a facade with a central colonnaded motif to which no axis leads on the other bank of the river, and there is even a kitchen behind part of the colonnade. In domestic architecture also there was a return to something more formal, as a reaction against the work of such men as Voysey and Baillie-Scott. However, in the case of buildings at Welwyn, at Wythenshawe and in other garden cities, garden suburbs and intelligently laid out housing estates, there is again, as there was in the 18th century, a deliberate contrast between the formality of the small-scale architecture and the relief which is given by trees.

TWENTIETH-CENTURY PICTURESQUE BUILDING[15]

[T]he "real determinants" of planning are exactly the forces which have brought to the front the valid argument in favour of the Picturesque in the twentieth century. [...] If one looks at the works of the pioneers of twentieth-century architecture, say as early as about 1925, Gropius's *Bauhaus* at Dessau or better still Le Corbusier's Stuttgart houses of 1927 and his Centrosoyus project of 1929, what are their aesthetic qualities? First those that everyone is familiar with; cubic shapes, no mouldings, large openings and so on. But, in addition, [...] a mixture of materials, synthetic and natural, rough and smooth, and, beyond that, the free planning of a whole quarter, with [...] differentiation of vehicular traffic and pedestrian ways, with interaction between landscape and building (the tree inside the Pavillon de l'Esprit Nouveau), and between buildings of different shapes and heights. Do not these qualities define the difference between the free exercise of the imagination stimulated by the disciplines of function and technique (e.g., Wright's "in the nature of materials") and academic rule of thumb, within whose strait-jacket architecture was confined before the modern movement set it free? And do they not show that, albeit unconsciously, the modern revolution of the early twentieth century and the Picturesque revolution of a hundred years before had all their fundamentals in common? The qualities of the modern movement were not developed to please the eye, but because without them no workable, no functioning, no functional architecture is possible in our age. Impose symmetry, impose axiality and grids, impose rules even where the artist is feeling his way, and you reduce usefulness. Le Corbusier was already following the new principles in the years in which Mr. Hussey wrote *The Picturesque* (1927)[16] and Sir Kenneth Clark *The Gothic Revival* (1928).[17] The two events had superficially nothing to do with each other, and only some years later, in the [*Architectural*] *Review,* was it argued that no other existing aesthetic theory fits the demands of modern architecture and planning so well as that of Price and Knight.

Fig. 22

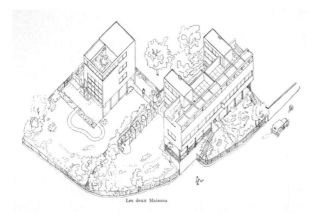

Les deux Maisons

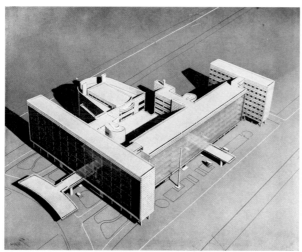

Fig. 22. Above: Le Corbusier's two houses at Stuttgart, 1927. Below: His Centrosoyus project, Moscow, 1929

History: Town Planning and Urban Design

EIGHTEENTH-CENTURY PLANNING[18]

"Their greatest reach of imagination is employed in contriving figures where the beauty shall be great, and strike the eye, but without any order or disposition of parts, that shall be commonly or easily observed,... and where they find it... they say the Sharawaggi is fine or is admirable, or any such expression of esteem." Sir William Temple is writing of the Chinese, but every word of what he says could equally well be applied to the subtle art of conscious or unconscious visual planning in our own country between 1720 and 1820. It is, alas, a lost art now, and one that must be recovered if the reconstructed England of after the war is not to be a dead place to live in—whether it be killed by academic or by Utopian specifics.

Frenchay Common, near Bristol, is one of hundreds of Georgian commons. **Fig. 23** It was never planned; size and disposition of houses were caused by conditions of property, very old, one can assume, and quite accidental. The fact that the aesthetic outcome of this process of growth is so curiously attractive, at least to the English eye, is equally accidental. But it is no less real for that reason.

It can be studied by the contemporary planner in the spirit in which he would study a specially happy configuration of, say, hills, a river and groups of trees—simply as a study in pattern. [...] But the value of a Georgian ensemble ought to be considered not only on the merit of its individual parts but also on those of composition.

Frenchay Common *or workaday sharawagg*

The photographs were taken by Dell & Wainwright, the plan was drawn by Mr. J. W. Tanner. More information on Frenchay can be found in the late C. H. B. Elliott's Winterbourne, Bristol (1936).

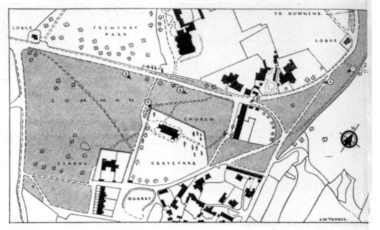

" Their greatest reach of imagination is employed in contriving figures where the beauty shall be great, and strike the eye, but without any order or disposition of parts, that shall be commonly or easily observed, . . . and where they find it . . . they say the Sharawaggi is fine or is admirable, or any such expression of esteem." Sir William Temple is writing of the Chinese, but every word of what he says could equally well be applied to the subtle art of conscious or unconscious visual planning in our own country between 1720 and 1820. It is, alas, a lost art now, and one that must be recovered if the reconstructed England of after the war is not to be a dead place to live in—whether it be killed by academic or by Utopian specifics.

Frenchay Common, near Bristol, is one of hundreds of Georgian commons. It was never planned ; size and disposition of houses were caused by conditions of property, very old, one can assume, and quite accidental. The fact that the æsthetic outcome of this process of growth is so curiously attractive, at least to the English eye, is equally accidental. But it is no less real for that reason.

It can be studied by the contemporary planner in the spirit in which he would study a specially happy configuration of, say, hills, a river and groups of trees—simply as a study in pattern. That, in addition, it holds a message to those watchful for the preservation of Britain's beauty spots need hardly be added. Georgian building does not fall under our outdated scheduling system. Of individual houses there may indeed be so many that to protect all of them would mean paralysing all planning. But the value of a Georgian ensemble ought to be considered not only on the merit of its individual parts but also on those of its composition. In the case of squares that has gradually become an accepted principle. Knock down one house and replace it by a tall office building, and the whole square is valueless. That the same applies to the loose grouping of a Common cannot be said too emphatically. Knock down one tree and everything may change its significance. This subtle correlation between objects, architectural and otherwise, on an English Common is indicated on this and the following pages by means of a conducted tour.

1 The Common is approached from the north, that is from Downend. Pas one of the lodges of the Frenchay Park Estate—the other lodge lies away i the west, near the main road—we get a first glance of the cluster of hous connecting the outer with the inner Common. The picture is dominated by magnificent sycamore. The tree sets the scale. Houses—all of approximatel the same height—keep to about two-fifths of the height of the tree. .The churc spire to the left, instinctively assumed to be taller than trees, gives a feeling distance to come, as one approaches the houses and a gap between them hardl yet recognisable. Note the contrasts in texture (from right to left) of hedg stone wall, brick wall and iron fence of the four nearest houses. Note also th outlandish cedar and cypress trees, young and sheltered in the first garden.

2 Now we approach this same group of houses. The elements of the compositi are now the rectangle of walls as a background to the two sycamores—the turn out to be two, not one. The main house, " Frenchay House," with its bro bay window, is all covered with ivy, dark against the cream front on the right a the fawn pedimented front on the left. The iron fence, with its wooden boardi behind, adds an oddly modern note. This whole set of façades lies on the be of the road. Following it we are drawn towards the dark hollow on the left, t chasm through which we have to pass if we want to reach the church and t open common beyond.

26

Fig. 23. Plan and photographs of Frenchay Common, near Bristol, showing key locations of Pevsner's early photographic tour

PICTURESQUE VILLAGES

Pevsner's notes for Part III indicate that he intended to continue the historical portrayal of early-nineteenth-century planning with the contribution of Nash and the picturesque village of Blaise Hamlet (1811) and later villages constructed from the then-popular pattern books, such as Edensor.[19] Pevsner identified these two projects for inclusion as the significant examples of early-nineteenth-century picturesque town-planning. Due to the unavailability of an appropriate text for this part, the reader is referred to two of Pevsner's early articles relating to the subject, both published in Architectural Review *under his pseudonym Peter F. R. Donner before the* Visual Planning *manuscript was begun. The first is "The End of the Pattern-Books"; the second, "Edensor or Brown Comes True."[20]*

ENGLISH PLANNING AFTER THE INDUSTRIAL REVOLUTION[21]

England suffered from the blight of bad land-use earlier than other European countries, because she had undergone the Industrial Revolution earlier than others, and because her faith in tolerance on the one hand, in private enterprise on the other, had prevented her from checking the fatal effects on the appearance of towns of the rapid growth of industry and urban population. When the reaction came about 1870–1912, (and it came earlier than on the Continent too), it took characteristically enough the form of a return to the Picturesque, and quite understandably it looked to the picturesque practice as much as, or more than, to the picturesque principles. So the result—a result to be proud of—was the garden suburb and then the garden city. They succeeded in the blending of small-size housing with nature and the application of the principle of variety to the layout of streets, the provision of footpaths and so on. But they failed in not being truly urban.

NINETEENTH-CENTURY PLANNING IN ENGLAND[22]

The contention that the sudden fall in the European importance of English architecture really took place shortly after 1900 is [...] confirmed by the development of townplanning.

In the planning of estates, especially garden estates, called garden cities or garden suburbs, England was ahead during the second half of the nineteenth century. From the fifties [...] the beginnings of modern planning of workmen's flats and small workmen's houses can be traced. [...T]he first planned estates of small houses [were due] to progressive manufacturers (Saltaire, Sir Titus Salt, begun in 1853). The earliest estate of friendly, middle-class houses was erected at Bedford Park, London, through the initiative of J. T. Carr (1875 and following years);[23] [...] Shortly after Bedford Park, Port Sunlight and Bournville were started, both garden estates for members of the staff of a big firm.[24] Port Sunlight was built for Lever's from 1888 on, Bourneville for Cadbury's from 1895 on.

The idea of the independent garden city was put forward by Ebenezer Howard in his famous book *Garden Cities of To-morrow* (1898).[25] It was taken up by the founders of Letchworth. The plan of this garden city (begun in 1904) is due to R. Unwin and B. Parker. The same architects are responsible for the layout of the Hampstead Garden Suburb (1907).

These English estates strongly influenced the Continent. Krupp's started their first workers' estate in 1891. The first independent garden city in Germany, Hellerau, near Dresden, was begun in 1909[....]

Burnham in Chicago began the movement for the erection of monumental Civic Centres in the United States, a movement that conquered England after

1900. In Germany, Camillo Sitte's book *Der Städtebau* (1889)[26] pleaded against the hollow grandeur of Neo-Baroque squares and roads, and proposed picturesque arrangements of medievalising buildings around irregular squares. Both Sitte and Burnham still thought in terms of individual pieces of architecture.

NINETEENTH-CENTURY PLANNING: SITTE AND VISUAL PLANNING[27]

Sitte teaches something that still needs as much emphasis today as it did in the last century. He teaches visual planning as opposed to drawing-board planning, and the informal as opposed to uniformity and regimentation. His technique in putting across his message on the other hand is still that of the nineteenth century. He goes to the past, to the Middle Ages and Renaissance, chiefly in Italy, shows how certain principles were successfully developed, and then recommends the adoption of the same principles to his own contemporaries. His analysis of Italian city squares is superb, sensitive and observant of effects lost on most spectators, including architects. His knowledge of European towns is startling too. He uses Brescia, Autun, Stettin and Boolswert with equal familiarity, and the only deeply regrettable thing is that he evidently never had an opportunity to travel in England. What splendid examples he would have found in Oxford and Cambridge or at Bath.

The outcome of his analyses of fourteenth to sixteenth century squares is the proof that before the Baroque (Sitte uses the word already in our sense) symmetry was the one thing carefully avoided.

It is indeed his *bête noire*. "The notion of symmetry," he writes, "is propagating itself today like the spread of an epidemic. The least cultivated are familiar with it, and each one feels called upon to have his say about the involved artistic matters" (p. 32).[28] In the first half of the book the placing of buildings and monuments in relation to squares (never in their centre), the entry of streets into squares, and the grouping of squares (Piazza della Signoria Florence, Piazza and Piazzetta Venice, etc.) are discussed.

After that conclusions are drawn for our own time. The first of these is that "the vitality of the glorious old models should inspire us to something other than fruitless imitation" (p. 72). There are some other equally important No's following this first: warnings against "forced spontaneity" in irregular, accidental-looking layouts (p. 72), and against the assumption that accident on its own will ever lead to aesthetically valuable results (p. 82). Even more surprising in its topicality are the warnings against the replacement of individual creation in planning by "public administration . . . with official discipline" (p. 82), and the plea that before starting to plan a district[,] surveys are needed of future uses, probable population development, historic buildings worth preserving and public buildings required.

TWENTIETH-CENTURY PLANNING: UNWIN AND VISUAL PLANNING[29]

Town Planning in Practice by Sir Raymond Unwin [. . .] was every student's textbook, from the time when it first appeared in 1907 until a few years after the second war.[30] [. . .] There are two reasons for this eclipse. Unwin had become for the new young the label for garden city and garden suburb exclusively, and they wanted to hear of true urban planning. To satisfy this demand architects of the generation between Unwin's and that of the students of about 1950 and after provided new books: Thomas Sharp his Pelican already in 1940 (before the Scott and the Uthwatt Reports and the Abercrombie and Forshaw plan for London),[31] Frederick Gibberd his *Town Design* in 1953,[32] Gordon Logie his *Urban Scene* in

1954.[33] In addition the townscape policy of the *Architectural Review* made itself felt, with its plea for informal visual planning, for the *genius loci,* for controlled accident and for intricacy, surprise and the other categories of the Picturesque in the English eighteenth century. Some key features were *Sharawaggi* (January 1944),[34] the Precinct of St. Paul's (June 1955)[35] and *Westminster Regained* (November 1947).[36] The Festival of Britain of 1951 demonstrated this townscape policy in action, and it has in certain respects become the official policy of the Ministry of Housing and Local Government, as their current manuals and guides show.[37]

I had recently occasion for historical reasons to go back to *Town Planning in Practice,* and this re-reading was a surprise indeed. Unwin was no doubt a visual planner par excellence, even if he remained a practical man as well and could write with conviction: "Drainage will not run uphill to suit the prettiest plan" (p. 140). But there is in his book already an illustration of the plan of the Oxford High and a sequence of shots to illustrate how the various vistas follow each other—in fact the Sharp device of his *Oxford Replanned* of 1948.[38] Unwin's sources for performances of this kind are known, he never concealed them: Sitte's *Der Städtebau* of 1889 republished in America—which is symptomatic—as recently as 1945,[39] and Stübben's *Der Städtebau* of 1907.[40] Sitte had been made known to England by T. C. Horsfall in 1904,[41] and that is how Unwin first heard of him, i.e., after he had planned Letchworth. Sitte deals chiefly with *places,* as Unwin called them, in medieval towns, the lessons to be learnt from their seemingly arbitrary irregularities, varied building lines, blocked vistas, general sense of enclosure, and asymmetrical placing of incidents. Unwin took all that over, even if he mostly exemplifies it in terms of the village, the suburb and the small country town. But there it is all the same, and a Florilegium can serve to reintroduce a great visual planner.

"Town Planning to be successful must be the outgrowth of the circumstances of the site and the requirements of the inhabitants" ([p.] 138). "The designer's first duty, then, must be to study his town, his site, the people and their requirements" ([p.] 140). "A City Survey"—Geddes is here acknowledged (*City Development,* 1904)[42]—"should be prepared before a plan of new development is made.... The city which seeks to design its future developments must...know itself" for the sake of "the preservation of its individuality of character (in) its enlarged self" ([p.] 146).

"Many ancient towns derive exceptional beauty from their enclosure by ramparts or walls.... To this is due the absence of that irregular fringe of ...half-spoiled country which form such a hideous girdle around modern growing towns." ([p.] 154). "Many of the old unhealthy slums are, from the point of view of picturesqueness and beauty, infinitely more attractive than the vast, ugly, dreary districts growing up around our big towns" ([p.] 4). "We should secure some orderly line up to which the country and town may each extend and stop definitely" ([p.] 163), for "it is not an easy matter to combine the charms of town and country; the attempt has often led...to the destruction of the beauty of both" ([p.] 164). So what it needed is "areas...closely built upon, surrounded by other of open spaces...rather than scattering our buildings and spaces" ([p.] 164). Unfortunately, however, the planner in practice must find solutions "which do not clash with strong prejudices on the part of the future householders. This will often lead to a greater degree of openness...than from a purely architectural point of view might be desirable" ([p.] 293). Readers of the [*Architectural*] *Review* will here remember comments made on New Town prairie planning.[43]

Illus. 98.—An imaginary irregular town.

Illus. 157.—Buttstedt, View from Standpoint H on plan.

Illus. 266.—Imaginary sketch of village scene where the buildings are square with each other on a road curving as shown on Illus. 265.

Fig. 24. Three illustrations from Raymond Unwin, *Town Planning in Practice*. Top: an imaginary irregular town. Middle: view of Buttstedt—a German town analyzed in detail. Bottom: an imaginary village where the buildings are square with each other on a curving road

There are other aspects of this plea for enclosure which go beyond the domestic. Buildings in general, including cathedrals and town-halls "are not seen to best advantage when seen in isolation" ([p.] 198). It is only when we are enabled…to measure them by their relation to and contrast with the (surrounding) houses, that we realize the full splendour of their dimensions ([p.] 207). Here for the readers of the [*Architectural*] *Review* Sir William Holford's precincts of St. Paul's will come to mind.[44]

Exactly as remarkable are Unwin's remarks on the contrived accident which is what Sitte and he were advocating. Unwin writes: "The town-planner must be on his guard against the supposition that it is easy to design accidents" ([p.] 260). Much as we admire the irregular *places* of medieval towns, "it must not be thought that any open space is a true *place,* or that, because successful places are formed of all kinds of irregular shapes…any shape will do" ([p.] 194).

Indeed, and here we begin to move away from Unwin the topical to Unwin the man of his moment, *Town Planning in Practice* is not entirely devoted to the praises of the irregular and the informal. The book—as the actual plans of Letchworth and the Hampstead Garden Suburb, as laid out by Parker and Unwin, confirm—is not a wholly anti-formal book. It advocates a *juste milieu.* Straight roads are reasonable as the main thoroughfares for direct access and to make it easy to grasp the principal pattern of a town ([p.] 112), but between them must be intimate narrow lanes and pedestrian passages ([p.] 208). So Unwin draws in one case ([p.] 253) a set of regular road junctions and contrasts them with irregular ones from German Sitte-esque town-plans to show that the visual advantages in both cases can be the same.

Fig. 24

But that comment refers to town centres only, and Unwin was, there can be no doubt, essentially a planner of residential areas. C. P. Wade's pretty drawings to *Town Planning in Practice* are drawings of cottages, of small towns, small *places,* nothing over two storeys. When Unwin speaks of suburbs he does not mean Bloomsbury. He says: "There may be said to be two styles of work: the picturesque and formal or symmetrical.… To the picturesque style of architecture irregularity of site and lack of symmetry in arrangement offer no difficulty. English domestic architecture very largely belongs to this class" ([p.] 368). So that leaves the Georgian century clean out and that more than anything else made students turn away from Unwin's book after the last war and forget a great all-rounder in urbanism.

TWENTIETH-CENTURY PLANNING[45]

At the beginning as well as at the end of the pedigree of [modern estate planning] stands—as in many other aspects of twentieth-century architecture—the great and elusive figure of Le Corbusier, a stimulus as well as a danger.

Fig. 25

His *ville contemporaine* of 1922 established the vision of twenty-four identical skyscrapers rising above uniform lower blocks. The layout is rigidly formal and symmetrical, a Versailles for the three million people of a twentieth-century city. Only parks and gardens are treated freely and picturesquely, but, it seems, without much attention or gusto. The *plan voisin* of 1925 has more of that, at least in the perspectives, but the general rigidity remains in spite of the fact that now this absolutist pattern was to be imposed on the centre of Paris. No compromise of existing features and new features is tolerated. In a later more concrete planning scheme, that for Nemours of 1935, Le Corbusier used in addition about twenty high slabs in staggered tiers.

Meanwhile Sweden had started from the other end. The Co-op estate on the

Fig. 25. Page from Nikolaus Pevsner, "Roehampton: LCC Housing and the Picturesque Tradition," *AR* 126 (1959): 22

island of Kvarnholm near Stockholm planned by Olaf Thunström in 1927, was informal, sympathetic to the rock and pine landscape and combined mill, elevators and different types of housing in a happy *ensemble*. Whether Gropius and Maxwell Fry knew of this when, in 1935, they made their plan for an Isokon estate at St. Leonard's Hill near Windsor is not recorded. It does not seem necessary to assume it; for the *genius loci* of England certainly acted with vigour on Gropius, and the idea of a picturesque English estate endowed with modern instead of Palladian blocks might well have appeared independently.[46*] The buildings here are two eight- or nine-storeyed slabs and one lower range at right angles. That the AA boys who put forward their splendid and astonishing scheme for Faringdon in 1938[47*] had studied Gropius's project goes without saying. Theirs is larger, more varied and remarkably prophetic with its mixed arrangement of high and low ranges and its intelligent use of the landscape elements of the site. [...]

In the years between Kvarnholm and St. Leonard's Hill, in 1932–33, Baudouin and Lods had built their bleak estate of fifteen-storeyed point-blocks and three-storeyed blocks at La Muette, Drancy—an estate of 1,200 flats—and in Holland J. F. Staal had erected a single point-block at Amsterdam[48*] and van Tijen, Brinkman and van der Vlugt a single high slab at Rotterdam.[49*] The point-block as such was not innovation, nor was the high slab. Dr. Sekler in his excellent little book on *Das Punkthaus*[50*] very prettily traces the conception back to Chambord and illustrates an eight-storeyed point-block by Hoeger of Hamburg dated 1911. High blocks of flats go back even in England at least as far as Queen Anne's Mansions in London with its fourteen storeys (1876–88 by E. R. Robson of the London Board Schools), and high slabs—still in severely parallel lines—were Gropius's recommendation at the CIAM Congress of 1930.[51*]

During the war these various themes were worked through with much intelligence and understanding in Sweden, one of the few countries in which building continued. Here, in 1942–45, amongst other things, the *parti* of clusters of point-blocks was developed. Among the earliest is Backström and Reinius's Danviksklippan. In these schemes architects learned to appreciate the effect of grouped skyscrapers arranged in an orderly, not a chaotic American, fashion. But not one of these wartime schemes in Sweden is on a really large scale.[52*] Yet one can be sure they form the principal inspiration for English work after the war.

Polemic

THE PICTURESQUE AND CONTEMPORARY ARCHITECTURE[53]

We have now almost reached the present day, and the problems of today in architecture and planning. [...] I feel, however, that some of you might [want] a few words on what I regard as topical application of what I have so far put to you entirely historically.

Let me say, first of all, that I do not regard the Picturesque as a patent medicine for all problems, or even for all the problems, all the ills, of today. It seems to me, however, that the functions of buildings have become infinitely more complex than they were right down to the early 19th century. It is not only that the architect has to build types of buildings of a kind that architects of repute never dreamed of before 1800, and that he has therefore to study different and complex functions for very many kinds of building, whereas up to 1800 the architect of repute was almost wholly a palace builder, a house builder or a church builder, with perhaps an occasional town hall thrown in. The more complex the function of a building becomes, the more difficult, I should think, must it become to impose on it a strict formality, a strict symmetry, all that smoothness and balance and harmony which rule out the Picturesque. Mind you, I don't say that they can't be imposed, but it becomes a very great thing if it is possible to impose them, and certainly much more of an effort nowadays than it ever was before.

I have also the feeling that, as the spirit of the age always tends to be reflected in its architecture, so the style and tempo of the life today, the style of our clothes and even of the letters we write, are of a more dynamic and a less formal and less leisurely kind, and that makes it even harder to impose a formality of the Roman kind or of the Palladian kind on architecture. That is why I am sure that the principles of the Picturesque in architecture have really a message today.

If I say picturesque architecture, I hope I need not add that does not mean arranging buildings asymmetrically and leaving all the rest to accident. Of course I agree with Uvedale Price's advice "to prefer impropriety to timid monotony," and even to prefer "the incongruous to the insipid." But that certainly does not mean that an architect should go out of his way to be improper or incongruous. I mention that because it is one of the arguments sometimes used against the possibilities of picturesque architecture today. If, however, you take the principles which were formulated a hundred and fifty years ago, the principles of variety, of intricacy, of the connection of the building with nature, of advance and recess, swelling and sinking, and of contrasts of texture, you will find that a great many of these principles are principles which you would apply to the idiom which has developed during the last twenty to thirty years. [...]

And one more thing: as in the 18th century so today these criteria apply not only to the individual building, but also to the problems of the connection of

Fig. 26. The *Architectural Review* plan by Gordon Cullen for the precinct of St. Paul's

buildings; that is, the problems of planning. The application there is, I think, really very complicated; but, from what little I know of the immense intricacies of these problems, I would think that such rigid and arbitrary solutions as those suggested by the Royal Academy plan of 1942 for London cannot really serve any useful purpose. If the circus at Hyde Park Corner has to be widened to a very considerable extent for traffic reasons, it really seems too easy and elementary just to duplicate the Hyde Park Corner screen and the Duke of Wellington's house. I do not think such application of the most primitive of ideas of balance, and so on, can work. In another plan of the Royal Academy the surroundings of the St. Paul's were re-designed with a duplication of the deanery on the other side of the cathedral.

As against this treatment of London planning problems I should like to refer to a plan worked out by the *Architectural Review* for the precincts of St. Paul's and published about a year ago.[54] It is not that I want to go into detail, or could do so, **Fig. 26** but it seems to me to be an example of a very useful and promising way in which the planner can proceed from what is necessary and functionally advisable—from such things as traffic necessities, the planning of special areas for special trades, the amenities of the pedestrian, and so on—to an attempt to create, by satisfying these needs, something which has a very great aesthetic interest, and something in which such principles as the variety of heights, and of levels, the blending of architecture with nature, the bringing in of an irregular, loose arrangement of landscape in conjunction with the very complicated pattern of traffic needs and the needs of users find an expression which tends to show that picturesque architecture has a very important function today. It is in that sense that I would plead it for today, not as the only existing type of architecture but as a type of architecture [. . .] which is neither a whim nor a romantic escape back to the 18th century but a sound policy, and the hard rather than the soft way of dealing with contemporary problems of architecture and planning.

TOWNSCAPE AND THE PICTURESQUE[55]

As this discovery [of the commonalities between the picturesque and modernism] was made, it became clear that it had a special application to planning in a town. Here the architect, instead of creating variety, has to achieve it by means of a mixture of what he finds on the site and has reasons to preserve, with what he designs himself. So the variety of shapes and materials within the individual building now grows into a larger variety of new and old elements within any one townscape.

That is what townscape meant, when the term was coined. To make townscape requires an architect wholly in sympathy with today, but at the same time sensitive to the character of a site and the character of what he finds standing on it when he starts.

Townscape is a word formed on the pattern of landscape.[56] If we speak of landscape we think first of all of a painting. A landscape painting is a piece of land seen through the artist's eye. He sees not only individual objects but the whole together under the aspect of its aesthetic values, or he may use objects not in reality together and compose them in such a way as to arrive at an aesthetically valuable whole. The same applies to townscape. Townscape is the whole of urban scenery [...] made especially so as to create an aesthetically valuable whole.

[I am] not going to deal with individual buildings or indeed with any aspects of planning except visual planning. That does not mean that I under-estimate the importance of the more usually remembered aspects of planning such as housing, slum clearance, traffic regulation, etc. They are indispensable, but visual planning is also indispensable, and if the whole of a town is in the end not visually pleasing, the town is not worth having. [...]

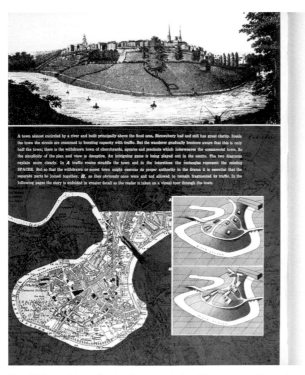

Fig. 27. Spread from Gordon Cullen, "Midland Experiment: Shrewsbury," *AR* 115 (1954): 322–23.

townscape manifesto

'If I were asked to define Townscape I would say that one building is architecture but two buildings is Townscape.'

    Gordon Cullen, *Prairie Planning in the New Towns*, Architectural Review, July, 1953.

'All the individual objects that we see in an urban scene are elements in town design, for they all influence the visual pictures, both by their appearance as single objects and by their appearance in juxtaposition with one another.'

    Frederick Gibberd, *Town Design*, 1953.

'Townscape aspires to practices more organic than was dreamed of by Victorian town-planning, which treated a town as a museum of separate exhibits, a lantern-slide lecture. The key to our modern conception of Townscape lies in the fact, the simple but surprising fact, that the items of the environment cannot be dissociated the one from the other. Further, the effects of juxtaposition are in themselves as exciting as the objects juxtaposed—often more so.'

    G. Cullen, *Immediacy*, Arch. Rev., April, 1953.

'The English genius has always lain in the production of harmony *in variety*. That has characterized our political and social life as well as our architectural forms throughout the long course of our history. And while in the last hundred years the physical expression of the native genius has been so vitiated that there was neither harmony nor variety in our town building, the genius is within us still if we care to give it again its freedom of expression.'

    Thomas Sharp, *English Panorama*, 1950.

'It may not be amiss for the architect to take advantage *sometimes* of that to which I am sure the painter ought always to have his eyes open, I mean the use of accidents; to follow when they lead, and to improve them, rather than always to trust to a regular plan . . .

'. . . Variety and intricacy is a beauty and excellence in every other of the arts which address the imagination; and why not in architecture?'

    Sir Joshua Reynolds, *Fifteen Discourses*.

'Consult the genius of the Place in all . . .' Alexander Pope, *Epistle to Lord Burlington*.

theory

A TOWN, LIKE A MAN, IS MORE THAN THE SUM OF ITS PARTS.

IT IS A PLACE WITH A PERSONALITY OF ITS OWN. This has always been known—The Romans gave this personality a name, *genius loci*.

TOWNSCAPE IS THE CONSCIOUS ART OF DEVELOPING THE CHARACTER OF A GIVEN PLACE.

IT IS THE COMPLETION OF THE TOWN PLANNING PROCESS, since it gives to the accumulated labours of all the other branches of town design—sociology, traffic circulation, industry, housing, hygiene—the face and bearing of a living organism.

ITS AIM IS TO ENHANCE THOSE QUALITIES, whether in a new town or one that has stood two thousand years— its problems include plumbing and refuse disposal but only as by-products of this higher organism, the emphasis here being on the body rather than its organs, the end-product not the by-product. A truism, but one that has been ignored for a century. All municipal officers today, however devoted, are specialists, exercised about the organs. No one worries about the end-product.

IN THE LAST RESORT ORGANS ARE WORTHLESS UNLESS THEY ADD UP TO A PLEASING END-PRODUCT. Wherever a town has personal qualities no matter what: contour topography, street pattern, colour, drama, nobility, cosiness, homeliness, surprise, intimacy, shock, anything that gives it individuality, the activities of the townscaper are flung into the battle of safeguarding, preserving, enhancing, developing them.

BUT HE DOES NOT WANT TO MAKE TOWNS INTO MUSEUMS—preservation is the fate of corpses, and townscape is concerned with living, bustling organisms that grow and change with the needs of their citizens. The universal standard object—be it motor-coach, traffic light or advertisement for a branded product—which has invaded the town

Fig. 28. "Townscape Manifesto," 1953 or 1954

As regards the planning of individual buildings, it is known that architects purely from the point of view of serving well-defined functions arrived at plans and elevations, which were not monumental in the old sense, that is symmetrical, but which consisted of groups of ranges or blocks composed in an informal, asymmetrical way. You can take as an early example in England the Impington Village College near Cambridge by Walter Gropius and Maxwell Fry, but there are, of course, hundreds of other examples. If one now looks at Townscape in the twentieth century what I am pleading for is a happy harmony between what functionalism demands and what tradition in England endorses. That should give this country its great chance in the evolution of a twentieth-century townscape.

But in order to create such effects and, even more, in order to demand them, it is necessary to become aware of the attractions of townscape in the past and present, wherever they exist. Towns and villages are much too much looked at purely as an assembly of individual buildings, and the minor details of urban furnishing are overlooked as consistently as are the relations between individual buildings. Those are the things which anybody interested in townscape must watch, and if they are not watched the visual attractions of towns and villages will disappear. [The *Architectural Review*] has in the course of the last year conducted a campaign in conjunction with the Extra Mural Department of the University of Birmingham, emphasising the townscape characters and problems of four west midland towns (Ludlow, Evesham, Bewdley, Shrewsbury) and putting forward positive suggestions as to how they ought to be preserved and developed. One outcome of this campaign   **Figs. 27, 28** has been a specially printed Manifesto[57] to tell the lay-man what townscape is and how it can be safeguarded.

MODERN ARCHITECTURE, NATIONALISM AND INTERNATIONALISM[58]

The architectural style of the twentieth century is international, whether we like it or not. Communications being what they are, local materials are no longer an advantage, and the new materials—steel and reinforced concrete, aluminium and plastics—have no local characters anyway. The functions of buildings also, and even the social conditions from which they arise, are largely the same. Nearly all important new buildings are in and around cities and are designed for large numbers of users: office blocks, hospitals, schools, factories, housing estates and so on. Only ideologies differ, and if the public buildings of Russia and eastern Germany do not look more or less the same as ours, the reason is that architecture "establishes a nation," as Sir Christopher Wren put it, and that the countries behind the Iron Curtain wish to go on record as ideal, heroic nations. As for the West, a certain democratic sameness must be accepted. [...]

That the style of the twentieth century by and large is a style that one can call neutral may be regrettable, but social premises being what they are, it is unavoidable. Grandeur as well as expressionism are not called for where functions are neutral. On the other hand, this seeming neutrality is a challenge to refine within the narrow bounds of the almost mandatory grid and parallelepiped. Proportion today is once again taken seriously, and details are treated with delicacy and discrimination. Moreover, the alleged rigidity and regimentation of the grid and the parallelepiped can be overcome by grouping.

When we turn to modern architecture—whence comes the style which we may label the style of our own age as we can label Gothic or Renaissance?[59] And how has the style spread? Its origins go back to Frank Lloyd Wright in America, to Perret and Garnier in France, Peter Behrens in Germany, and Adolf Loos and Hoffman in Austria. Independently all these men saw the possibilities of the new building materials, concrete, steel and glass, and developed a new aesthetic of construction. They preferred the flat to the pitched roof, the horizontal window line to the vertical, the smooth surface to the decorated. The style they evolved—whose various elements were fused by Gropius the famous German architect, by Oud the Dutchman, or by Le Corbusier in France—appears essentially homogeneous and shows few national variations. How does this happen? and should we welcome it? [...]

Now modern communications have obvious advantages, but there are also some disadvantages. For while modern inventions pass from land to land, from continent to continent with amazing speed, individual, provincial, national personality may easily be crushed and overwhelmed in the process.

Many people welcome this. Their argument is that architecture today has become scientific and that science is international. Look, they say, at building materials. In other ages there were districts known for their slate, their timber, their limestone or their marble. Today we can transport building materials anywhere. We can cut the hardest stone, as if it were cheese. We employ an increasing amount of synthetic materials whose use is not tied to any locality. And this is a blessing (they hasten to add), for nationalism is to blame for all wars of the twentieth century, and wars destroy culture. Hence nationalism in architecture is to be annihilated.

All this sounds convincing enough, but it is in my opinion not the whole truth. In the first place international uniformity in architecture seems at present to arise more from the use of materials than from the spirit that underlies it. Of course a building in China can look exactly like a building in the United States or in Spain. But you cannot turn an American into a Spaniard. The essence of [Spanish] character and the essence of American character are distinct, and this is an enrichment for the world.[60] [...]

No one has demanded of poets, of Shakespeare, Goethe or Racine, that they should speak in any but their native tongues. Why then, in the case of modern architecture, should we ask that it deny the various traditions which are found in the different cities of its birth? I certainly do not mean by this that we should return to the imitation of earlier styles. Nothing could be worse. Luckily the period of imitation has gone once and for all, though the Blimps of all countries will not admit it. No living architecture or literature was ever achieved by imitation. And of all centuries, our own, with its gigantic increase of new building materials, is the one that can least tolerate the imitation of styles. In the past no age ever avoided the task of evolving an original aesthetic form for its technical achievements. Shall our own be the first to go down to history as an example of such aesthetic cowardice? We have the free use of steel and concrete. It would be the greatest error not to make use of these openly and unashamedly, everywhere. Or perhaps not quite everywhere. For the concrete surface does not, for example, stand up satisfactorily to English weather. Le Corbusier and his followers have praised this material to the skies, but concrete houses, office blocks and factories in England are inclined after a short time to look bedraggled. Unless it is possible to paint the concrete every couple of years, and until some new surface is found for concrete which will make it impervious to weather, it does not seem advisable to use it generally in our climate. Matters are different in Italy or France.

Thus climate alone offers sufficient grounds to differentiate architecture along national or local lines. It is but common sense to build large windows where we need all the available sunlight, and small windows, or windows facing narrow courtyards where we wish to protect ourselves from the heat. Hence modern architects in Brazil hit on the idea of that new and original kind of sun-blind which is such a distinctive feature of their facades.

But it is not climate alone, which determines the differences in national architecture, still less is it the terrifying twentieth-century myth of race. (We easily forget today that Holbein was a German and van Dyck a Fleming.) Why are Edinburgh, Bath and Dublin so different? Why in Italy has Rome its own peculiar essence—its *romanita;* whilst in Florence the air seems crisper and clearer? Cities, provinces, nations, they all have their individualities recognizable in their architecture. Alas that so much of it is now lost for ever.

If neither climate nor race be the cause behind the individuality of Rome, Paris or Vienna, whence does it come? The answer is: from its history and tradition.[61] Climate and race are only single threads in the fabric woven by these great forces; it is from a common heritage of experience, vision and knowledge, that the final garment of a city, its architecture, is composed. And we should accept this truth and reinforce it; which is not to say we should support imitations in architecture, but rather that we should sustain the spiritual individuality behind Bath or Dublin without imitating the architecture of Wood or Gandy.

The problem of our own time is to find an accepted language variable according to areas and countries, a style of our own clearly embodying our own demands, and yet rooted in the civilization and aesthetic feeling of each province and each people. Just as both the Gothic period and the Renaissance began with an international phase, so in our day we must pass through an international phase. Its task will be accomplished when all possibilities of mere imitations of past styles have finally vanished. When that point is reached—and no sooner—when the modern style has become the mother tongue generally understood, then, and only then, will it be strong enough to branch out into the wealth of different idioms so ardently to be hoped for.

This is, to my mind, the architectural programme that lies before us together with the most gigantic task of rebuilding which has ever faced mankind. And if European rebuilding is to have any aesthetic merit, the architects of all countries must be united in the same profound understanding for the new spirit as they have had in the past; they must comprehend both the spirit of Europe and the spirit of their individual countries.

GENIUS LOCI, FUNCTIONALISM AND VISUAL PLANNING[62]

[The] *rus in urbe* is indeed eminently English, but, when it comes to the problems of to-day, it has little to contribute. Our problems are those of improvements in towns, including the metropolis, and the laying out or, as it is now called, the planning of new towns or new parts of towns. But even with regard to these urgent problems, so much more serious and portentous than those of the country house and its grounds, the English Picturesque theory—if not its practice—has an extremely important message. We are in need of a policy of healthy, attractive, acceptable urban planning. There is an English national planning theory in existence which need only be recognized and developed. It is hidden in the writings of the improvers from Pope to Uvedale Price and Payne Knight. The first line quoted from Pope [...] ran: "Consult the genius of the place in all." The genius of the place, the *genius loci,* is a mythological person taken over from antiquity[63*] and given a new meaning. The *genius loci,* if we put it in modern planning terms, is the character of the site, and the character of the site is, in a town, not only the geographical but also historical, social and especially the aesthetic character. If one wants to plan for the City of London, one must be sensitive to the visual character of the City. The same exactly would apply to Cambridge, or to a small town with much character such as Blandford, or with little character such as Slough.

Now this kind of consideration is tantamount to treating each place "on its own merit," and it is therefore an eminently English treatment, even if its Englishness has been forgotten in the nineteenth century and still needs rediscovering now. It is the same attitude applied to visual planning as it is applied, or so one hopes, to their day-to-day work by the Home Office and the Ministry of Pensions. "Each case on its own merit" is the humane principle to act on, and [. . .] may indeed be called the principle of tolerance in action, and there is no more desirable element of Englishness than tolerance. [. . .]

In planning and architecture to-day "each case on its own merit" is called functionalism, and if present-day urban situations are treated functionally, it is obvious that the result would not look like "the mockery of princely" towns such as Versailles, with symmetry enforced on streets and buildings. The informal—this is a better term than the irregular; for the *regulae,* the rules, were not absent in English landscaping, only they were of a subtle kind—the informal then is at the same time the practical and the English.

The difference is summed up in the phrase "*genius loci.*"[64] [. . .] Paul Nash, in 1933,[65] must have been the first to restore to it that meaning which the eighteenth-century planners had endowed it with. It is a twofold meaning, when applied to the architectural tasks of the twentieth century. One refers to the fact that each country (on the rich soil of its traditions) will find its own suitable variations on the theme of the universal style of a period. The other refers to the fact that each individual task must be treated on its own merits, according to its own locus and usus. [. . .]

That is the functional function of the Picturesque, meaning the Varied, the Intricate, the On-its-own-Merit, in the twentieth century. [. . .]

The real point at issue [. . .] is the one I have tried to deal with under *genius loci,* the issue between feeling and principle—both equally valid, indeed complementary, though contrary, stimuli to art. It happens that the first half of the twentieth century was a period of innovations, that the old principles of academy and Beaux Arts were no longer acceptable or indeed applicable. The artist had to feel his way, explore, risk, and often fail, but the architect doing the same succeeded—succeeded in reaching the safe ground of locus and usus. For him at this moment the Picturesque movement, the first feeling-your-way theory of art in European history and far the greatest contribution England has made to aesthetic theory, is, as I maintain, supremely significant. For the town planner it is more than significant, it is the life-line by which he can defeat chaos.

PLANNING AND PRESERVATION[66]

So this is a plea for two things which are really one: for visual planning instead of expediency planning, and for the preservation of your history. French planning often makes preservation impossible or, if as in the centre of Paris preservation is decided on, makes modern renewal impossible. English planning allows for both, and he would be a routine architect who for the sake of his shopping centre or administrative centre would not accept the challenge of good older buildings remaining, i.e., of history in stone or brick remaining to tell their story.

I assure you, in the hands of a good architect, I mean in the hands of a city architect [...] in the hands of those whom the council on his suggestion might commission, the mixture of good old and good new, whether in the streets of the centre or in the suburbs of old mansions, and new housing, would be a blessing.

It is the mixture of old and new, sensitively managed that I call an environment.

[England] has not suffered from wars as have all the others in Europe.[67] Hence the number of old buildings wholly or partly preserved is prodigious. [...] What is one to do about their preservation, and what is the effect on the work of the modern architect of so much that is traditional? Struggles to preserve certain buildings, certain groups of buildings, never cease. [...] Sometimes the battle is won and one is pleased, sometimes it is lost and one is infuriated, but occasionally it is lost and one finds in the end that one ought to be pleased; for what has taken the place of the old is as good or better, and in addition alive in the sense in which only the buildings of our own day can be alive. [...]

Much less justifiable is the resistance of county councils and rural and even urban district councils to the admission of modern buildings on the ground that they would not fit in with the old. It is unjustifiable not only because the old is only rarely as perfectly of a piece as, say, at Corsham,[68] but also because the stylistic uniformity they require is scarcely ever a visual asset. Original with imitation marry less well than original seventeenth with original eighteenth century, and the same applies to original twentieth. This is not a recommendation for ruthlessness. The new ought to be kind to the old, even respectful to it. It is sometimes a mere matter of the choice of materials and nothing else, or of floor heights and the like. There is far too little courage displayed in this field by architects, let alone the councils. English cathedrals nearly always frankly display the periods in which they were built: one can easily recognize the styles of 1080, 1200, 1400, 1520 at Winchester.[69] The French, the German and the Italians, on the other hand, like their cathedrals all of one piece. This country has always enjoyed the variety of parts. The Oxford and Cambridge colleges are a case in point: many buildings in many styles, not one huge uniform design like the École Militaire in Paris or the Lycées. [...]

In returning to the relations of new to old on a larger scale than that of the individual building or group of buildings, it is worth pointing out that the case of the one new house in an old village is in fact no rarer than that of the one old house on a new estate. While the former nearly everywhere has to overcome resistance, the latter has nearly everywhere met with all the required sympathy, which is proof that the planner of estates can be trusted aesthetically and that councils cannot. Examples are the Georgian mansions on the L.C.C. Roehampton estate and the village church of Latton in the middle of Harlow New Town. The finest of all examples, if circumstances allow, will be Sir William Holford's precincts of St. Paul's. This was a demonstration once for all of the often unrecognized fact that worthwhile buildings are seen to best advantage set against a neutral background and not a background weakly competing with themselves. [...]

It was stated earlier on that the style of architecture of the twentieth century is neutral. At Roehampton it is, but the conjoint action of architecture and setting are not; they are relaxed, human, and visually as well as intellectually inspiring. It was also stated that our style of architecture is international and that national characters have little chance of survival. Roehampton and similar L.C.C. estates

[...] prove the opposite. The old—that is, the internationally appreciated English tradition of the picturesque—reasserts itself in the new.

Examples

INTRODUCTION[70]

So there is plenty of precedent to make use of in our situation to-day—not by copying but by applying the same principles, the same great English principles. The situation in planning in all countries to-day calls for two things in particular, both totally neglected by the nineteenth century: the replanning of city centres to make them efficient as well as agreeable places to work in, and the planning of new balanced towns, satellite towns, New Towns, which are towns and not garden suburbs with odd shopping centres as urban exclaves and a trading estate along the railway. Planning is of course largely a matter of economics, sociology, traffic engineering and so on, but it is also a visual matter, and if in the end the city centre or new town is not visually satisfactory—not only in its buildings but as an urban whole—it is a failure.[71*]

These are urgent problems for all countries, but what has been said about English character shows that no country is aesthetically better provided to solve them and thereby leave its imprint on other countries than England. If English planners forget about the straight axes and the artificially symmetrical facades of the academy and design functionally and Englishly they will succeed. There are in fact promising omens in many places already, the consistent policy of the *Architectural Review* over the last twelve years and more, resulting in sketch plans for the City, the area round the Houses of Parliament, and several small towns,[72*] Sir Hugh Casson's and Mr. Misha Black's layout of the 1951 exhibition on the south bank of the Thames, then the design by Sir Hugh Casson and Mr. Neville Conder for the Faculty of Arts precinct of Cambridge University, the Holden

Fig. 29. Design for the centre of Harlow New Town by Frederick Gibberd

and Holford plan for the City of London, the LCC and the Holford plans for the Barbican area in the north part of the City, and—in the flesh as it were—certain aspects of the Harlow New Town by Mr. Frederick Gibberd and several LCC housing estates designed by Dr. J. Leslie Martin and his department.   Fig. 29

These are the things eagerly studied by architects from abroad, but they are also things that still need support, support against ignorance and shortsightedness, and against the stupid prejudice that such new-fangled ideas as would give England modern and worthy town and city centres must be outlandish. It has, I hope[,] been demonstrated how thoroughly inlandish they are.

VISUAL PLANNING AND THE CITY OF LONDON[73]

Metropolitan planning—and this brings me, at long last, to the City of London—is as a rule regarded as social planning, and that is quite right; but the best social plan does not necessarily secure satisfactory aesthetic results, and, while we want healthy and socially-planned towns and cities, we also want something for our eyes to enjoy. The pleasures of the eye are not everything, but they are something which we deserve to have when we live in towns; they are not only one of the amenities but one of the necessities of the good life. I am not competent to deal with the social side at all, and therefore I am confining my remarks to the visual side.

The danger is that the application of visual planning may lead to something like the Royal Academy plan for London; that is to say, it may lead to something as formal and symmetrical and Parisian as that plan is. The Royal Academy plan carried symmetry so far that existing buildings were duplicated to secure it; in opening up St. Paul's, the deanery was to be duplicated. I regard this as a danger, for two reasons: it is not the right historical approach, and it is not the right functional approach.

The historical side is supposed to be my pigeon, and on that I would say that, although such planning is perhaps in harmony with Christopher Wren's plan of 1666, it is entirely out of keeping with that very great tradition of urban planning which existed in this country in the eighteenth and early nineteenth century. An example of that is Barry and Pugin's Houses of Parliament, where there is a symmetrical front, but the sky-line is deliberately varied by the introduction of all kinds of shapes, towers and spires, to create that very variety which is given by Christopher Wren's spires, and which seems wholly opposed to the symmetry of the riverside facade.

When you look at the present grouping of buildings in the City you find this same tendency applying everywhere. You finds odd lanes and corners, with buildings of different dates placed at different angles, and contrasts between light and shade, smooth and rough, high and low, wide and narrow, buildings of the Wren period and buildings of the nineteenth century, with well-lit lanes leading suddenly into dark passages. You find in a curious, vernacular way what you find in an aesthetically much more deliberate way in the collegiate lay-out of Oxford and Cambridge. These are, in the City of the nineteenth century, accidental effects, but they are accidents for which we have to be grateful, not because we should imitate them but because, as every artist knows, accident can be a very great stimulus. In that sense, these odd vistas in the City are a very great stimulus indeed, showing   Fig. 30
what possibilities there are.

When the modern movement started in the architecture of individual buildings, the architect found himself confronted with an approach different from that

The first view, strangely enough, seeing what has gone before, is an almost purely monumental one; in its day, though revealed only by the blitz, the greatest view in London. We throw it into the Peep-Show as a proof of good faith, or as a reminder that arrogant modernists are not too proud to like a vista now and then, even when there's a baroque monument at the end of it. The odd thing is that this, the greatest classical view in London, has been ignored by the R.A. planners, which seems unnecessarily perverse of them. We refer to the scene from the altar step of Bow Church, from which, through the West Window and door, can be seen, unbelievably beautiful on a fine day, the dome and east end of St. Paul's. There isn't another view in London to compare with this product of the blitz, and as it wasn't there before, so it won't be there after, unless, which is highly unlikely, someone who matters decides to fight for its retention. Bow's own interior, roofless and fire-marbled, is today that rare thing a piece of pure architecture, more architectonic indeed than when it was entire, but the ruling-off, locking-out process is in full swing, and the west door, open for the last year or two, now has Yale locks to keep you out, so that the view's brief moment has been successfully cut short by the wise and good, but not highly understanding men who have authority over it. From Bow, forcing your eyes away from those gratuitous effects of the blitz which make the open spaces, the church towers, the cliff and sea-scapes round the Cathedral so tantalizing to the visual planner (but we shall return to them later), make your way across Watling Street and down Garlick Hill, where blue-chinned skinners and furriers, speaking all the languages under the sun except English, are doing business on the street—and what a street—and with a glance inside the open door of St. James', Garlickhithe, at Jimmy Garlick in his glass case, pull up for the next halt, or the second step of the peep-show, at St. Michael's Royal, College Hill. Just above is the home of Dick Whittington—the big merchant houses of his day occupied the part of the City immediately north of Thames Street—but it is not Dick Whittington's home we want to see (anyway it isn't there), but the grouping of the buildings above St. Michael's. Quite a simple street scene, remarkable for nothing more than a combination of Baroque doorways and pedantic classicism, but the little street slopes down (at the present moment) to an open view of the river, and the tucked-away effect of the little church and the urban architecture, all good orthodox stuff, yet not exhibited, hidden, feels right. In this scene the hoots of tugs mingle with church bell chimes on the historic water-front of the world's port.

Authentic London. When you want academic, classical, Royal Academy stuff, this, surely, is the London way to go about it, the cosy way; relying not on monumentally uniform elevations or the carrying on of cornice lines or on text-book over-whiteness (how unenglish, how ill-bred), but on a contrast of academic opinions, a polite discord, like the dinner table of cultivated dons, each obstinately odd beneath a suave convention of good manners.

That is one kind of urban visual set-up, classical in detail though in essentials picturesque, which

St. Paul's from Bow Church

At St. Michael's, College Hill

St. James', Garlickhithe

6 **concerning the motifs of the Picturesque City**

This tour of City sights keeps in the main to the less publicised intimate corners, which give the City that particular Londonish flavour. Though not unfamiliar to the City worker, they are not regarded as important ingredients in the City picture. Yet, un-spectacular and often dingy, they are fragments of the vigorous idiom which has evolved through the ages as a suitable expression of City life; as such they must be respected. Probably only a fraction can be preserved. Yet if part has to go, it should not be for something less authentic.

171

Fig. 30. City Peep-Show

of the nineteenth-century architect. He found that in order to design a functional building he had to consider the use of the building, and not only to design facades. The outcome of that, as everybody knows, is the predominance of informal, asymmetrical planning in the individual building belonging to the modern movement, whether it be a school, a hospital, a civic centre or anything else.

It seems to me that if the planner deals strictly with the functional side of his job, he will probably find the same thing. If we ask ourselves what nowadays is the function of the City of London and what actually happens there, we shall find that most of the business is transacted and most of the contracts are made by people walking short distances to meet each other, standing about, meeting in pubs, meeting over lunch. It is entirely a pedestrian system of contacts, so that obviously the right functional pattern in the re-planning of the City is as far as possible to keep the fast traffic away, and to have only, as far as it can be done, service roads inside, and precincts for pedestrians, with pedestrian links connecting them. Even now the City is largely a place for pedestrians, and there is no reason to make the district round the Bank into a centre for fast traffic. A much more smoothly functioning City could be brought into being by the use of what is best in the tradition of English town planning—this collegiate layout which has been developed in England more convincingly, more ingeniously and more imaginatively than anywhere else, this bold mixing up of old and new which is found in the Colleges and the Inns of Court. The old City of London is anything from Mediaeval churches to Victorian pubs, and the buildings which would remain, sticking out at odd angles, would provide a good deal of Price's irritation and incongruity.

Fig. 31. Illustration by Hugh Casson of the *Architectural Review*'s plan for the City of London

There is no reason why one should attempt in the new architecture to keep to any imitation of an old style; on the contrary, during the past centuries the very mixing up of what was brand new and what was old has come off most successfully. To show you what might be done, the A[rchitectural] A[ssociation] is showing some drawings by Hugh Casson which give a very good idea of what the City of London of the future might look like. ...

Fig. 31

A very bold scheme will be necessary to give a new lease of life to the City. Whether that scheme will be bold in the Royal Academy sense or in the sense which I have tried to outline I do not know; but I would say "Give me Hugh Casson every time," and I would not say that the vision shown in his drawings is Utopian. As a matter of fact, the appointment of William Holford, seems to indicate that the stars are favourable.

THE PRECINCTS OF ST. PAUL'S: SIR WILLIAM HOLFORD'S PLAN[74]

Why should *The Housing Centre Review* take notice of Sir William Holford's plans for the precincts of St. Paul's? There is no housing or hardly any housing involved. Yet the way in which Sir William has handled the specific, extremely intricate problems of his area has implications which are of great importance to readers of this *Review,* because they reach into any major task of urban planning. The treatment of any centre of a New Town or of a neighbourhood, the treatment of any old manor house or old church to be surrounded by new housing and new shopping will benefit from a close study of Sir William's ingenious and sensitive solutions. Sir William's proposals for the neighbourhood of St. Paul's are a compendium and should be regarded as such by anybody actively or passively concerned with urban, central planning, though in such immediate proximity to a major architectural monument the problem is of course posed on a scale not likely to be met again.

What the Holford Plan demonstrates is very briefly this.

(1) If an area possesses a building which forms its natural focal point or climax, it is helped more by contrasting surroundings than by attempted conformity. Sir William has no colonnades, or symmetrically placed colonnaded office buildings. His proposed buildings are all in the idiom of the twentieth century. Wren's columns and pediments and generous curves are given intensified poignancy by this contrast with the verticals and horizontals and cubes of today. Similarly the bulk of the cathedral is brought out ideally by the great variety of new low and high buildings around.

(2) Urban elements of planning can be treated as subtly and variedly as were the landscape elements in English eighteenth-century layouts in the country. The Picturesque garden is indeed, historically speaking, the ultimate source of the Holford Plan, though the transposition into urban terms had already taken place at the time of the John Woods of Bath and John Nash. The planning of Bath and of Regent Street and Regents Park are the classic English example of how to achieve the subtlest effects of variety, contrast and surprise—that is those very criteria which had been established by Alexander Pope for the design of gardens. These informal English effects are exactly as valuable as the French effect achieved in terms of symmetry and uniformity.

(3) The elements which Sir William, as the creative descendant of Pope and Uvedale Price, of the Woods and Nash, uses, are manifold. The most

important of them is contrived vistas of a subtler kind than the straight avenues of Paris and Washington, leading to a portico or an obelisk. Then there are contrasts of narrow and wide, of closed-in and open, and also contrasts of levels. One may take as an instance the raised terrace to the north of the west facade of St. Paul's. It is raised to allow for an underground garage below where on two levels cars can be parked and it affords a brilliant view to the south towards the highly Baroque northwest tower of the cathedral, in utter contrast to the view in the opposite direction, where there is a group of office buildings with one point block higher than ten storeys. Equally rewarding is a walk along the north flank of the cathedral, through the returned Temple Bar, past Wren's chapter house into a shopping close of great intricacy and on to the trees of the old churchyard which are left unmolested.

(4) Urban intricacy benefits from a mixture of architecture with trees and lawns. How true that is can be experienced in the City, when one suddenly discovers an old churchyard tucked away behind a big office building. But it is an error to think that the only possible application of picturesque principles of planning is by means of introducing greenery. Stones and glass can be composed just as picturesquely as trees and shrubs. In fact, central areas should not be diluted by too much of the elements of the open country. Verdure ought only to be introduced occasionally to add interest and relief. A garden city is a perfectly acceptable twentieth-century conception, but there must be a place in it for city as well as garden, and city means closeness and compactness. Therefore:

(5) Spaciousness and close confinement have both their functions in urban planning. The congestion of a small Italian hill town—but even that has almost without exception the sudden contrast of a piazza, be it in front of a church or the town hall—is not more objectionable than the dilution of a New Town, where terraces of cottages are kept far too far apart across

Fig. 32. Plan for the precinct of St. Paul's by William Holford

the road, and accents of the type so brilliantly developed in the Holford Plan are totally impossible.

Fig. 32

These are five principles inherent in the Holford Plan. But to tabulate them like this deprives them of the life which they possess in their demonstration in Sir William's beautifully made large model. Sir William is emphatically not a drawing-board planner. In his mind the principles here summarized have clearly become so completely second nature that one moves with perfect ease through the model and never becomes fully aware of the degree of purposefulness and usefulness which it embodies. This seeming naturalness is the highest aim that any planning in a town can pursue. I cannot remember ever having seen it achieved in English twentieth-century planning quite so successfully as in the Holford Plan.

THE FACULTY OF ARTS PRECINCT OF CAMBRIDGE UNIVERSITY[75]

The third of July should become a day of celebrations and junkettings for the Cambridge patriot; for on that day this year the Committee for the Sidgwick Avenue site recommended to the University the approval of Sir Hugh Casson's and Mr[.] Neville Conder's development scheme. The scheme is equally outstanding as a piece of planning and, in its sketch suggestions, as a piece of architecture. Neither can be extolled too much.

Fig. 33

As for planning we have amongst us the Downing site as a painful example of what can happen to a spacious site, if for lack of an accepted and adhered to plan it becomes cluttered up with far too many buildings arranged on no better principle than that of loose symmetry and designed without any consideration for each other. By the Second World War everyone knew what a failure this university development had been, and, indeed such recent buildings as the Engineering Laboratory and the Chemical Laboratories are designed on their own, at one go, and in a contemporary spirit. Yet the one overpowers Scroope Terrace, the other

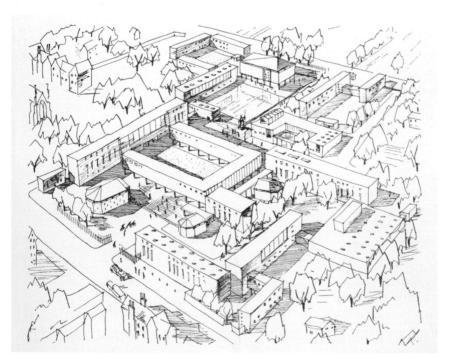

Fig. 33. Aerial sketch of Hugh Casson and Neville Conder's Faculty of Arts Precinct, Cambridge University

Lensfield Road—in both cases because new buildings are placed too close to the centre of old Cambridge to which its Regency streets and houses belong as much as its mediaeval core. That was a planning mistake, no fault of the architects.

Now that mistake is not going to be made again. The Sidgwick Avenue site is far enough away to give ample unimpeded space for the present and many years to come. It is, moreover, nowhere near monuments of a past which, against their will, might have been made to stake claims for imitation. Gibbs—to repeat a truism for the n'st time—did not imitate King's Chapel, nor Wren the facade of Pembroke, nor did Waterhouse imitate anything at Cambridge or, indeed, in England. But that danger exists, and Sir Hugh Casson has not succumbed to it, nor has his enlightened committee. No imitation of, or compromise with Newnham (exceedingly pretty and appropriate though its older parts are) and with Ridley on the south, and Selwyn on the west, and, thank God, none with the north either—that means with the University Library and its heavy symmetrical bulk, a classical composition shorn of classical detail in its business parts.

Instead, Sir Hugh and Mr. Conder have designed an intricate group of courts, as varied in size and as unexpected in visual effects as the old colleges are—the key principle of collegiate planning observed, but no details copied. [...]

Cars, of course, are only allowed to wait on the periphery, a periphery by the way treated very ingeniously to avoid complete openness as well as the horror of the long prison wall, and the main inner spaces are all reserved for those who walk, stand round or sit round. That is as it should be, and it is expressed by a kind of causeway raised two feet which crosses the site from south to north and forms one of the chief features of the design, and also by covered ways, passages below buildings and plenty of squares of all sizes and kinds. One square has an oblong sheet of water as its centre, one is turfed, others are paved, with or without trees, and apart from paving, the addict to floorscapes will be able to enjoy cobbles, tarmac and setts.

This close interest in detail is characteristic of the plan. Sir Hugh and Mr. Conder are obviously thinking in terms of human beings ready to appreciate the scale, the variety and the minutiae of what surrounds them. The terms of reference of the planners excluded precise architectural detailing of the individual buildings. Yet Sir Hugh suggests at least that some should be dark, some light, some brick, some limestone, and he shows the agreeable pattern which that would make, a pattern carefully devised to harmonize with the height pattern of four-, three-, two-, and one-storeyed buildings. Nothing higher than four storeys is intended; that is probably why Sir Hugh places so much importance on the Library tower. The new site itself could, however, do with an accent of its own, the Lecture Theatres used by Sir Hugh as such will hardly be powerful enough, and Sidgwick Avenue by the time the buildings are up will be in great need of visual strength, more of it than one would assume now.

For I am as convinced as when I wrote about it eighteen months ago in *The Cambridge Review* (and Sir Hugh kindly refers to the article)[76] that by then the Backs will be fronts, because important university and college buildings will stand as consistently to the west of the Backs as they now stand to their east across the river. The Backs will then be the campus of the university, a campus in the best English picturesque tradition, leafy, informal and variegated, and the sites near the University Library will have to hold their own against the sequence of delights from St. John's (Sir Hugh's old College) to Queens'. **Fig. 34**

Garden Hostel certainly won't, but the Casson plan would. I say "would"

Fig. 34. Sketch of part of the precinct designed for the Faculty of Arts of Cambridge University by Hugh Casson and Neville Conder

advisedly, because, as pointed out before, the architects were not requested to submit more than a plan and a block model, and the report makes it clear that the plan would work and result in something visually pleasing whatever architecture the individual buildings would exhibit. That is pathetic; for it implies a conception of architecture as something applied at a later stage to a plan, or, more generally speaking, a conception of a plan that has so little style that any architectural style will do with it.

Now that cannot be regarded as true by Sir Hugh nor by any other good architect, although it may just be by a committee. What is true is that, within a style, much personal expression remains possible. Twelve different architects may well design twelve different buildings outlined by Sir Hugh, but they could not possibly do it one with mullioned and transomed windows and a high-pitched roof, and the next with giant Ionic columns and a pediment. That would wreck a plan which is so sensitively working towards a balance of unity and variety. Too much unity, that is pompous symmetry, is no more explicitly excluded than too much variety, that is the admission of any style in any building. Sir Hugh's admirable sketches elucidate that point. They are admirable not only as drawings, but also for revealing just enough and concealing just enough of the architectural character which he was not meant to detail but could not help to visualise. It is worth following at leisure the conducted tour devised and illustrated by him, and described in the report. But when you have done that, may I recommend that you embark on your own tour, working out your own probable day-to-day progress through these buildings and imagining the sensations you would receive? I, for instance, tried to follow my distant successor from his lecture theatre [...] into the water square to his own faculty (he will no doubt have one for the teaching of the history or art and architecture exclusively). [...] He has to go on then, my successor, under the *pilotis* of Modern Languages, past the turfed court swarming with undergraduates, under the *pilotis* of English and Moral Science, and so into the haven of his pleasant seclusion. And there we can leave him settling down to prepare his next lecture, the one which is to deal with the Festival of Britain, 1951, and its Influence on the Architecture of the later Twentieth Century in England.

FESTIVAL OF BRITAIN[77]

The English have a reputation in the world as a serious, loyal and somewhat dull people, relying on practical experience and lacking boldness, fascination and imagination. In the last fifteen years, when England participated with its pavilions in the international exhibitions—1937 in Paris and 1939 in New York—this reputation was confirmed by a ponderous, correct and unimaginative architecture.

This year's London exhibition demonstrates the danger of making definitive judgements of a people based on their philosophy, literature and figurative arts. The English spirit certainly did not lack audacity at the time of Drake and Raleigh, nor imagination and fantasy at the time of Shakespeare and Donne, or even at the time of Shelley and Keats. The English spirit—that which today we are too quick to consider eternal and unchangeable—is in fact a product of the mid-nineteenth century. It was shaped by Queen Victoria and Prince Albert and the religious movements of their time, by Dr. Arnold—responsible for the standards and conventions of the public school system—and by Ruskin with his moralizing way of judging art and architecture. In the eighteenth century the English knew to appreciate Roubiliac's exquisite rococo tombs in Westminster Abbey, but William Morris—who maintained that for him the writings of Ruskin had been "a true revelation"—defined those monuments "as the most horrendous examples of false art to be found in the entire world" (open letter to the director of the *Daily News,* 30 January 1869). In the eighteenth century, together with Roubiliac, we also find the lively scepticism and elegance of Berkeley and Hume in philosophy; in architecture we find the Gothic and Greek revivals—the will, that is, to build in different styles according to personal taste—and the art of gardens. This art—a purely English creation, in stark contrast to the French grandiosity and formalism of Versailles, just like English liberalism is in contrast to French absolutism—this spontaneous, complex and romantic art is England's greatest contribution to European art.

What are its principles? It was discussed in many writings by many authors and above all in one of exceptional perspicacity, too little known outside England: *An Essay on the Picturesque* by Sir Uvedale Price (first essay 1794, definitive edition 1810). Here are some citations—all, mind you, referring exclusively to the art of gardens:

> [A]lthough smoothness be the ground-work of beauty, yet that roughness is its fringe and ornament, and that which preserves it from insipidity....One principal charm of smoothness, whether in a literal or a metaphorical sense, is, that it conveys the idea of repose; roughness, on the contrary, conveys that of irritation, but at the same time of animation, spirit, and variety.[78]
>
> Repose is always used in a good sense; as a state, if not of positive pleasure, at least as one of freedom from all pain and uneasiness: irritation, almost always in an opposite sense, and yet, contradictory as it may appear, we must acknowledge it to be the source of our most active and lively pleasures.[79] Any winding road...must necessarily have some degree of intricacy; but in a dressed lane every effort of art seems directed against that disposition of the ground...the whole, in short, has such an appearance of having been made by a receipt, that curiosity, that most active principle of pleasure, is almost extinguished.[80]

According to the idea I have formed of it, intricacy…might be defined [as], that disposition of objects, which by a partial and uncertain concealment, excites and nourishes curiosity.[81]

but if I were obliged to determine between insipid congruity, and incongruity which produces…striking effects, I should not hesitate in preferring the latter.[82]

Impetuosity, irritation, intricacy, surprise, incongruence: all qualities that few people would associate with English art and architecture. And yet the great European importance of the present exhibition on the South Bank of the Thames, right in the heart of London, is that it revealed, in rigorously modern architectural terms, the rebirth of this English concept of the picturesque. The exhibition was not planned by a single individual, even if there was a director of architecture, Hugh Casson. This man, about forty years old, was in charge of the layout of the area—a congested site between County Hall and Waterloo Bridge—and he was also the one who coordinated and stimulated, more than designed, even if he personally studied many of the minor, but nonetheless important, connecting elements. The general layout does not have major cross-axes in the Beaux Arts tradition. It is intricate, complicated and full of surprises. Before the inauguration of the exhibition it was feared that there would be a disagreeable sensation of overcrowding in such a small area, but this did not turn out to be the case. The pavilions were sometimes oppressively crowded, but the open spaces, the squares and the connecting passageways were never more than pleasantly animated. The individual pavilions were freely conceived, like the general layout. They were designed by a number of architects, but in a common language that revealed a common sentiment. There was no architect of outstanding renown among them; no academic, no Sir. They were of all ages, from such well-known modern architects as Maxwell Fry (born in 1899), Wells Coates (born in 1895) and R. D. Russell (born in 1904), to Powell and Moya (born in 1920–21).[83]

This common language is perceptibly different from that of two decades earlier. Gone is the hardness, the inflexible angularity, the aloof dogmatism of the beginning of the modern movement; gone is the excessive insistence on the social and scientific aspects of architecture.

Fantasy and romanticism have come back, but not through an imitation of style. In effect, allusions to the past are completely missing from the South Bank exhibition. However, in Battersea Park, just a couple of miles away, these allusions have returned, albeit in a new and singular way. Here we find a street of shops, with two symmetrical towers at the end, designed by the painter John Piper and the cartoonist Osbert Lancaster in a burlesque-regency, rococo-gothic style. The street is made entirely of cane, including the statues on top of the towers: a diverting and witty game in the spirit of Brighton Pavilion rather than a serious reassessment of the architecture of 150 years ago.

But in the central zone of South Bank any compromise with the past was rightly excluded. Rather, one senses a joyful lightheartedness, almost a suggestion of irresponsibility, especially in the works of the youngest architects. It is true that the elements are still substantially the same as those introduced by the pioneers of the modern movement: a lot of glass, light metal structures, and a daring use of spatial interpenetration. The effects of the different levels inside and outside the pavilions in fact account for some of the most emotional experiences to be had by anyone visiting the exhibition. Inside the pavilions, the visitors are channelled

Fig. 35. The Festival of Britain, 1951. A general panorama by night looking toward the Transport Pavilion, and, behind it, the Royal Festival Hall

in such a way that the various streams of people can be seen moving along at different levels without any apparent connections. And outside, access to the Royal Festival Hall—a vast building standing permanently at the centre of the exhibition area—is by way of elevated walkways.

Fig. 35

The Royal Festival Hall, designed by Leslie Martin and R. Matthew for the London County Council, is London's first entirely modern official building. This reveals how reluctant England was to accept the new language and how recent was the change of spirit—if one can call it such. The building is not a simple compromise. The principal auditorium, with its zig-zag rhythms of cantilevered boxes—bizarre effect, though perfectly legitimate from the point of view of function—seems a little abstruse from both exterior and interior. But the articulation of the foyers, stairs and halls is daring and free, as in the nearby pavilions of the exhibitions. The great hall for 2000 spectators seems suspended in mid air because it rests on *pilotis* around which the space of the vestibule flows uninterruptedly. The unexpected views in every direction are enchanting—here, as in the whole exhibition—a principle derived (no doubt unconsciously) from the English theory of the picturesque.

The same principles emerge in the layout of the exhibition, in the way that visitors are channelled through the spaces. There are no two symmetrical buildings: the principal arteries unexpectedly narrow and then unexpectedly widen, they turn corners and suddenly reveal a familiar panorama of London across the river. Similar effects can be experienced inside the buildings. The important Sea and Ships Building (by the architect Basil Spence) is not even a real building. It is nothing but a composition of walls, solid or transparent, and roofs or vaults beneath which are found the displays. The love of the outdoors, so typical of England, is intensely felt here. And it culminates in the transformation of the fluvial landscape into a seascape, ingeniously achieved and a lively reminder to the visitor of Great Britain's insular nature and seafaring traditions. [...]

In the vicinity of the river are mainmasts, lookouts and so on, all made in authentic naval fashion, and a restaurant has placed some tables outside on a long and narrow terrace over the river, which unmistakeably recalls a ship's bridge. Similar in spirit is the hemicycle above one of the entrances on top of which is built a group of cantilevered offices. Nearby is one of the greatest successes of the exhibition: a high wall hiding a large railway station. This wall is constructed of a framework of tubular aluminium covered with variously coloured sheets, resulting in a three-dimensional composition of panels angled with respect to the length of the wall. How much the young architects have learned from Moholy-Nagy, Gabo and other abstract metal sculptors! [...]

Finally, the contribution of the fine arts also demonstrates remarkable inventiveness and total lack of ostentation. There are no painting or sculpture exhibitions. Instead, painters and sculptors displayed their works in squares and in streets between pavilions, on pavilion walls and inside the pavilions themselves. The effect is successful architecturally and further helps to create asymmetrical accents and a variety of interests, although perhaps the austerity and ethical seriousness of Henry Moore do not lend themselves to this kind of treatment, and certainly not for exhibition in the midst of huge crowds.

But from the point of view of the picturesque layout—which is what I thought was the most interesting aspect to investigate in this note about the exhibition—paintings and sculptures are as useful as the many minor elements of external furnishings, all of which were prepared with the greatest of care: the ponds with rocks and pebbles, the lights, the wastebaskets, the signposts, the variety of pavements, the planters that serve to guide and barricade visitors' access, and the enormous variety of wall surfaces. I believe that it is this message of variety, spontaneity and, above all, liberty that will secure the London Exhibition of 1951—celebrating its first centenary—a place in the history of international exhibitions.

ROEHAMPTON: LCC HOUSING AND THE PICTURESQUE TRADITION[84]
Standing securely in a modern European tradition of town planning that reaches back into the early twenties, and equally securely in an English landscape tradition that goes back almost two centuries further, the LCC's Roehampton Estate is one of the masterpieces of post-war residential design. [...]

The plan is characterized by the absence of any centre in the academic sense. If a centre can be named, it would be the rising lawn of Downshire Field, a negative, picturesque, informal centre. How it is reached, how the groups of point-blocks are experienced variously, can only be appreciated in the form of a perambulation, and such a perambulation has been [...] made more persuasive by the accompanying pictures.

Fig. 36

The elements which make up the character of this vast, yet not inhuman, composition are the point-blocks and the high slabs, the mixture of high and low and the placing of the all the buildings in landscape. [...]

Fig. 37

Whatever the sources of its planning and architecture, the combination of the two is highly individual and moreover eminently English. The setting of a cubic type of building in the landscape is eighteenth-century tradition and has once before made a deep impression everywhere abroad. The informal but highly thoughtful grouping of buildings is equally English and has established Bath as the opposite of Nancy in eighteenth-century town planning. Benefiting from this civilized Georgian tradition the architects of the Roehampton Estate succeeded in combining human scale with vast extent—a feat no French nor any

123

123 and 124. *Picturesque Principles applied to urban conditions:* The Roehampton Estate of the London County Council, designed by Dr. J. Leslie Martin and the Council Architects' Department.

124

176

Fig. 36. The Roehampton Estate of the London County Council, designed by Dr. J. Leslie Martin and the Council Architects' Department

ALTON EAST, ROEHAMPTON

11, 12 and 13 (opposite), three views of Alton East, showing the three contrasts on which the aesthetic success of the estate depends: high and low, trees and building, curved and straight. The buildings in this case are point-blocks, four-storeyed blocks of flats and two-storeyed cottages.

Fig. 37. The three views of Alton East, Roehampton, showing the three contrasts on which the aesthetic success of the estate depends: high and low, trees and building, curved and straight. The buildings in this case are (above, left) point-blocks, four-storeyed blocks of flats and two-storeyed cottages

ALTON EAST, ROEHAMPTON

14 and 15, according to how the photographer places himself an urban effect can be experienced or one belonging to the tradition of the English garden suburb.

16, two of the most thrilling views of the Roehampton Estate are that of Alton East from the approach to London on the Portsmouth Road and that of Alton West from Richmond Park illustrated above.

ALTON WEST,

Fig. 38. Views of Alton East, Roehampton. According to how the photographer places himself, an urban effect can be experienced or one belonging to the tradition of the English garden suburb

Italian or Dutch architect has been able to achieve. The effects accomplished at Roehampton range from the cosy to the violently startling. [...]   Fig. 38

There has been, as everyone knows, a great longing among architects after the war to get away from rationalism and to recover fantasy. Ronchamp is as much a sign of this as the Neo-Liberty of Italy, the chunky concrete of the English brutalists as much as the chequerboard patterns of fenestration of the English non-brutalists or the arbitrary patterns in screen walls inside and outside the Americas. Roehampton demonstrates the possibility of up-to-date sanity. It is not necessary to cover the surfaces of buildings with arbitrary bits. Planning and siting ought to serve the purpose of creating that sense of variety, contrast and relief which everyone wants. Buildings can remain rational, as they ought to, if they are sensitively grouped and if they are placed in juxtaposition with lawn and trees. That is what distinguishes the best mid-twentieth-century schemes from those of the twenties and thirties.

Conclusions[85]

[L]et me tell you in conclusion [...] how I got interested in the English eighteenth-century Picturesque and what value in my opinion this not so usual approach may have.

Some time after the beginning of the Second World War the *Architectural Review* lost its principal editor J. M. Richards (now Sir James Richards) to the Ministry of Information. He suggested me as his—temporary—successor and moved to Cairo. I did what I could, and this would have been entirely in matters of contemporary building, if it had not been for the co-owner of the *Review*, H. de Cronin Hastings. He is a brilliant man who likes to stay in the background. He had read Christopher Hussey's *The Picturesque*,[86] the great classic of the movement. [...] I also had of course read the book—even several years before I settled down in England, but purely as a piece of English art history. It was de Cronin Hastings who dropped a remark in his studiedly casual way indicating that surely Hussey's *Picturesque* and our day-to-day work for the *Review* were really the one and same thing. This is what set me off. With de Cronin's blessing I started on a book whose subject was just this aside of the great pathfinder. In the end the book was never written, and instead only a few papers on the Georgian Picturesque came out, all but one in the *Review* (1944–48), and one which was the longest and went into the *Art Bulletin* (1949). As my thought in these years developed, I realised that the missing link between the Picturesque and twentieth-century architecture was the picturesque theory chiefly of Uvedale Price, but also Payne Knight and Repton, and even Reynolds.

Price's categories are Variety, Intricacy, Irregularity, Contrast, Surprise, Irritation and Accident. Of these Reynolds in his Discourse of 1786 had the first three and the last. But whereas Price applies his categories to landscape, Reynolds uses them for arguing about townscape. He prefers the accidents of town growth to the regularity of town planning which later, he said, can easily lead to weariness. [...]

Now if you think of the situation of architecture in the twentieth century, it is a familiar fact that twentieth-century architecture was created in opposition against Beaux-Arts composition, or in Central Europe against the neo-Baroque and in England against the Wrenaissance. The Beaux-Arts, the Wrenaissance and the neo-Baroque all went in for symmetry and hence no surprise nor any irregularity.

But the new style was more than the introduction of new elements of form and composition principles. Architects such as Gropius—think of the Bauhaus building—laid it down that to create a successful building, i.e., a building which functions well, the architect must start from an investigation of the function of his building getting down to such details as the production lines in a factory, the movement lines in a hospital and so on. Once this process is accepted as the basic necessity of architecture, then it will come as no surprise to anyone that the result of the process can only very rarely be symmetrical. Instead the architect has to start from an asymmetrical group and convert it into something aesthetically valuable. This applies to town planning as much as to individual buildings. In town-planning Camillo Sitte in 1889 had analyzed medieval towns and their details as the very opposite of Versailles or Karlsruhe planning, and Sir Raymond Unwin had refined Sitte in applying his doctrine to the situation today. In his best estate, the Hampstead Garden Suburb in London, begun in 1907, he combined Picturesque planning with a few main axial roads planned straight.

As for the individual building, you can almost pick any recent compositionally complex group at random, and you will find variety, intricacy, contrasts. The late Walter Gropius's Bauhaus of 1925–26 I have already mentioned. In England the new universities are the best example and the Greater London Council's housing schemes, notably Roehampton. Public housing in the United States lags behind, and this is the one reason why over [t]here I try always to preach the application of Visual Planning principles instead of the pernicious gibberish of sociological planning.

My examples, you will have noticed, are not up-to-the-minute. But if you take more recent architecture, the style has certainly changed from Falling Water to Paul Rudolph and the Boston City Hall—and the change does not please me—but whatever the value of the new formal elements, genuine or gimmicks, the principles of Uvedale Price still hold sway.

NOTES

1. These two quotations were identified for inclusion in Part III and are held in Nikolaus Pevsner papers, box 25, folder "Visual Planning (Notes: General Points)." Pevsner later published them as the prelude to his "C20 Picturesque: An Answer to Basil Taylor's Broadcast," *AR* 115 (1954): 227.

2. This section is drawn from Nikolaus Pevsner, *The Englishness of English Art: An Expanded and Annotated Version of the Reith Lectures Broadcast in October and November 1955* (London: Architectural, 1956), 167–68. The lines quoted are from Alexander Pope, Epistle IV, to Richard Boyle, Earl of Burlington.

3*. *See N. Pevsner: London, Except for the Cities of London and Westminster (The Buildings of England), Harmondsworth, 1952, p. 217. Also the Architectural Review, vol. 103, 1948.* These citations refer to Nikolaus Pevsner, *London: Except the Cities of London and Westminster* (Harmondsworth: Penguin, 1952), 217; and Nikolaus Pevsner, "Humphrey Repton: A Florilegium," *AR* 103 (1948): 53–59.

4*. *See S. Lang, in the Architectural Review, vol. 104, 1948.* See Susan Lang, "The English Cathedral Close," *AR* 104 (1948): 189–92.

5. See the typed quotations titled "Extract from: *Encyclopaedia of Gardening*. Loudon," Nikolaus Pevsner papers, box 25, folder "Visual Planning (Notes: Part III)."

6. This tour has not been included in the selection for Part III, as Pevsner only mentions the area once in his notes, and it does not appear again either in any of his contemporary articles or in those from the years following, which suggests that it may

have been a preliminary thought. In addition, Pevsner did not prepare any text to accompany the photographs, with the exception of the instructions to the photographer. See Nikolaus Pevsner papers, box 25, folder "Visual Planning (Notes: Part III)." For the illustrations, photographic instructions, and accompanying plan of Ladbroke Grove, see Nikolaus Pevsner papers, box 25, folder "Visual Planning…(Illustrations: Ladbroke Grove)." This folder contains twenty-two black-and-white photographs and a plan showing the area and the position from which the photographs were taken, along with the instructions for the photographer.

7. See Nikolaus Pevsner papers, box 25, folder "Visual Planning (Notes: Part III)." In these notes, Pevsner also pointed to Hubert de Cronin Hastings's equation of landscape and urban scenery, an idea most clearly articulated in the urban design studies of Gordon Cullen, which were most likely commissioned by Hastings. See, for example, Gordon Cullen, "Hazards, or the Art of Introducing Obstacles into the Urban Landscape without Inhibiting the Eye," *AR* 103 (1948): 99–105.

8. This section is drawn from Nikolaus Pevsner, "Visual Planning and the City of London: A Paper Read before the A. A. by Dr. Nikolaus Pevsner," *Architectural Association Journal* 61, no. 699 (1945): 33.

9. The reader will notice minor discontinuities and overlaps here with regard to the development of picturesque architecture from the eighteenth and into the nineteenth century. Part III was to begin where Parts I and II had finished their descriptions, that is, at the beginning of the nineteenth century. For Pevsner's more continuous treatment of the subject, refer to Nikolaus Pevsner, "The Picturesque in Architecture," *RIBA Journal* 55 (1947): 57; and Nikolaus Pevsner, "Richard Payne Knight," *Art Bulletin* 31 (1949): appendix 1.

10. This section is drawn from Pevsner, "The Picturesque in Architecture" (note 9), 57.

11. Pevsner's notes for Part III contain the full excerpt of Pevsner's quotation from George Gilbert Scott's section on "Buildings in Towns":

> One very valuable element in street-architecture is the individualizing of the houses, giving, so far as possible, to each its own front clearly marked out from those of its neighbours, rather than grouping them into masses. I do not insist strongly on this, as there are difficulties about it, but I wish to call attention to the fact, that where every house has its own individual design, the prevailing character of the architecture is of necessity *vertical,* while if the houses be uniform, or grouped into large masses, it is almost as sure to be *horizontal:* and I need hardly say that the difference in the effect produced is prodigious. The fact that in most of our streets, as Cheapside, the Strand, Oxford-street, etc., each man has built his house as he liked, and that the whole is consequently cut up into vertical strips, is the one thing which redeems them from that abject insipidity which we see paramount in Gower or Harley-street; but if every one of these vertical divisions had a beautiful design of its own, differing in height, in outline, and in treatment, and terminating in a good sky-line, our streets would at once become as picturesque and pleasing as those of the great mediaeval cities.

George Gilbert Scott, *Remarks on Secular and Domestic Architecture, Present and Future* (London: John Murray, 1858), 174. See Nikolaus Pevsner papers, box 25, folder "Visual Planning (Notes: Part III)." Pevsner also employs this quotation in Pevsner, "Richard Payne Knight" (note 9), 311.

12. For Pevsner's discussion of Shaw's work, see Nikolaus Pevsner, "Richard Norman Shaw, 1831–1912," *AR* 89 (1941): 41–46.

13. This refers to Charles Locke Eastlake, *A History of the Gothic Revival* (London: Longmans, Green, 1872), 143.

14. For this point, see Nikolaus Pevsner, "A Short Pugin Florilegium," *AR* 94 (1943): 34.

15. This section is drawn from Pevsner, "C20 Picturesque" (note 1), 228–29.

16. Christopher Hussey, *The Picturesque: Studies in a Point of View* (London: Putnam, 1927).

17. Kenneth Clark, *The Gothic Revival: An Essay in the History of Taste* (London: Constable, 1928).

18. This section is drawn from [Nikolaus Pevsner,] "Frenchay Common or Workaday Sharawaggi," *AR* 98 (1945): 26.

19. See Nikolaus Pevsner papers, box 25, folder "Visual Planning (Notes: Part III)."

20. Peter F. R. Donner [Nikolaus Pevsner], "The End of the Pattern-Books," *AR* 93 (1943): 75–79. Peter F. R. Donner [Nikolaus Pevsner], "Edensor or Brown Comes True," *AR* 95 (1944): 39–43. The latter article is a follow-up to the former, which was on Richard Brown's pattern book of villa architecture published in 1841. It is a review and tour of the architecture of the village named Edensor, which was laid out around 1838 to 1839, "with every cottage in a different style." Pevsner wrote, "The main street of Edensor fulfils all the requirements of picturesque village planning, as set out in such books as P. F. Robinson's *Village Architecture* of 1830." Pevsner's interest in such villages was not limited to them being an example of picturesque planning but also due to the use of the pattern books and the implicit variety of styles. He relished the statement of one of the cottage architects, John Robertson, who said of his own work, "[it has] no merit from an architectural point of view." Pevsner noted not only the buildings' picturesque qualities, with their "incongruities and absurdities," but also his interest in their combination: "the surprise of Norman, Italianate and Tudor rubbing shoulders." Pevsner condemned the emerging "antiquarian historicism" of the architecture of the early Victorian period, stating his preference for Nash's Blaise Castle village architecture, which "comes off, because it looks so sweetly sham." Toward the end of the article, Pevsner cited Pugin's critique of the pattern book approach to architecture and planning, published in his book *The True Principles of Pointed or Christian Architecture: Set Forth in Two Lectures Delivered at St. Marie's, Oscott* (London: J. Weale, 1841). Pevsner quoted Pugin in stating, "Does locality, destination, or character of a building form the basis of a design nowadays[?]…No, surely not. We have Swiss Cottages in a flat country [and] Italian Villas in the coldest situation."

21. This section is drawn from Pevsner, *Englishness of English Art* (note 2), 178–79.

22. This section is drawn from Nikolaus Pevsner, *Pioneers of the Modern Movement: From William Morris to Walter Gropius* (London: Faber & Faber, 1936), 166–68. Pevsner continued his portrayal of the development of early-twentieth-century town planning in opposition to the English situation with reference to German planning and figures involved in *Stadtbaukunst* (the art of city building).

> Most German towns own a great deal of the building land within their
> boundaries and try—helped by legislation—to acquire more. Theodor
> Fischer, one of the most energetic young architects, was elected city architect
> for Munich in the nineties; the periodical *Der Städtebau* began to appear

in 1904; towns such as Nürnberg, Ulm, Mannheim, Frankfort, worked out comprehensive schemes for the development of centre and suburbs. The town-planning exhibition held at Berlin in 1910 can be taken as the final summing-up of these tendencies as they flourished before the war (pp. 168–69).

Pevsner's note to the final sentence stated, "Cf. W. Hegemann: *Der Städtebau,* Berlin 1911–13. With regard to the outstanding position of Germany in pre-war townplanning, Mr. H. I. Triggs in his book on townplanning (London, 1909, p. 39) writes: 'Nowhere has the subject of townplanning received more careful attention than in Germany, where for many years the foremost architects of the country have given much thought to the subject, and where the State practically compels municipalities to own land for public improvement...'" (p. 223 n. 20). This note refers to H. Inigo Triggs, *Town Planning, Past, Present, and Possible* (London: Methuen, 1909). It is worth comparing this passage on the development of town planning to those of later editions of *Pioneers* (note 22), such as the third edition of 1960.

23. Bedford Park was designed by Norman Shaw; see Pevsner, "Richard Norman Shaw" (note 12), 46.

24. See Nikolaus Pevsner, "The First Garden City," review of *Sixty Years of Planning: The Bournville Experiment,* by the Bournville Village Trust, *AR* 92 (1942): 128.

25. Pevsner refers to Ebenezer Howard, *To-morrow: A Peaceful Path to Real Reform* (London: Swan Sonnenschein, 1898). This was later published as Ebenezer Howard, *Garden Cities of To-morrow: Being the Second Edition of "To-morrow: A Peaceful Path to Real Reform"* (London: Swan Sonnenschein, 1902).

26. Camillo Sitte, *Der Städtebau nach seinen künstlerischen Grundsätzen: Ein Beitrag zur Lösung modernster Fragen der Architektur und monumentalen Plastik unter besonderer Beziehung auf Wien* (Vienna: Graeser, 1889).

27. This section is drawn from Nikolaus Pevsner, "A Pioneer of Town-Planning," review of *The Art of Building Cities,* by Camillo Sitte, *AR* 100 (1946): 186. The occasion for this review is the publication of the first English-language edition of Sitte's *Der Städtebau.*

28. Pagination is from Camillo Sitte, *The Art of Building Cities: City Building According to Its Artistic Fundamentals,* trans. Charles T. Stewart (New York: Reinhold, 1945).

29. This section is drawn from Nikolaus Pevsner, "History: Unwin Centenary," *AR* 134 (1963): 207–8.

30. Raymond Unwin, *Town Planning in Practice: An Introduction to the Art of Designing Cities and Suburbs* (London: Adelphi, 1909).

31. Pevsner is referring to Thomas Sharp, *Town Planning* (Harmondsworth: Penguin, 1940). Pevsner's personal library contains a copy of this book with uncharacteristically heavy markings, suggesting a heavy reliance on Sharp and his work in the formulation of his own position. See also George M. Young, *Country and Town: A Summary of the Scott and Uthwatt Reports* (Harmondsworth: Penguin, 1943).

32. Frederick Gibberd, *Town Design* (London: Architectural, 1953).

33. Gordon C. Logie, *The Urban Scene* (London: Faber & Faber, 1954).

34. The Editor [Hubert de Cronin Hastings,] "Exterior Furnishing or Sharawaggi: The Art of Making Urban Landscape," *AR* 95 (1944): 3–8.

35. This appears to be a mistake and most likely refers to the special issue of the *AR* from June 1945; see "A Programme for the City of London," special issue, *AR* 97 (1945): 157–96.

36. Gordon Cullen, "Westminster Regained: Proposals for the Replanning of the Westminster Precinct," *AR* 102 (1947): 159–70.

37. See Frederick Gibberd, William Holford, and Thomas Sharp, *Design in Town and Village* (London: H. M. S. O, 1953). See also the *AR*'s special issues on the Festival of Britain and the development of London's South Bank: Gordon Cullen, "Bankside Regained: A Scheme for Developing the South Bank of the Thames with an Eye to the 1951 Exhibition," *AR* 105 (1949): 15–24; "Royal Festival Hall," *AR* 109 (1951): 336–94; and "South Bank Exhibition," *AR* 110 (1951): 72–138.

38. See Unwin, *Town Planning in Practice* (note 30), 265–75. Compare Thomas Sharp, *Oxford Replanned* (London: Architectural, 1948), 21–26. In light of the discussion in Part I, note 7, this is a curious reference, considering that the sequence to which Pevsner refers is much the same as his own for the Oxford High. See Part I of this volume.

39. Sitte, *Art of Building Cities* (note 28).

40. This is not the correct date of publication; the first edition of Stübben's book appeared in 1890. Joseph Stübben, *Der Städtebau,* vol. 4, *Handbuch der Architektur* (Darmstadt: Bergsträsser, 1890).

41. T. C. Horsfall, *The Improvement of the Dwellings and Surroundings of the People: The Example of Germany* (Manchester: Univ. Press, 1904).

42. Patrick Geddes, *City Development: A Report to the Carnegie Dunfermline Trust* (Edinburgh: Geddes, 1904).

43. Pevsner is referring to two articles: J. M. Richards, "Failure of the New Towns," *AR* 114 (1953): 28–32; and Gordon Cullen, "Prairie Planning in the New Towns," *AR* 114 (1953): 33–36.

44. Presumably Pevsner is referring to the editorial on William Holford's plan for St. Paul's: "St. Paul's," *AR* 119 (1956): 294–98.

45. This section is drawn from Nikolaus Pevsner, "Roehampton: LCC Housing and the Picturesque Tradition," *AR* 126 (1959): 21–22.

46*. **See [the *Architectural Review*], vol. 77, 1935, pp. 188 etc.** Pevsner is most likely referring to the collage showing a modern slab building in the place of the Blenheim Castle. The page numbers of his citation appear to be incorrect. See W. A. Eden, "The English Tradition in the Countryside. III. The Re-Birth of the Tradition," *AR* 77 (1935): 194–95.

47*. **Their names were as follows: Planning: Elizabeth Chesterton, P. L. Cooke, R. V. Crowe, D. Duncan, A. Pott, P. M. Thornton, J. Wheeler. Housing: A. J. Brandt, R. L. Davies, D. S. Gladstone, J. C. de C. Henderson, A. W. Nicol, P. Saxl, F. L. Sturrock. See *Focus,* No. 1, 1938.**

48*. **Daniel Willink Plein, 1931.**

49*. **Bergolder Flats, 1934.**

50*. **Vienna, 1952.** Eduard F. Sekler, *Das Punkthaus im europäischen Wohnungsbau* (Vienna: Dokumentationszentrum für Technik & Wirtschaft, 1952). See also Nikolaus Pevsner, review of *Das Punkthaus im europäischen Wohnungsbau,* by E. F. Sekler, *AR* 117 (1955): 340.

51*. ***Rationelle Bebauungsweisen,* Frankfurt, 1931, p. 30.** *Rationelle Bebauungsweisen* (Frankfurt-am-Main: Englert & Schlosser, 1931).

52*. **The largest probably is Reimersholm by Forbat & Egler with 888 flats.**

53. This section is drawn from Pevsner, "The Picturesque in Architecture" (note 9), 57–58.

54. It is quite possible that Pevsner was a coauthor of this scheme, as he was editor of the *AR* in this period. The plan is attributed to "Hugh Gordon-Peter," and

the accompanying text mentions both Hugh Casson and Gordon Cullen by name. Presumably, "Peter" refers to Peter F. R. Donner, Pevsner's pseudonym within the *AR*. See Hugh Gordon-Peter, "Plan for the St. Paul's Area: The Plan," *AR* 100 (1946): 142–45.

55. The two following paragraphs are from Pevsner, "C20 Picturesque" (note 1), 229.

56. This paragraph and the remainder of this section is from Nikolaus Pevsner, "Townscape," address at Annual Meeting of the Council for Visual Education, *Journal of the Institute of Registered Architects* 10 (1955): 39, 41–42.

57. Pevsner held a copy of this manifesto; see Nikolaus Pevsner papers, box 52, folder "BBC Talk on Holford's Plan for the precinct of St. Paul's, 1956 (correspondence, notes, material)." This four-page manifesto is printed on brown cardboard with yellow highlights and was most likely published in 1953 or 1954, as it contains references to *AR* articles from 1953, and Architectural Press publications from 1953. It was not published in the *AR* and was most likely produced for popular distribution.

58. The first two paragraphs of this section are from Nikolaus Pevsner, "Why Not Harmonize the Old and the New?" *The Times*, 3 July 1961, xxii–xxiii.

59. The remainder of this section is taken from Nikolaus Pevsner, "Modern Architecture and Tradition," *Highway*, August 1947, 228–32. This article was originally intended for publication in German as "Neue Baukunst und Bautradition," the typewritten galley proofs for which are held in Nikolaus Pevsner papers, box 25, folder "Pevsner (Nikolaus) Neue Baukunst und Bautradition (1947)." An earlier article by Pevsner carried much the same argument for a national variation of modernism; see Nikolaus Pevsner, "Homes of the Future," *Europe* (1944): 58–59.

60. The text continues here with recourse to urban planning and national differences and greatly resembles Pevsner's discussion in the foreword and Part I of the *Visual Planning* manuscript:

> Let me illustrate this point with an example taken not so much from architecture as from town planning. London and Paris have a long tradition of town planning. In Paris the dominating tradition has been that of the *rond-point,* the central place from which radiate long straight avenues, in a clear and logical pattern. This tradition, which goes back to the time of Henry IV, reached its summit with Louis XIV at Versailles, was resumed in the Paris of the Revolution and of Napoleon, to be carried to a second culmination under Napoleon III and his architect Haussmann. To this tradition we owe the Arc de Triomphe and the adjoining boulevards in Paris, with the magnificent view round the Place de la Concorde, round the Madeleine and round the Opéra. These broad streets, their sharp angles, all this clear rational design, is truly and inevitably French.
>
> London seen through French eyes must look an incredible muddle. Piccadilly Circus is hopeless considered as a *rond-point* on the French model. The streets meander in at any old angle, Regent Street drifts off round a bend and takes a further bend a little higher up. Not even a main street like Piccadilly follows a straight course. There is not a single view of the Parisian kind, and no street follows a logical plan.
>
> Yet London has things unknown to Paris, the Temple, Lincoln's Inn and Gray's Inn for example (or as much of these as remain since the destruction

wrought in air raids) with their squares of varying types and with walks, trees and smooth lawns quite informally [ar]ranged. Here are intimate and grand courts or 'quads' rhythmically free and apparently casual in lay-out, surrounded by closely [ar]ranged rows of forbidding looking brick houses. This is one of the main notes of London planning. The other is the square generally surrounded by private houses each with its own facade (in contrast to the rigid uniformity of all the houses fronting the Place Vendôme in Paris). But all London houses harmonize, for their fronts are modest and not showy. Perhaps, compared with the inventive and inexhaustible variety of the Viennese eighteenth-century palaces and houses, they may seem a little dreary. But after all, they are characteristic of London, of English character and of the English tradition.

It is perhaps unnecessary to add that to France we owe the artificial garden on the Versailles plan, whilst the English landscape garden (known throughout Europe as "the English garden") produces asymmetrical grouping of trees, natural lakes and winding paths, such as we see in the very centre of London in Hyde Park or Regent's Park. England is also responsible for the conception of the Garden City. It would certainly be misguided to fit London into a Parisian mould as many people desire, and as even that great architect Sir Christopher Wren wished to do after the Great Fire, impressed as he was by the Paris he had recently visited. The vigour of the French pattern would merely look stiff and academic in London. Equally foolish would be to turn Paris into an imitation of London for the pictorial qualities of London would look insignificant and trivial in Paris.

Pevsner, "Modern Architecture and Tradition" (note 59), 229–30.

61. In a later article, Pevsner did soften this opinion to include geography as a determining factor of national differences in architecture:

Geography is the second. But while climates are reflected in the actual design of buildings, geography influences the way in which they impress us. The same building will appear different in the plain of the Middle West and in the varied, rolling, fragmented landscape of Southern England. Architecture for . . . social reasons . . . tends to increase in size. The private house of architectural value still plays an important part in Italy and California and of course the Commonwealth; in England and most continental countries it is a rarity. How can England reconcile the large units that enclose our corporate activities with her small scale? Moreover, England's landscape is man-made and made largely by aesthetic man. There is little in a natural state and little of purely utilitarian layout. What to the visitor constitutes English scenery is the work of the eighteenth century improvers. Is this an asset or an obstacle in modern architecture?

Pevsner, "Why Not Harmonize" (note 58), xxii.

62. The first three paragraphs of this section are drawn from Pevsner, *Englishness of English Art* (note 2), 168, 177.

63*. **Virgil: *Aen*. VII, 136, and in other places.**

64. The next three paragraphs are drawn from Pevsner, "C20 Picturesque" (note 1), 229.

65. This is most likely a reference to an essay by Paul Nash that dealt with one of Pevsner's central themes: that of the relationship between art and geography, and in particular, his use of the concept of *genius loci*. See Paul Nash, "Paul Nash," in Herbert Read, ed., *Unit 1: The Modern Movement in English Architecture, Painting, and Sculpture* (London: Cassell, 1934), 77–81.

66. The next three paragraphs are drawn from Nikolaus Pevsner, "Environment and History: Have We No Respect for Our Heritage? After Horton Hall, Horton Old Hall and Bierley Hall, What Next?" *Milestone: The Monthly Magazine of Bradford Junior Chamber of Commerce* 3, no. 9 (1970): 5.

67. The remainder of this section is drawn from Pevsner, "Why Not Harmonize" (note 58), xxii–xxiii.

68. The article published a photograph of this building; the caption read, "Corsham Court in Wiltshire, an unspoiled sixteenth century building." Pevsner, "Why Not Harmonize" (note 58), xxii.

69. This is a view also put forward by Pevsner in a later article dealing with "anti-scrape" and preservation, the conclusions of which are particularly relevant for the greater idea of visual planning. See Nikolaus Pevsner, "Scrape and Anti-Scrape," in Jane Fawcett, ed., *The Future of the Past: Attitudes to Conservation, 1174–1974* (London: Thames & Hudson, 1976), 34–53.

70. This section is drawn from Pevsner, *Englishness of English Art* (note 2), 179–80.

71*. **See J. M. Richards, "The Failure of the New Towns," *The Architectural Review*, vol. 114, 1953, and in reply to it Lionel Brett, ibid., p. 119.** See Richards, "Failure of the New Towns" (note 43); and Lionel Brett, "New Towns: Failure of the New Towns?" letter to the editor, *AR* 114 (1953): 119–20.

72*. **See features in the *Architectural Review*: Precinct of St. Paul's, vol. 97, 1945; St. Paul's Area, vol. 100, 1946; Westminster Regained, vol. 102, 1947; Houses of Parliament, vol. 108, 1950; Basildon Town Centre, vol. 114, 1953; Midland Experiment: Ludlow, Bewdley, vol. 114, 1953; Evesham, Shrewsbury, vol. 115, 1954.** These refer to the following editions respectively: "A Programme" (note 35); Gordon-Peter, "Plan for the St. Paul's Area" (note 54), 124–50; Cullen, "Westminster Regained" (note 36); Gordon Cullen, "Basildon Town Centre," *AR* 114 (1953): 245–50; Gordon Cullen, "Midland Experiment: 1. A Case Study: Ludlow," *AR* 114 (1953): 171–75; Donald Dewar Mills, "Midland Experiment: Bewdley," *AR* 114 (1953): 319–24; Gordon Cullen, "Midland Experiment: Evesham," *AR* 115 (1954): 127–31; and Gordon Cullen, "Midland Experiment: Shrewsbury," *AR* 115 (1954): 322–30. The "Houses of Parliament" citation appears to be an error, as no such feature has been found.

73. This section is drawn from Pevsner, "Visual Planning" (note 8), 33–34. This talk was delivered by Pevsner on 27 November 1945 and refers chiefly to an anonymous plan put forward in the *AR* in June 1945; see "A Programme" (note 35). As mentioned above, some of the illustrations for this plan were attributed to Hugh Casson and later reworked for the special edition of the *AR* in November 1946: Gordon-Peter, "Plan for the St. Paul's Area" (note 54). See figure 26, the authorship of which is discussed in note 54 above.

74. Nikolaus Pevsner, "The Precincts of St. Paul's: Sir William Holford's Plan," *Housing Centre Review* 5 (1956): 71–72. This article is a shorter version of the broadcast by Pevsner, titled "A Setting for St. Paul's," which aired 6 May 1956 on BBC radio on the Home Service. It also bears a heavy resemblance to the editorial article in the *AR* of June 1956. See "Plan for the St. Paul's Area" (note 54). See Nikolaus Pevsner, "A Setting for St. Paul's Cathedral," *Listener*, 10 May 1956, 594–96; reprinted in

Pevsner on Art and Architecture: The Radio Talks, ed. Stephen Games (London: Methuen, 2002), 240–49.

75. Nikolaus Pevsner, "The Sidgwick Avenue Site," *Cambridge Review* 75 (1953): 88–89. In 1958, Pevsner again wrote on the subject of Cambridge planning proposals in "Churchill College—Some Considerations: Passions Not Aroused," *Varsity* (Cambridge), 17 May 1958, 6–7. In this article, Pevsner repeats many of the opinions expressed in his earlier articles on the planning of Cambridge University.

76. The article Pevsner refers to is Nikolaus Pevsner, "The Cambridge Campus of the Future," *Cambridge Review* 73 (1952): 391–92. Two years earlier, Pevsner had contributed another article concerned with planning proposals for Cambridge in his "Visual Aspects of the Cambridge Plan," *Cambridge Review* 71 (1950): 510–13.

77. This section is excerpted from Nikolaus Pevsner, "Il Festival di Londra," *Comunità,* 12 October 1951, 48–51, and was kindly translated from the Italian by Sabine Eiche.

78. Uvedale Price, *Essays on the Picturesque, as Compared with the Sublime and the Beautiful: And, on the Use of Studying Pictures, for the Purpose of Improving Real Landscape,* 3 vols. (London: printed for J. Mawman, 1810), 1:115.

79. Price, *Essays on the Picturesque* (note 78), 1:126–27.

80. Price, *Essays on the Picturesque* (note 78), 1:24.

81. Price, *Essays on the Picturesque* (note 78), 1:22.

82. Price, *Essays on the Picturesque* (note 78), 2:230.

83. Sir Phillip Powell, 1921–2003; and John Hidalgo Moya, 1920–94.

84. This passage is drawn from Pevsner, "Roehampton" (note 45), 21, 35.

85. This section is drawn from Nikolaus Pevsner, "Conclusions," in idem, ed., *The Picturesque Garden and Its Influence Outside the British Isles* (Washington, D.C.: Dumbarton Oaks, 1974), 119–21.

86. Hussey, *The Picturesque* (note 16).

Selected Bibliography

This bibliography contains works by Nikolaus Pevsner either cited in this volume or loosely related to the *Visual Planning* manuscript.

Archival Sources

Nikolaus Pevsner papers, Getty Research Institute, Los Angeles (acc. no. 2003.M.34)

Publications

1933

"Fritz Schumacher." *Gottinger Tageblatt*, 16 February, 5.

1934

"Das Englische in der englischen Kunst: Die retrospektive Austellung britischer Kunst in der Londoner Akademie." *Die Deutsche Zukunft: Wochenzeitung für Politik, Wirtschaft und Kultur*, 4 February, 15.

1936

Pioneers of the Modern Movement: From William Morris to Walter Gropius. London: Faber & Faber.

1937

"C. F. A. Voysey. An Appreciation." *AR* 82:36.

1941

"Criticism." *AR* 90:68–70, 91–92. Published under the pseudonym Peter F. R. Donner.

"London Life." Review of *The Streets of London through the Centuries*, by Thomas Burke. *The Spectator*, 24 January, 93–94.

"Meine Kollegen, die Schuttschipper." *Die Zeitung*, 1 September, 3. Published under the pseudonym Ramaduri.

"Schuttschipper-Psychologie." *Die Zeitung*, 25 September, 3. Published under the pseudonym Ramaduri.

"Richard Norman Shaw, 1831–1912." *AR* 89:41–46.

1942

"Criticism: Treasure Hunt." *AR* 91:23–25. Published under the pseudonym Peter F. R. Donner.

"The First Garden City." Review of *Sixty Years of Planning: The Bournville Experiment*, by the Bournville Village Trust. *AR* 92:128.

"Heritage of Compromise: A Note on Sir Joshua Reynolds Who Died One Hundred and Fifty Years Ago." *AR* 91:37–38.

An Outline of European Architecture. Harmondsworth: Penguin.

"Works and Planning: The New Ministry's Multiple Tasks: Research for Reconstruction." *The Times*, 18 November, 5. Published anonymously.

1943

"The End of the Pattern-Books." *AR* 93:75–79. Published under the pseudonym Peter F. R. Donner.

"A Harris Florilegium." *AR* 93:51–52. Published under the pseudonym Peter F. R. Donner.

"The Lure of Rusticity." *AR* 93:26. Published under the pseudonym Peter F. R. Donner.

"Review of the Exhibition." Review of an exhibition of students' work at the Architectural Association at Bedford Square, London. *Architectural Association Journal* 58, no. 674: 82–83.

"A Short Pugin Florilegium." *AR* 94:31–34.

1944

"Cincinnati Looks at Strawberry Hill." Review of *Horace Walpole, Gardenist: An Edition of Walpole's "The History of the Modern Taste in Gardening" with an "Estimate of Walpole's Contribution to Landscape Architecture,"* by Isabel Wakelin Urban Chase. *AR* 95:56. Published under the pseudonym Peter F. R. Donner.

"Edensor or Brown Comes True." *AR* 95:39–43. Published under the pseudonym Peter F. R. Donner.

"The Genesis of the Picturesque." *AR* 96:139–46.

"Homes of the Future." *Europe*, 58–59.

"Price on Picturesque Planning." *AR* 95:47–50. Published anonymously.

1945

"Act 2: Romantic Gothic. Scene 1: Goethe and Strassburg." *AR* 98:155–59.

"The English Eccentrics: Land of Follies in Architecture." Review of *British Architects and Craftsmen*, by Sacheverell Sitwell. *TLS: Times Literary Supplement*, 14 July, 325–26.

"Frenchay Common or Workaday Sharawaggi." *AR* 98:26–27. Published anonymously.

"Visual Planning and the City of London." Summary of a talk to the Architectural Association. *Architects' Journal* 102, no. 2655:440, xliv.

"Visual Planning and the City of London: A Paper Read before the A.A. by Dr. Nikolaus Pevsner." *Architectural Association Journal* 61, no. 699:31–36.

1946

"Basic Architecture." Review of *Style and Composition in Architecture*, and *Good and Bad Manners in Architecture*, by Trystan Edwards and John Tirranti. *AR* 99:156. Published under the pseudonym Peter F. R. Donner.

"A Pioneer of Town-Planning." Review of *The Art of Building Cities*, by Camillo Sitte. *AR* 100:186.

"Reflections on Ruins." BBC radio talk broadcast on Home Service, 3 May. Published as "Bombed Churches as War Memorials?" *Listener*, 16 May, 639.

"Rococo to Romanticism." Review of *The Creation of the Rococo*, by Fiske Kimball. *TLS: Times Literary Supplement*, 23 March, 133–34.

Visual Pleasures from Everyday Things: An Attempt to Establish Criteria by Which the Aesthetic Qualities of Design Can Be Judged. London: Published for the Council for Visual Education by B. T. Batsford.

1947

"The Architecture of Washington." BBC radio talk broadcast on Third Program, 10 July. Published as "Greece, Rome— and Washington: Nikolaus Pevsner on the Need for a New Style in Monumental Architecture." *Listener*, 17 July, 93–94.

"Lavedan Continued." Review of *Histoire de l'urbanisme*, vol. 2, *Renaissance et temps modernes*, by Pierre Lavedan. *AR* 102:103.

"Modern Architecture and Tradition." *Highway*, August, 228–32.

"The Other Chambers." *AR* 101:195–98.

"The Picturesque in Architecture." *RIBA Journal* 55:55–61.

"Richard Payne Knight." Radio Talk broadcast on Third Program: BBC. Broadcast, 16 January. Published as "An Eighteenth-Century 'Improver': Nikolaus Pevsner on Richard Payne Knight." *Listener*, 30 January, 204–5.

1948

"Humphrey Repton: A Florilegium." *AR* 103:53–59.

"Der Monumentalbau und unsere Zeit." *Blick in die Welt*, no. 20:13–15.

1949

"Judges VI, 34." *AR* 106:77–79.

"Reassessment 4: Three Oxford Colleges." *AR* 106:120–24.

Review of *Amsterdams Bouwkunst en Stadsschoon*, by J. G. Wattjes and F. A. Warners. *AR* 106:196.

Review of *Tony Garnier*, by Giulia Veronesi. *AR* 106:196.

"Richard Payne Knight." *Art Bulletin* 31:293–320.

"Sir William Temple and Sharawaggi." Cowritten with Susan Lang. *AR* 106:391–93.

1950

"The Humane Builder." Review of *Grundlagen für das Studium der Baukunst*, by Fritz Schumacher. *TLS: Times Literary Supplement*, 14 July, 432.

"Visual Aspects of the Cambridge Plan." *Cambridge Review* 71:510–13.

1951

"Il Festival di Londra." *Comunità*, 12 October, 48–51.

"The New Chambers." Review of *The New Chambers's Encyclopaedia*, by George Newnes Ltd. *AR* 109:121–22.

Nottinghamshire. The Buildings of England. Harmondsworth: Penguin.

Review of *Capability Brown*, by Dorothy Stroud. *Cambridge Review* 72:432–34.

1952

"The Cambridge Campus of the Future." *Cambridge Review* 73:391–92.

"Downing College." *Cambridge University Medical Society*, Easter, 1–2.

London: Except the Cities of London and Westminster. The Buildings of England. Harmondsworth: Penguin.

"Schinkel." *RIBA Journal* 59:89–96.

"Town-Planning." Review of *Towns and Buildings*, by Steen Eiler Rasmussen. *TLS: Times Literary Supplement*, 4 April 1952, 239.

"Town Planning: Pioneer of the Pedestrian Network." *AR* 112:57.

1953

"The Sidgwick Avenue Site." *Cambridge Review* 75:88–89.

1954

"Art in Use: Inhabited Sculpture." *AR* 116:331–32.

"C20 Picturesque: An Answer to Basil Taylor's Broadcast." *AR* 115:227–29.

"Towers in the City? I Say Yes." *Evening Standard*, 24 November, 16.

1955

"The Englishness of English Art: The Genius of the Place. The Last of Seven Reith Lectures." *Listener*, 1 December, 931.

"Townscape." Address delivered at the Annual Meeting of the Council for Visual Education. *Journal of the Institute of Registered Architects* 10:39–42.

"Townscape: Metropolitan Promenade." *AR* 118:330–31.

1956

The Englishness of English Art: An Expanded and Annotated Version of the Reith Lectures Broadcast in October and November 1955. London: Architectural.

"On Finding Oneself out of Date." *Architects' Journal* 123, no. 3175:77–78.

"Hogarth's Thoughts on His Art." Review of *The Analysis of Beauty*, by William Hogarth. *TLS: Times Literary Supplement*, 20 January, 32.

"The Precincts of St. Paul's: Sir William Holford's Plan." *Housing Centre Review* 5:71–72.

"Topography: Frith and the Irregular." *AR* 120:191.

"Welcome to Professor Martin." *Cambridge Review* 78:136–37.

1957

London, I: The Cities of London and Westminster. The Buildings of England. Harmondsworth: Penguin.

1958

"Churchill College—Some Considerations: Passions Not Aroused." *Varsity* (Cambridge), 17 May, 6–7.
"Criticism: Backyard Mentality." *AR* 124:409–12.

1959

"The Classical Ideal." Review of *The Ideal City in Its Architectural Evolution,* by Helen Rosenau. *AR* 126:145.
"Roehampton: LCC Housing and the Picturesque Tradition." *AR* 126:21–35.

1961

"Modern Architecture and the Historian or the Return of Historicism." *RIBA Journal* 68:230–40.
"Why Not Harmonize the Old and the New?" *The Times,* 3 July, xxii–xxiii.

1962

"Topography: Wiltshire Surprises." *AR* 132:365–67.

1963

"Achievements in British Post-War Architecture." *Building, Lighting, and Engineering,* no. 34:40–41, 48.
"History: Unwin Centenary." *AR* 134:207–8.

1966

"Cityscape: Only East Germany Rivals D.C. in Paralysis of Architecture." *Washington Post,* 16 January, G9.

1967

"Nikolaus Pevsner: 1967 Gold Medalist." *RIBA Journal* 74:316–18.
"The Royal Gold Medal: Nikolaus Pevsner." *RIBA Journal* 74:9–10. Published under the pseudonym Peter F. R. Donner.

1968

Studies in Art, Architecture and Design, vol. 1, *From Mannerism to Romanticism.* London: Thames & Hudson.

1969

"The Pleasures of Ruins." Review of *Fascination of Decay,* by Paul Zucker. *TLS: Times Literary Supplement,* 28 August, 946.

1970

"Environment and History: Have We No Respect for Our Heritage? After Horton Hall, Horton Old Hall and Bierley Hall, What Next?" *Milestone: The Monthly Magazine of Bradford Junior Chamber of Commerce* 3, no. 9:5.

"Foreword." In John Barr, ed., *Sir Nikolaus Pevsner: A Bibliography,* vii–xi. Charlottesville: Univ. of Virginia Press.
"Obituary. Christopher Hussey: 1899–1970." *AR* 148:130.

1971

"Elusive JMR." *RIBA Journal* 78:181.
"The Objects of Nineteenth-Century Vienna." Review of *Die Wiener Ringstrasse—Bild einer Epoche,* edited by Renate Wagner-Rieger. *TLS: Times Literary Supplement,* 21 May, 599.

1974

"Building a Better Berlin." Review of *Schinkel's Berlin,* by Hermann G. Pundt. *TLS: Times Literary Supplement,* 11 January 1974, 24.
Oxfordshire. Cowritten with Jennifer Sherwood. The Buildings of England. Harmondsworth: Penguin.
"Ein Nachwort: Deutsch-englische Wechselbeziehungen." In Ludwig Grote, ed., *Die Deutsche Stadt im 19. Jahrhundert: Stadtplanung und Baugestaltung im industriellen Zeitalter,* 311–14. Munich: Prestel.
The Picturesque Garden and Its Influence outside the British Isles. Edited by Nikolaus Pevsner. Washington, D.C.: Dumbarton Oaks.

1976

"Scrape and Anti-Scrape." In Jane Fawcett, ed., *The Future of the Past: Attitudes to Conservation, 1174–1974,* 34–53. London: Thames & Hudson.

2002

Pevsner on Art and Architecture: The Radio Talks. Edited by Stephen Games. London: Methuen.

Illustration Credits

Every effort has been made to identify and contact photographers whose work may still be in copyright, or their estates. Anyone having further information concerning copyright holders should contact the publisher so that this information can be included in future printings.

The materials illustrated on the following pages are held in the Nikolaus Pevsner papers at the Getty Research Institute: pp. 8, 11, 66–72, 74–81, 82 (bottom), 83–88, 94–98, 165, and 180. All photographs reproduced from the Nikolaus Pevsner papers are courtesy the Getty Research Institute.

The following sources have granted additional permission to reproduce illustrations in this book:

Introduction

Visual Planning and the Picturesque

(London: Cruchley, [ca, 1830]). Courtesy the Huntington Library

Fig. 5   Guildhall Library, City of London

Figs. 6, 7   From Emmanuel Héré, *Plans et élévations de la Place royale de Nancy et des autres édifices qui l'environnens bâtie par les ordres du roy de Pologne, duc de Lorraine* (Paris: Ches François, Graveur Ordinaire de Sa Majesté…, 1753), n.p.

p. 94   Reproduced from the 1930 Ordnance Survey map with the kind permission of the Ordnance Survey

pp. 95–98   Photo by Aerofilms LTD. © English Heritage. NMR. Aerofilms Collection

Fig. 8   From John Summerson, *John Nash, Architect to King George IV* (London: Allen & Unwin, 1935), n.p. © The Trustees of the Estate of John Newenham Summerson

Figs. 9–13   From Thomas Hosmer Shepherd and James Elmes, *Metropolitan Improvements; or, London in the Nineteenth Century…* (London: Jones, 1827), after pp. 99, 92, 23, 27, 20, respectively. Courtesy Getty Research Institute

Fig. 14   Country Life

Fig. 15   Conway Library, The Courtauld Institute of Art, London. Photograph by A. F. Kersting

Fig. 16   From Nikolaus Pevsner, *Studies in Art, Architecture and Design* (London: Thames & Hudson, 1968), 1:111

Fig. 17   From Nikolaus Pevsner, *Studies in Art, Architecture and Design* (London: Thames & Hudson, 1968), 1:121

Fig. 18   Photograph of the Louvre by Compagnie Aérienne Française; photograph of Buckingham Palace by Aerofilms Ltd. © English Heritage. NMR. Aerofilms Collection; and photograph of Salisbury Chapel © *The Times*/NI Syndication Limited

Fig. 19   Photo: Erich Auerbach

Fig. 20   Detail of Richard Horwood's *Plan of London*, 1813

Fig. 21   From Alfred Barry, *The Life and Works of Sir Charles Barry, R. A., F. R. S., etc.* (New York: Benjamin Blom, 1972), before p. 293

Fig. 22   © 2010 Artists Rights Society (ARS), New York/ADAGP, Paris/FLC

Fig. 23   From Nikolaus Pevsner, "Frenchay Common or Workaday Sharawaggi," *AR* 98 (1945): 26. Plan drawn by J. W. Tanner. Architectural Press Archive/RIBA Library Photographs Collection

Fig. 24   From Raymond Unwin, *Town Planning in Practice; an Introduction to the Art of Designing Cities and Suburbs* (London: T. F. Unwin, [1919]), [Ills.] 98, 157, 266

Fig. 25   Architectural Press Archive/RIBA Library Photographs Collection

Figs. 26, 27   © Gordon Cullen. Courtesy the Estate of Gordon Cullen

Fig. 28   Reproduction of front page of "Townscape Manifesto." Architectural Press Archive/RIBA Library Photographs Collection

Fig. 29   Courtesy Gibberd Studio

Fig. 30   From "A Programme for the City of London," special issue, *AR* 97 (1945): 171. Architectural Press Archive/RIBA Library Photographs Collection. Photograph by E. O. Hoppé. © 1945/2009 Curatorial Assistance, Inc., Pasadena/E. O. Hoppé Estate Collection

Fig. 31   From "A Programme for the City of London," special issue, *AR* 97 (1945): 189. Architectural Press Archive/RIBA Library Photographs Collection. Copyright Hugh Casson. Reproduced with permission of the Casson Estate

Fig. 32   From "St. Paul's," *AR* 119 (1956): 294. Architectural Press Archive/RIBA Library Photographs Collection. Photo: Heinz Zinram

Fig. 33   *Cambridge Review* 75 (1953): cover

Fig. 34   Copyright Hugh Casson. Reproduced with permission of the Casson Estate

Fig. 35   Architectural Press Archive/RIBA Library Photographs Collection

Fig. 36   From Nikolaus Pevsner, *The Englishness of English Art* (London: Architectural, 1956), 176. Architectural Press Archive/RIBA Library Photographs Collection. Photos: John Pantlin

Figs. 37, 38   From Nikolaus Pevsner, "Roehampton: LCC Housing and the Picturesque Tradition," *AR* 126 (1959): 26–28. Architectural Press Archive/RIBA Library Photographs Collection. Photo: Toomey

Index

Page numbers referring to illustrations are in *italics*. Page numbers followed by n indicate information in endnotes.

Visual Planning and the Picturesque

Nikolaus Pevsner

Edited by Mathew Aitchison

Introductory text by John Macarthur and Mathew Aitchison

Mathew Aitchison received his doctorate in architecture from the University of Queensland in 2009. The research toward his dissertation, "Visual Planning and Exterior Furnishing: A Critical History of the Early Townscape Movement, 1930 to 1949," was carried out in conjunction with the Technical University Berlin and focused on mid-century British architectural and urban design discourses, a subject on which he has published several papers. He has taught architecture at the Technical University Berlin, the University of Queensland, Syracuse University, and at Queen's University Belfast, where he is currently lecturer in architecture and urban design. In addition to his academic work, he has practiced as an architect in Australia, Germany, Holland, and Ireland, and has received awards for competition entries. He has held fellowships at both the Center of Metropolitan Studies Berlin and Syracuse University's School of Architecture, where he organized an exhibition and conferences. Over the past two years, he has also been engaged in the establishment of an international center for architectural and urban design in Berlin, a city in which he has lived predominantly since 1995.

John Macarthur is head of the School of Architecture at the University of Queensland and director of the research group ATCH (Architecture, Theory, Criticism, History). He is also a visiting professor at RMIT (Royal Melbourne Institute of Technology) University. Macarthur studied architecture in Queensland before taking a PhD at the University of Cambridge. He writes on the cultural history and aesthetics of architecture and is an active critic of contemporary architecture in Australia. He is a former president of the Society of Architectural Historians, Australia and New Zealand, and currently the chair of its editorial board. His work has appeared in *Assemblage, Architecture Research Quarterly, The Journal of Architecture, Architectural Theory Review,* and *Oase.* His book, *The Picturesque: Architecture, Disgust and Other Irregularities,* was published by Routledge in 2007 and examines the picturesque in the light of its later uptake and use, notably by Nikolaus Pevsner, and it draws in part on the research presented in this volume. He is currently working on projects on the twentieth-century reception of baroque architecture, on criticism and aesthetics, and on the architecture of Queensland.

Other books featuring the holdings of the Research Library at the Getty Research Institute:

Printing the Grand Manner: Charles Le Brun and Monumental Prints in the Age of Louis XIV
Louis Marchesano and Christian Michel
ISBN 978-0-89236-980-5 (hardcover)

Walls of Algiers: Narratives of the City through Text and Image
Edited by Zeynep Çelik, Julia Clancy-Smith, and Frances Terpak
Copublished with the University of Washington Press
ISBN 978-0-295-98868-9 (paper)

The Getty Murúa: Essays on the Making of Martín de Murúa's "Historia General del Piru," J. Paul Getty Museum Ms. Ludwig XIII 16
Edited by Thomas B. F. Cummins and Barbara Anderson
ISBN 978-0-89236-894-5 (hardcover)

Allan Kaprow—Art as Life
Edited by Eva Meyer-Hermann, Andrew Perchuk, and Stephanie Rosenthal
ISBN 978-0-89236-890-7 (hardcover)

China on Paper: European and Chinese Works from the Late Sixteenth to the Early Nineteenth Century
Edited by Marcia Reed and Paola Demattè
ISBN 978-0-89236-869-3 (hardcover)

Art, Anti-Art, Non-Art: Experimentations in the Public Sphere in Postwar Japan, 1950–1970
Edited by Charles Merewether with Rika Iezumi Hiro
ISBN 978-0-89236-866-2 (hardcover)

Lucien Hervé: Building Images
Olivier Beer
ISBN 978-0-89236-754-2 (hardcover)

Had gadya: The Only Kid: Facsimile of El Lissitzky's Edition of 1919
Edited by Arnold J. Band
ISBN 978-0-89236-744-3 (paper)

Aldo Rossi: I quaderni azzurri
Aldo Rossi
ISBN 978-0-89236-589-0 (boxed set)

Devices of Wonder: From the World in a Box to Images on a Screen
Barbara Maria Stafford and Frances Terpak
ISBN 978-0-89236-590-6 (paper)

Making a Prince's Museum: Drawings for the Late-Eighteenth-Century Redecoration of the Villa Borghese
Carole Paul
ISBN 978-0-89236-539-5 (paper)

Maiolica in the Making: The Gentili/Barnabei Archive
Catherine Hess
ISBN 978-0-89236-500-5 (paper)

Russian Modernism
Compiled by David Woodruff and Ljiljana Grubišić
ISBN 978-0-89236-385-8 (paper)

In Preparation

China in a Frame: Photographs 1839–1937
Edited by Jeffrey Cody and Frances Terpak

Designed by Stuart Smith

Coordinated by Amita Molloy

Type composed in Times, Verlag, Stymie, and Schadow on Gold East Matte